FIFTY-TWO OF THE BEST

Selected highlights from the first five years
of
Rod Fleming's World

PlashMill Press

Published in 2017 by PlashMill Press, Friockheim, Scotland.

Copyright© 2012-2017 Rod Fleming

All rights reserved.

All names in this publication have been changed to protect the identities of the real people.

ISBN:

All photographs except pages 42, 64, 98 and 209: Rod Fleming

To all my longsuffering readers and fans who have sustained me for so long. Thank you all and I hope you enjoy this. I'll be honest, if I'd known how much work it would be…

Rod Fleming, Molinot, France

2017

Contents

Humour

1. Sticks, Ice-Creams and Specks of Dust	1
2. Archaic Humans Discovered in Scotland	4
3. Wot? No Rabbits? - The Brither	6
4. In France, Everything Shuts at Twelve	9
6. Gendarmes, Police and Faulty Speedos	13
7. The Church of Hedonism	18

Sex and Gender

1. Transgender - Is there really an increase?	23
2. The thought or image of oneself	33
3. The history of buggery.	42
4. Girly-boy beauty	49
5. Autogynephilia: Sex as a Woman	56
6. Not Men: bekis in the Philippines	64
7. Autogynephilia Explained	76
8 Brain Sex?	82
9. The Man Who Would Be Queen	88
10. Jennifer Laude, Victim of Hate	98
11. Pansexual: the human norm	102

Politics

1. We Live in Interesting Times   107
2. Swivelly-eyed Brexit panic.   111
3. The British Project: the sun goes down   115
4. Cameron's Phony Referendum   119
5. Super-emasculated men and autogynephilia   124
6. Scene from an Imaginary Western   129
7. Socially aware, libertarian, scientific, secularist   134
8. The first of our 3 Ps is Pot; marijuana   138
9. Je suis Paris   144

Islam.

1. Qandeel Baloch: killed by Islam.   149
2. Dar al-Harb: The Islamic stimulus for war.   153
3. War with Islam: ideology, not people   158
4. Unli sex: the foundation of Islam   163
5. Sharia: Halal and Haram   168
6. Why Islam Cannot Change   172
7. Muslims we Must Support: Maajid Nawaz   181
8. The Realpolitik of Islam   185
9. Islam: a danger to society   193

Religion

1. The 'Ontological Argument'= busted.	199
2. Christians is Bitchin'	206
3. Hot Cross Buns – Cakes for the Goddess	209
4. Ley-lines: how an English Gent launched the New Age movement	212
5. God proposition: god true or god false?	217
6. Is Witch-burning Back? The Religious Right Is.	220
7. The Storytelling Ape	225
8. Jesus? I have a better story than that...	229
9. Singing the World into Being	231
10. Pursuing the Goddess	234
11. Something Greater	237

Travel

1. Boracay, A Hidden Tropical Paradise	242
2. Philippines Diary: Jeepneys	252
3. Arayat Escapade	256
4. Manila: Skinny Cats, Transports of Delight and Beautiful Women	262
5. The Goddess in The Philippines	266
6. Ladyboys in Pattaya	271
Author's note	280

Humour

1. Sticks, Ice-Creams and Specks of Dust

A long time ago, when I lived in Arbroath in Scotland, my role before opening up the old Fleming Partners office was to do the school run. Our kids went to a small village school just outside the town itself and there was no bus.

On these runs I always tried to entertain the boys by talking about whatever came into my mind (and would not take more than 10 minutes.) So one day I explained why humans can see in colour and many animals can't. This is because, I said, there are two types of vision receptor cells, rods and cones. Cones see colour and rods see brightness – monochrome, in other words. (I do know it's a bit more complex than that, but these were primary kids.) Humans have both rods and cones, and many animals, like dogs, only have rods. So we see colour and they don't.

This went fine and was met with all the usual approval that could be mustered from a 5-year old and an 8-year old.

I liked to test the little buggers to see if anything I said stuck, so a couple of days later I asked, 'Why do we see colour and dogs don't?'

To which Silas, 5, shouted out, 'Because they don't have any ice-creams in their eyes, only sticks!'

To which there was general hilarity. But he was still right.

I personally think my kids are all geniuses but I am quite certain Silas is. That story, (which is true by the way) to me, serves to illustrate what genius really is; it is the ability to conceptualise an idea in a totally novel and unique way. All through his life, Silas has demonstrated an uncanny ability to understand and conceive of the world in ways which are just slightly – and some not so slightly – different from everyone else, yet which make perfect sense. And to his great credit, perhaps aided a little by his thoroughly anarchistic and non-conformist parents, he has maintained that unique and individual perspective.

Genius is not just being hugely intelligent, although it is partly that. Genius is being able to see the world in a new way, which allows new perspectives of understanding. Robert M Pirsig, in his novel 'Zen and the Art of Motorcycle Maintenance' talked of ideas as super-saturated solutions, clear liquid until a tiny speck of dust fell in, and then the whole would crystallise in instants, revealing structure, integrity, balance. Genius is that speck of dust, the application of which causes a whole system of ideas to suddenly appear. And it takes minds unafraid to think differently to apply it.

Da Vinci had it, Mozart had it, Newton had it, Einstein had it. It's not given to everyone, but it is given to far more of us than we realise. The trouble is that most children go through an education system that is designed to make them conform, rather than to celebrate their riotous, inchoate but absolutely brilliant minds; designed to snuff the sparkling flame of their unique vision and replace it with the dullness of the commonplace. We take the stuff of genius and turn it into the slurry of mere conformity, making fodder for the capitalist grist-mill and the patriarchal hegemony. We take our young minds and carefully, thoroughly, sanitise all the specks of precious dust.

One day we may have education systems which celebrate minds that conceptualise rods and cones as sticks and ice-creams; education systems which actually encourage people to think like that, which reward innovation and iconoclasm and discourage the trotting out of conventional wisdom. Education systems that not only allow young people to dare to be different, but which positively encourage it, that give out prizes for not being like all the others.

Perhaps one day we will have education systems, in other words, which exist for the benefit of both the students and humanity, and not for that of the career educators who make their living from the imposition of mind-numbing conformity, or for the benefit of a corrupt politico-economic system that is determined to destroy the planet in the pursuit of quick money, or for the preservation of privilege, and the maintenance of the status quo.

But that seems a long way off, and I wonder – will it come in time?

2. Archaic Humans Discovered in Scotland

Scientists all over the world are turning their attention to Scotland in the wake of a shock discovery that 'archaic' humans may be alive and well and living there.

The discovery came when one of them was filmed saying that they 'were not evolved to make political decisions'.

Professor of Anthropology Farquhar McFarquharson of the University of Aberdeen explained: 'All modern humans – *Homo sapiens* – have evolved highly sophisticated social behaviour including the ability to arrive at complex decisions within a formal political framework. The discovery of a population that lacks this ability, apparently living alongside more developed hominids, is very exciting.'

He went on to point out that while there had been numerous anecdotal reports of sightings of potentially archaic humans, notably in Sauchiehall Street after 'Old Firm' kickball matches, this was the first time a live specimen had been caught on film.

The subject of the surprise discovery is apparently known as 'Johann Lamont', and her revelation more than explains the disastrous state of Scotland's so-called 'Labour Party', which has been unable to make an intelligent political decision in several decades, and which, bizarrely, managed to elect someone 'not evolved to make political decisions' as its own leader.

Prof. McFarquharson continued, 'This raises really interesting possibilities. At first thought it seemed as if a pocket of Neanderthals (*Homo sapiens neanderthalis*) might have survived, when we all thought they had died out 30,000 years ago. But Neanderthals had developed social systems like ours and it seems likely that they were also able to make political decisions. That might mean that the group belongs to an even older hominid species, *Homo heidelbergensis*, which was thought to have gone extinct in Spain some 400,000 years ago, as a result of drinking too much Fundidor brandy.'

In Prof Mc Farquharson's lab, graduate students have been studying the film, which shows the archaic human talking to a modern human, all day. However, the task is so distressing that students can only watch the screens for twenty minutes at a time.

The Professor explained, 'To our eyes the subject is shockingly ugly, but of course to her own species she may be very beautiful. However, despite the difficulties in observing her, we have already established that she shows many morphological traits consistent with her being of an archaic hominid type, such as low forehead, beetling brow, massive jaw and so on. Initial tests on her speech patterns also reveal differences from modern humans.'

Meanwhile, Professor of Palaeontology at Edinburgh University, Dr Michael Scott, said 'I'm sanguine about this. There's a lot to be done to establish whether this is actually evidence of an enclave of archaic humans living in our midst, or whether it is some sort of genetic evolutionary throwback. It might even just be a wee nyaff who doesn't understand big words.'

Professor McFarquharson was undeterred, however. 'There's a Nobel Prize in it if this info is kosher, so it's into the Profmobile for me and away down to Glasgow. No other bugger's getting that limmer on the dissection – er, sorry, 'examination' table before I do.'

3. Wot? No Rabbits? - The Brither

Now my brother was a bit of a character. I'm not talking about my wee brother, here, or the big one I suddenly discovered I had in 2004 that no bugger ever told me about before (aye, we'll get to that.) I mean my other big brother Sandy, AKA Sye.

Sandy did things his own way. He ran a car breaking yard – and trust me, there is no more joyous place to spend your school hols than in a place like that – and he lived in a wee cottage in Arbroath, one of those sandstone ones. His wife was called Toos and she was Dutch.

Sandy was always coming up with schemes and one of these was inspired by Toos, who told him that people in Holland raised rabbits for the pot.

'Hm,' thinks he. 'I'll have a dod of that.' So off he goes and buys a pair of white rabbits from Thomson's the pet shop in the High Street. Well, Toos just laughed, because they have special rabbits for eating in Holland but Sandy never knew. So he put them in a hutch he'd nailed together in the back yard and waited.

The thing is, rabbits do two things. One is they, you know, like rabbits, and the other is, they eat their way through anything that isn't metal. They might even do that if they were hungry enough.

So the rabbits had a few clutches of baby rabbits, but they weren't really big enough to eat, you know. So Sandy got bored and turned to other things for amusement. Which I daresay we'll get to. Unfortunately, the rabbits also got bored and pulled a Colditz out of the hutch, having eaten their way through, and scattered. Like they do in the best POW movies.

Sandy – predictably – just shrugged his shoulders and went back to fixing whichever car he was up to his elbows in the guts of at the time. Probably a Jag. He liked Jags. And no more was said about the subject.

A few months later I was round at Sandy and Toos' house. I think it was a Saturday. Anyway I looked out the kitchen window and was pure amazed to see a thick covering of snow on the ground. I mean, I know it was Scotland, but it was the summer holidays.

Somewhat startled, I looked more closely and realised that the snow was moving. True. Moving snow. Except this snow had long ears and red eyes. There were hundreds of rabbits in the yard. Well, 92. I'll tell you how I know later.

The problem was that even though Sandy's yard had a stone wall round it, the rabbits just dug under, and pretty soon he was getting it in the neck from everybody in the street. Hannah Street, it was called. Anyway the neighbours were kinda het because where once there had been green and lush wee gardens, all set out neat, now it was scorched earth with droppings and mobile snow as far as the eye could see. Kinda like the Somme on a bad day.

After a while of this, Sandy got fed up of Toos nagging him about the moaning neighbours. So he decided Something Had To Be Done. Well. Sandy had a right straightforward view on life…

(Voice off: Like youse ya mean? Big lunk.)

No, I am not going to respond to that, not just now anyway. Just you hold your wheesht and I will go on with the story. Decorum and dignity and all that.

Anyway, Sandy had a direct take on life and he lived about a hundred yards from the port, so off he goes and chats up a couple of his fishermen pals, which involved an hour or so in the Ship. Inn, that is. And then, when it came to flinging-out time (the pubs closed at 2.30 in the afternoon in those days) all the three of them hied back to Hannah Street with a couple of dogs and a great big net.

The rest of the afternoon was filled with dogs barking, men swearing, not a few flying tackles on running rabbits, and a couple of hundred spectators cheering it all on, with their heads sticking over the top of the wall round the garden like Mr Chad; it was an away day for Arbroath and there wasn't much for entertainment, you know.

Toos, on account of my tender age, wouldn't let me take part in the procedures, which were basically three pissed men falling about, but it was mighty good fun to watch.

In the end, they got all the rabbits into the net – not all at once, like – and then into tattie sacks and up to Fleming the butcher (no relation) where they were exchanged for beer vouchers. That's how I know there were 92.

I think they got turned into potted haugh, well, the rabbit equivalent.

Now if you think that's a load of (rabbit) baloney, just go to Arbroath and ask some locals.

POACHING THE RIVER
ROD FLEMING
'wonderful' ...'a laugh a minute' ...'a real classic'
Read more about this cracking humorous adventure set in Scotland
ISBN: 978-0-9554535-0-2

If you liked that, why not rty one of my books about life in Scotland?

THE SPRING RUN
ROD FLEMING
More excitement than you can handle in this dramatic rom-com set in a Scottish village
ISBN: 978-0-9752612-5-9

4. In France, Everything Shuts at Twelve

A village in Burgundy, France.

One thing the guidebooks never bother to tell you about France is also one of the most important that you should know. In fact this piece of information is so important that my imparting it to you, as I am about to do, is worth the price I am eventually going to ask you for the book. So perhaps, if you've borrowed this from a friend, you should skip to the next chapter right now. (I jest.)

So what is this invaluable knowledge that no-one should travel in France without first having assimilated? Just this:

Everything Shuts At Twelve. For Two Hours. At Least.

That's it. Outside of the major metropolitan cities like Paris and Lyon, and maybe even Marseilles these days, if you ain't got whatever it is you were looking for by the time the midi rings, you can forget getting it until two o'clock at the earliest.

Believe me, you will not be in France long before you realise how much this immutable chronology affects life. All those thoughts of a nice long lie-in, a lazy, protracted breakfast, perhaps a little snoodling with your loved one and a pleasant shower afterwards followed by a quick trip into town to do the shopping…er, no. By the time you get into that town, say eleven-thirty, people are already making their ways home for lunch, the baker will have sold all of that nice bread you like, and your efforts to purchase the bare minimum, having already edited your shopping list from the thirty or so items it began with, which you intended to buy on a relaxed saunter around all those lovely artisanal shops you like the look of so much, will turn into a desperate, manic dash around the aisles of the local supermarket while the staff watch you with the regard of those who just know you're going to make them late for their break. You will be the only person in the checkout queue, dealt with frostily by the cashier, who can't close up the only till left open until you leave, and the door will be closed quickly enough to catch your heels by the manager, who will have been standing by it jangling his keys, alternately looking at his watch and you.

Think I'm kidding? Think again.

Once, while Moira and I were looking for our dream home, we had an accident. Well, I mean Calum had an accident, of the type that renders a two-year-old's lower garments fit for the bin.

In the ensuing panic, after I had screeched to a stop at the side of the road, Moira performed the emergency repair procedure – pants and nappies off, into the spare plastic bag and into the nearest poubelle; clear up the worst of the spillage with toilet paper, wipes to finish up (those of you with children know this already; those without – it awaits thee.)

When she had done, she rummaged in the mummy bag and then turned to me, eyes wide in alarm.

'Shit. I forgot the nappies.'

Indeed she had, as I quickly verified. Now anyone who has had children knows that it is sheer insanity to allow a two-year-old with a very obvious case of the Bombay (or should that be Burgundy?) Trots to sit in a car without a restraint device, and I don't mean a seat-belt, so we had to find nappies, and quickly.

'I think I saw a supermarket on the way into that last town,' said Moira, hopefully, so we wrapped Calum in our only remaining towel, strapped ourselves in and put pedal to metal, as they say. It was only then that I looked at the clock.

11.55.

Despite ripping through the quaint medieval town at a speed that I can only apologise for, slamming to a halt two metres outside the door of said supermarket in a prodigious cloud of dust and leaping out of the car like those posers in The Professionals, we were met with the face of doom, as the grim-faced manageress on the other side of the door turned her key with finality and shook her head. She began to turn away and I banged on the glass…..

'No,' I cried, and summoned up the best of my then limited French, 'Cas d'urgence!'

But this made no impression on the battle-axe, who shook her head again, pointed to her watch and mouthed 'Quattors heures et demi.'

Whatever my emergency was, it would have to wait another 150 minutes. Aghast as she began to turn away again, and now completely at a loss for words, I was once again reminded of the sheer brilliance of my wife in situations like this. Knowing that she could not hope to plead her case in French, she had slipped over to the car, unstrapped Calum, and now appeared with him in her arms; when she knew she had the dame's attention, she lowered the towel wrapped around him to show the lad's bare bottom, and just said one of the few French words she knew by heart, because she needed it so often. 'Couches!'

It was, of course, the master-stroke, an ace of trumps. No person born French with double-X chromosomes can resist a child, and whatever she might have thought of his clearly irresponsible Anglais parents, a child in need of nappies was a greater imperative; lunch would be delayed today. The battle-axe turned the key and allowed us in. She closed and locked the door, led us to the nappies section (no stopping for other fripperies) and then whisked us back to the checkout with great efficiency. She was really very sweet, if truth be told, and not a battle-axe at all, now that she was on our side. She even gave Calum a lollipop and smiled as she locked up after us.

Arnay le Duc, Burgundy.

That, however, is the only time I can remember the immutable rule being bent, and it was clearly an exceptional case.

This, incidentally, is why, again outside the major cities, commuting to work just does not happen in France, and that in turn, is one reason why there are so many houses for sale silly cheap in the countryside. It is imperative that one be able to get home for a civilised lunch, and no self-respecting French person would ever buy a house that did not permit this. Since the most that can reasonably be commuted, allowing for the necessary ninety-minute repast, even the way the French drive (and it pays not to get in their way at lunchtime) in a two-hour lunch break, is around twenty kilometres, or roughly twelve miles, there you have it; any house outside this distance of a reasonably-sized town is worth sweeties.

Arnay le Duc, Burgundy.

French Onion Soup!

'Hilarious'...'brilliant'...'better than Mayle'

Once there was a Scotsman who thought it would be a great idea to take his family to live in an ancient French country house...read all about it

ISBN: 978-0-9565007-3-1

6. Gendarmes, Police and Faulty Speedos

The kind of road the Gendarmes like.to hide on.

My friend Antoine the potter had a little incident with the Gendarmes from Bligny not long ago. Now before I begin this tale, I feel I should put to rest a belief that has become, apparently (according to my children,) current in the UK in the last few years.

This is that the Gendarmes in France are not real police. Well, they are, and this is a classic bit of Anglo-Saxon, er, confusion. I believe it has even been aired on Stephen Fry's television show; not that that would make it any more the truth.

So let me explain. Gendarmes are Police, right?

Firstly, the Gendarmes are indeed police, as understood by any Anglo-Saxon. The term literally means 'men at arms' and the Gendarmes are descended from the peacekeeping forces that first appeared in the Middle Ages, when local lords and later, town councils, would hire the biggest, toughest bruisers they could find and set them to breaking the heads of troublemakers, and then throwing them in the stocks.

I suggest you exercise caution before expressing any quaint notion that they might not be 'real' policemen. They have a long and proud history, tend to resent having it belittled, and a posh accent cuts no mustard here. Just saying.

I think the situation is complicated for Anglo-Saxons, well, the

English anyway, because although the Gendarmes are indeed The Law, there are Police police too. The chief differences are that the Gendarmes fall under the authority of the Ministry of Defence and the Police the under that of the Ministry of the Interior. Perhaps more useful to know is that while both are armed, the Police police can only shoot you if you attack them with lethal force, while the Gendarmes can legally shoot you if you should try to escape. That might one day be useful knowledge, so remember it.

British people are not used to this level of confusion, though the septic tanks might be. So let us list them in order of …..how does one express mechancité in English? Meanness, perhaps. Well, the least virulent are the Police Municipal. To a Brit, these are a bit like Traffic Wardens on steroids. They often drive around towns on Mobylettes or in little vans, and don't normally carry heavy ordnance. They can still hand out tickets and on-the-spot fines, though, and otherwise thoroughly ruin your day, if they want to.

Then there are the aforementioned Gendarmes, who are your common-or-garden, one-size-fits-all, regular Plod. They wear blue uniforms and carry automatic pistols. Their cars are blue, and have the word 'Gendarmes' on the side. Every town has its Gendarmerie, and that is where you go to file complaints, do any police-style stuff, and appear when you have been naughty. They are the primary enforcers of the law and investigators of crime. And they are as intolerant of transgressors as plod anywhere. Treat them with respect.

In major cities, they have do indeed have Police who call themselves Police. Possibly, if you never strayed outside central Paris, you would never see a Gendarme. But the city Police are really just the same as the Gendarmes, the uniformed ones anyway, with a fancy title. And outside of major cities, in the smaller cities, towns and countryside of France, the Constabulary are called Gendarmes and that is that. Says so right here in my trusty Collins Robert.

Going up a level, to the downright nasty, we come to the Police National. These were formed from the old CRS, or Compagnie Republicain de Securité, or, in other words, the riot police. These lads got a worldwide reputation for being black-enamelled bastards in 1968, when they were deployed to tear-gas and baton-charge the rioting French students during the Siege of the Sorbonne. They made the mistake of not nobbling the Media first. (If you are too young to remember this, kindly keep it to yourself.)

Anyway they went on being the CRS for a while after that, and then one day they became the Police National. Doubtless this was a PR gimmick, or maybe their intended victims were too smart to do anything illegal while they were around. But despite the name-change, they remain as tough, brutal and merciless as ever.

France is by no means a federal state; on the contrary, it is very much centralised, but the various brigades of Gendarmerie are responsible to local bodies, principally the Prefecture of the Departement in which they are active. The Police Nationale are organised nationally and are thus able to respond to issues that cross Departementale boundaries. These guys drive jam sandwiches rather than the discreet blue of the regular Gendarmes, and they also carry machine-guns. Do not mess with them.

On the roads, you will often see what look very much like police, with blue vehicles like the Gendarmes, but with Douane written on the side. These are actually Customs. They hang around the parking areas at the ferry terminals, and at the 'aires' or service stations on the motorways. They seem to really like machine-guns and very big dogs.

France is a Schengen country, which means that it has open borders; no Customs controls, unlike in England, where there is always some officious little shit with the title 'Customs' asking questions he (or she) has no business knowing the answer to, well, not in a free country anyway.

The Douaniers are not out to arrest you, beat the holy crap out of you or otherwise ruin your day, they just want your money, and the way to get them to take it is to not have the appropriate papers for whatever it is that you might have in your vehicle, also with you. Brits, of course, are brought up to leave their documents at home, as a security measure.

The opposite is true in France. You are expected to carry all the relevant documents, all the time. The sensible thing to do is to keep your receipts for everything you ever buy, your insurance, MoT, driving licence, dog licence, whatever, in a nice big bundle and stuff all of it in the glove box of your car.

That way there is a good chance you might actually have the receipt showing that the gallons of wine causing your car to ride on its bump-stops were bought legally, and if you don't, a slightly less good chance that the Douanier will give up halfway through the pile of confetti and wave you along.

By the way, the oft-quoted 'limit' of ninety litres for the amount of wine that a UK citizen can buy in France and bring home to guzzle, is a complete red herring. It is only a 'guide' thought up by those shits, sorry, nice people at the UK Customs. It is not in any way enforceable in law, and you can bring back as much cheap (or otherwise) glug as you like. The European Court has ruled on this. Same applies to cigarettes, if you have the evil habit. They have to actually prove that you intend to sell the stuff once you get back…..and you wouldn't do a thing like, would you? Oh, about Antoine's speedo

Anyway, to get back to Antoine and the Gendarmes. He told me one day that he'd just been stopped at the crossroads at Pont d'Ouche – a notorious plod hideout – for doing 120kph in a 90 zone. The Gendarme, as usual in these cases all stiff and haughty like, explained to him that he had been driving 30kph over the speed limit, and that the punishment for this was eighty Euros and a point off his licence. Antoine, after a moment's thought, politely countered that his speedo had been saying 90, and he had not gone past this. The Gendarme, sniffily, looked inside the car and shook his head.

'Your speedo is stuck at 90,' he pointed out. 'No wonder you didn't know you were over the limit. That's another forty Euros for the defective speedometer.'

Now this is where the logical mind of the Frenchman can be seen to best advantage. 'Ah,' says our potter, 'I see. But if I didn't know I was speeding, I couldn't have known I was going over the limit, as you say, sir. So how can you charge me for breaking it?'

At this the Gendarme, apparently, frowned, sucked a tooth, and went to discuss matters with his colleague. After a few minutes he returned, his mien grave. 'All right,' quoth he, 'You can either have the speeding fine or the defective speedo. Which is it to be?'

Antoine thought about this for about for seconds, and then made sure he had the details correct.

'It's eighty Euros and a point off the licence for the speeding, yes?'

The Gendarme agreed.

'And forty and no endorsement for the speedo?' Once again, the officer affirmed.

'Umm, okay, well, I'll take the speedo, thanks,' said Antoine, absolutely convinced there must be a catch. But there wasn't. The nice Gendarme (who wasn't such a bad lad after all, it seemed,) duly wrote out the faulty speedo ticket, and relieved Antoine of forty Euros, in cash.

'Get it fixed,' he said to Antoine, before saluting and waving him off.

I swallowed my beer slowly as I percolated this. 'That's amazing,' I said. 'In the UK they'd have hit you for the speedo, the speeding, and taken your car apart to find out whatever else they could fine you for as well.' I shook my head and cast my eye over his ageing SAAB, which was parked across the road. I could see a half-dozen vehicle faults without even standing up.

'Oh, bah non,' said Antoine. 'That would not have been reasonable.' He shrugged.

'But you've fixed the speedo?'

'No. Why? I already paid the fine.' Antoine shrugged again and swigged his beer. 'I'll do it for the next Controle Technique.' He chuckled. 'It was a damn good job he let me off with the speeding though. I only had forty with me and it's a long walk back from there. Plus they'd have impounded the damn car and I'd have had to pay to get it out again.'

Fortune favours the bold, even in France, it seems.

Croutons and Cheese!
Rod Fleming
Continuing the hilarious, madcap adventures of a family 'Lost in France'.
ISBN: 978-0-9572612-4-2

7. The Church of Hedonism

Funeral in Laoag, Philippines.

I'm going to become a Hedonist. No really, I am. Seriously. I am going to join the Church of Hedonism. Yup. Before this happens to me.

Of course, no such church actually exists and most religions seem to be mainly concerned with stopping people having fun. But anyway. If there isn't one, I think it's time we started one.

I am rapidly approaching that watershed in life, the dawn of my seventh decade. I don't have that much time to waste any more. A quick demographic of my parents' families suggests that if I remain a non-smoker, keep the drink to a moderate level and eat reasonably healthy food, I have maybe another fifteen years of active life and another five or so of winding down, before parting the mortal coil and becoming one with the Earth again.

That is not an awful lot of time. And I am beginning to resent every moment of it that is not spent, basically, having fun.

I don't have the option to defer the fun any more, like I once did. I can't look into a long, serene future when, sometime, I might be able to stop pissing myself off with other people's demands and move to a life of pleasure. And my marriage, for many reasons, broke up some years ago, so the idea of a serene old age rocking our mutual armchairs in front of the fire and making cups of tea, has vanished. I regret that but it is water under the old bridge.

My kids are old enough to look after themselves. When I was sixteen I left home and got a job. I'm not suggesting that my kids should do this, indeed I support them in their desires to study and live lives of their own. I'm not asking them to look after me in my old age. But much as I dearly love them, my material responsibility towards them will be drastically reduced when the last gets to be sixteen and can make the same choices I did. That will happen in a couple of months.

I've had to ask myself some searching questions. I've not always been a 'good' man, by the lights of many. But actually, anything I did that left anyone else a bit bruised was just business. My priority was my family and the home.

I don't have that any more. I'm not bitter; I have lovely kids, and I just spent an incredible ten days with my daughter. I plan to do a lot more of that. But I ask myself, would I enter into another commitment, now, that might take years to resolve, years I don't have? Would I enter into a relationship with someone who had or wanted to have children? The answer is that I'd be nuts to do so. Nuts. I have paid my genetic debt; my alleles are out there to replicate.

I certainly don't feel any loyalty towards a nation, either. I am proud to be Scottish, and very supportive of my country's culture, but I wouldn't lay down my life for it. For my children, yes, without question; but neither for a geographical nor a political entity, would I endanger myself, either now or in the past. It's as ridiculous a concept as I can imagine.

I don't feel I need to 'pay back' to my nation or culture. I didn't choose to be born Scottish, though I consider myself lucky to have been, and I owe it nothing other than my deep affection – and as for the absurd 'British' State, well, frankly, the sooner that's consigned to the dustbin of history, the better.

I've had a full life, and a lot of fun, many good times. If I were to die tomorrow, or be told that I had some hideous disease that would kill me soon, then I wouldn't enjoy the suffering, but I wouldn't feel bitter either. My life account is well in credit, and I would leave behind four wonderful people as my legacy. No. I couldn't complain. I have seen and experienced much that most people have never even glimpsed.

That, however, is no reason to rush my life to a conclusion. And if I am to be alive, I want to be enjoying it. My moral and pastoral responsibilities towards my children I will never deny or renege on. But other than those, and they are more a pleasure than a burden anyway, I am free.

Since realising this, more and more I see how much my previous life was conditioned by other people's demands. Many of these, like my children, I accepted fully and freely and without prejudice or regret, twenty-four years ago when I decided that yes I did want a family. Others were obligations I took on as a part of that, too. But a great many were just things other people expected me to do, because 'society' demanded it. Most of these were completely spurious and unhelpful, although I didn't see that at the time. But now, my only responsibilities are to myself, and to getting as much out of life as I can in the time that is left to me.

So what has all this got to do with the Church of Hedonism? Well I do think a moral code is important. Are we, without the control of official religion, completely without principles? Fortunately, as an atheist, and understanding Evolution, I know that our moral codes are innate, and that religions have simply hijacked these for the purpose of social control.

I remember, when I was very young, reading all I could about the esoteric religions of the East, indeed anything I could get my hands on, as I explored the mysteries of spirituality. I came across a phrase that I thought was the most apt statement of morality I had ever seen: Do as you will, as long as you harm no other.

It seemed then and now to be a very powerful, simple, and valuable code. Looking back on my life so far, the things I regret doing most, are the things that contravened it. Yet when I first came across it, this code – a perfect moral statement – was condemned, for reasons that I could never understand, and still don't, other than that it demands that we all be our own moral guides, our own consciences. Which, of course, the religious demagogues do not want us to do; they want to control us and to that end, prescribe codes which fit their own purposes, and pronounce upon the actions of others from on high.

I've not always lived up to that simple and honest code and I apologise. Looking forward, I would like to live more closely by it. And it really doesn't stop us having fun.

Sex and Gender

1. Transgender - Is there really an increase?

Phuket, Thailand. Midnight: Bangla Road is packed with tourists. They're mostly Westerners and Russians, but many Asians and a smattering of Indians. There seems a disproportionate number of unattached males. The music is very loud, and throbbing.

Outside the bars, on elevated stages, Thai girls are dancing provocatively. They're tall, fantastically beautiful, and seductive. They look, and move, like supermodels, but with better bodies. Then you realise: there are other Thai women here too, but they're short, cute and pretty, not at all statuesque or magnificent. Alongside Thailand's famous transwomen, they're all but invisible, like candles next to a searchlight. It's easy to see who has the attention of the gathered men.

On stage, one girl rolls her dress down to her hips so that her naked breasts and torso – she sports a delicate dragon tattoo on her back – are shown off, as she wriggles to the thrumming techno. Her body is as flawless as a Greek goddess' and her dance mesmerising as a Siren's: you just can't help but watch and smile at her exquisite insouciance. Her own grin is wide and genuine: she is no miserable sex-slave; this girl loves performing and is basking in the rapt attention of her audience.

Most of the girls here have already had Genital Reconstruction Surgery; they are as proud of their bodies as teenagers with a new car, and as enthusiastic about displaying them. Everywhere, the dancing kathoey engage the watching men; they call out to them, beckon with their hands, seduce with a flick of their luxuriant hair or a flash of dark eyes. Breasts, buttocks and even more are flaunted, always with an outrageous gesture of false modesty: bashful these girls are not.

Fifty and hundred-baht notes are flying onto the stages like confetti, and the more explicit the dancer the more she earns. A girl slips onto an empty bar stool beside a middle-aged Western man. As she does so she daintily rucks her dress up round her waist. Like many of the girls, and discovering this has not required guesswork, she's wearing no knickers. A moment later the man turns, smiles at her, looks down, and smiles even more. Business is about to be done.

This is the popular view of kathoey, as trans women are known in Thailand. As so often the case, however, this view is distorted, for the coyote dancers and bar girls are only a small fraction of the total. Nor are they by any means dominant even here, for there are far more natal women selling sex and titillation. Pattaya, for example, has an estimated 10,000 sex workers, of whom only 10% or so are kathoey.

Prostitution has very little stigma in Thailand, and a successful one can make £3000 or more a month, much more than a teacher or an office worker. Although prostitution is illegal, it is an entrenched part of Thai culture, and the main market is indigenous. Recent studies suggest that 75% or more of Thai men employ prostitutes. Visits are given as birthday presents, business sweeteners, even by wives to their husbands when they themselves are pregnant. The business is not the result of 'sex tourism', although that represents a lucrative addition to it.

Thai trans women do not become so in order to work in the sex trade. However, some are attracted to the job, partly because, like all Thais, they are expected to help support their families, partly because their hormones, breast implants and other surgery are expensive, and partly because of the pleasure they get from affirmation: one proof that they are beautiful women is that men will pay to be with them.

However, far greater numbers of trans women work in offices, banks, shops, salons, restaurants. They are models, showgirls, actresses, entertainers, even air-hostesses. Many are teachers; I know of one who is the 'headman' of her village. Others run businesses of all sorts, some with turnovers running into the tens of millions – of dollars, not baht.

Azumi. Pic Rod Flemin

Many have degree-level education or higher.

Though the numbers may appear high, Thailand is not a transgender paradise.

Discrimination is widespread, and families may reject them, unless they can send money home. Although proposed changes to the Constitution that might help have been reported in the Media, at present it remains impossible for a Thai to legally change gender. Since the production of an identity card is mandatory in many everyday transactions, having the wrong gender markers causes much distress and actual hardship to trans people. Many other petty and unnecessary obstacles confront them and complicate their lives.

However, any kathoey will say the same: 'I was born this way.' It is not a matter of choice. Often they began dressing as girls long before puberty, usually in secret, but not always.

Many Thai schools now have three toilets: male, female and kathoey. There is even a kathoey university. Being kathoey is no more a lifestyle decision than being transgender anywhere else: they just live in a society where they will, at least, not be ostracised, beaten or even killed for openly being what they are.

There remains some debate about why transgender occurs, despite the fact that it has a recorded history spanning some 6000 years, to the Eanna Temple of Inanna in Uruk in Sumer. In Rome, amongst the devotees of the Phrygian goddess Cybele, who was imported after the Punic Wars, ecstatic young trans girls called 'galli' would ritually self-castrate and then enter the service of the goddess.

This practice is maintained, today, by the transgender hijra of India and Pakistan. There is even evidence of the phenomenon in Palaeolithic burials. Whatever the cause, transgender has long been part of human culture.

A genetic cause would explain, in a way that no other hypothesis can, why both homosexual behaviour and transgender identities appear to be similarly prevalent in all human populations, at about the same rate, throughout history.

However, the suggestion that either homosexuality or transgender might have this cause has long been objected to by social conservatives who argue that any non-hetero sexual behaviour or transgender identity must be a reproductive cul-de-sac because it does not lead directly to reproductive sex.

This completely ignores the inconvenient fact that same-sex behaviours have been observed in over 400 different species of other animals. These observations voided most of the social conservatives' arguments but were unexplained. This was finally resolved in 2014 when researchers at the University of Portsmouth, led by Dr Diana Fleischman, established that same-sex bonding had indeed proved to be an evolutionary asset.

The team found that sex was not exclusively, in the populations studied, used for reproduction, but instead for a gamut of other functions that included reinforcing the bonds that held the group together and assisting the survival of the young. These helped the survival of the whole group, which in humans and the other species observed, is made up of closely-related individuals. Better group survival confers an advantage for the individuals within the group and explains why these phenomena may have a genetic cause. The 'evolutionary cul-de-sac' argument was finally, definitively, torpedoed.

Complex or simple though the underlying stimulus may be, transgender is very easy to treat. You give the patient the gender and body she or he needs, and that's it. Many trans folk don't even require sex reassignment, just hormones and cosmetic work.

So why is it often so hard for them to get help from their doctors that they self-medicate with drugs bought on the Internet? There lies the rub: the difficulty is not in making life better for the individuals, but in accepting them at all.

What all trans people want is to be treated with respect as the gender they feel themselves to be. Thailand's Buddhist culture provides that. Kathoey are thought to have been adulterers in a previous life. Since reincarnation happens to everyone, and treating kathoey unfairly might impact on one's own status in the next life, people are usually polite to them. No one wants to come back as a slug, after all. And in a culture that believes in an infinite number of reincarnations, everyone has both once been, and will be, themselves transgender. Kathoey are living reminders that karma can be tough.

Transgender challenges conventional notions of sexuality. The popularity of transgender pornography on the Internet proves that many men are attracted to trans women; but at the same time, society still insists that a man who has sex with someone born male has thrown away all his status. He's gay, that's it, end of: you know how it is…..sleep with one little ladyboy…he'll never be able to show his face down the pub or the golf-club again; now he's 'playing for the other team'.

Angel.

So men are on the horns of a dilemma, attracted to trans women, yet tortured by the horrible angst that says penis, past or present, means they are other men, and for a man to desire sex with one is the greatest taboo of the patriarchal hegemony.

This dilemma, often exacerbated by alcohol, can be lethal for trans women. Men, who've been pawing them all night, suddenly realise what they're doing and can't handle it; in order to redress the offence to their masculine status, they beat the girl up, or worse.

Sometimes, men go further, have sexual relations with a trans woman, and only turn violent when they realise they are about to be discovered by their peers. They may attack the woman to prove how 'manly' they really are: as the subsequent trial proved, this is why and how Gwen Araujo died the horrible death she did. But Gwen's tragedy is not unique or even unusual; trans women die at the hands of male attackers with shocking frequency, as we see only this week.

Zeta and friend.

As well as this, 'gender-bending' upsets how we relate to others. We are conditioned to see gender as a male/female binary. When someone appears to be one thing but is, or might once have been, another, or is in between, we become confused. It's as if they're trying to trick us; but they're not, they're just being who they are. None of this, however, is the fault of trans people: it's our own social conditioning that's to blame. Indeed, they are the victims of great injustice; yet so few of us are prepared to recognise that.

Brandon Teena, Gwen Araujo and more recently Filipina Jennifer Laude, Mercedes Williamson and many others were not alone in having their young lives ended by vicious, intolerant men. In Brazil, over a hundred trans women were murdered in 2012, and beatings and killings take place everywhere, all the time. Nearly all the victims were in their teens or early twenties, who had a right to be allowed to live out their lives– a right that society did nothing to defend.

This year, a shocking uptick in killings of trans women in the USA is causing great concern; it is almost as if the more progress trans people make towards acceptance, the more determined the transphobic extremists are to silence them.

While the killers and beaters themselves are most culpable, every one of us, in not speaking out and acting against the transphobia that spurs them on, is accessory both before and after the fact. Our sin may be of omission, but this blood is still on our hands.

The media often carries articles mocking prominent men for dalliances with trans women. Mainstream 'entertainment' has a nasty track record of insulting trans people for a cheap laugh. Most distressingly, in the comments sections of news reports on the murders of trans people, for example Jennifer Laude, a horrible undercurrent of hate is prevalent. Trans people, it says, are dishonest and trying to trick others, and their deaths are their own fault. This is a blatant victim-blaming that would not be tolerated under any other circumstances.

Any time the subject of transgender comes up, people express distaste or worse, not to mention the overt disapproval of a grim hegemony of social conservatives from pulpit to politics.

All of this leads directly to transphobic violence by a technique called 'othering'. Trans people are not like us, it says, and so it's all right to mock, slander or beat them. This intimidates not only trans people, but the rest of us too. Any man, or woman, who dares to defend them also risks mockery, abuse and violence. The inference is obvious, and ever the threat of cowards and bullies: stand up for those we despise and we will turn on you next.

Attitudes towards homosexuality have come a long way, over the last thirty years, in Western Europe, although it would be foolish to suggest that all prejudice has been eradicated. Governments have had to legalise 'same-sex' marriage and put in place laws against discrimination against gays in the workplace and elsewhere. However we must not forget that in large parts of the world, atrocious levels of discrimination and violence, often sanctioned by church and state, are levelled at people solely for the crime of loving each other.

This better treatment of gays within more enlightened cultures has not led to an explosion in numbers. Alfred Kinsey, sixty years ago, long before the liberalisation of anti-gay legislation, found that 8% of American men had been 'exclusively homosexual for at least three years', and research published in 1995 found a range between 6-10%. At least nine other peer-reviewed studies concur.

Removing the judicial sanctions did not lead to a substantial increase in actual prevalence, because there is a base rate, which appears constant. All that changes is how open people are about their orientation.

There is a big difference between homosexual individuals, of either gender, and transgenders; it is far easier for gay men and women to blend in. This is not because trans people are necessarily easy to spot, but because by definition, their lives must change. The families of many gay people might never know, but it's hard to keep a gender transition so well hidden.

Because of this, trans people may either attempt to hide or suppress their natures, or break all ties with their pasts and disappear,

Lovi at Manila Harbour.

to live in so-called 'deep stealth'. If they feel rejected or discriminated against, they are more likely to do so. This causes problems with estimating their numbers, and allowed some to suggest the prevalence was very low.

The American Psychiatric Association (APA), on the basis of a small study in Germany in the 1960s, for decades insisted that the prevalence for male to female transgender was around 1:30,000, and this figure was widely accepted. Other groups in the USA have slightly higher estimates;

all are at least 1% but none more than 5%.

In Thailand, the majority of trans women do not seek SRS; the sensual sirens of Bangla Road represent only a small fraction of the total. Many have no choice, since the surgery is so expensive. Others simply do not feel that they need to go further.

There are around twenty Thai clinics offering SRS procedures, which can be found through a web search. Those that publish figures suggest they carry out 150 to 200 surgeries per annum each, but perhaps half of these are on non-Thais. That would suggest that over the last twenty years, around 40,000 of the Thai transgender population have had the surgery. Although it is immensely difficult to find accurate figures, most estimates suggest that 1-2% of the Thai adult male population is transgender.

Ladyboys in Malolos

The truth is all over Thailand; far from being vanishingly small, the numbers of trans people are high enough to be obvious, when they feel secure enough to be themselves.

So, if we treat trans people better, we should expect to see more. But, like gay men and women, they won't over-run the place. The statistical estimates and the evidence from Thailand above strongly suggest that transgender prevalence will stabilise around 1-2%, given similar social tolerance. That's far less than some, more visible minorities.

Other than seeing slightly larger numbers of tall, glamorous women and small, fine-boned men, nothing will change; the sky will not fall on us for treating other people with decency and compassion. Speaking out against transphobia whenever and wherever it arises will cost us absolutely nothing more than the loss of some absurd prejudices, and perhaps a fair-weather friend or two. Shining the light of public disapproval into the dark places where transphobic hatred festers would do our souls good, too. We could take credit for protecting vulnerable people, and we wouldn't have to go to war or drop bombs on anyone to do it. We'd just have to call time on the transphobic bullies, as we have already begun to do on racists and homophobes.

We should applaud the good things that trans people bring, in forcing us to be more accepting of difference, in showing that personal resolution and fortitude are keys that can open any door, in the undemanding tolerance, resilience and good humour in the face of adversity that so many exhibit themselves, and in having the courage to walk a difficult and lonely path.

The Warm Pink Jelly Express Train
ROD FLEMING

```
Sex.Sleaze.Trannies.Passion.Love against love itself.
     A man caught between passion and reason,
   a woman caught  between herself and the world.
```

ISBN: 978-0-9565007-2-4

2. The thought or image of oneself

Few clinical definitions, established by obscure researchers in obscure institutions, referring to an obscure subject, can have caused more brouhaha than Ray Blanchard's definition of autogynephilia as 'a man's paraphilic propensity to be sexually aroused at the thought or image of himself as a woman.'

But what does it actually mean?

> 'Paraphilia is any intense and persistent sexual interest other than sexual interest in genital stimulation or preparatory fondling with phenotypically normal, physically mature, consenting human partners; if a paraphilia causes distress or impairment to the individual or if its satisfaction entails personal harm (or the risk of such harm) to others, it is considered a paraphilic disorder.' Guy E Brannon, MD

A paraphilia is 'sexual interest other than sexual interest in genital stimulation or preparatory fondling with phenotypically normal….. partners.' Ahm…..What the fuck does that mean?

What is 'phenotypically normal' anyway? According to the trusty Oxford, the only dictionary I use:

Phenotype: noun. Biology. The set of observable characteristics of an individual resulting from the interaction of its genotype with the environment.

(In this case 'individual' means singular organism and 'environment' is meant to indicate the hard, physical one, not the social one.)

Rly? I went to school with a girl who had six toes. She was pretty cute. I am sure she fell in love, got married, had kids and in doing so, had a whole heap of sex with one or more men. Were they paraphilic because she was 'phenotypically abnormal'?

Branner either means something else or he has a logic problem. Suppose I have sex with a woman dressed as a man or a boy might. Say my girlfriend. She likes to slob around the house in an old t-shirt and a pair of training pants 'cause it's comfy. If I get the hots and tell her 'On the bed, honey, now', is that paraphilic? I is confused.

Clothes are not a part of a biological phenotype. Gender is not a part of a biological phenotype. So sex with someone conforming to gender norms not consistent with social expectations according to their birth genitalia, is that a paraphilia, Doc?

Of course it's bloody not. It's just sex.

Now the good doctor goes on: 'physically mature…partners'. Oh yes, so all those teenage pregnancies are a result of paraphilias. Nothing to do with teenage boys being randy little fuckers. Got it.

'Consenting partners.' OK that I buy. Preparatory fondling?

Eh? I like it when she sucks my balls. Is that 'preparatory fondling'? What about mutual masturbation that does not lead to coitus? That's a paraphilia? Who knew? What about I tickle her feet, she likes that – fetish?

Give us all a break and say what you mean: 'missionary sex only'.

Only a sexually fucked-up, Western person could come up with that. This definition of what is non-paraphilic sex would please the Pope.

Paraphilic disorders.

The American Psychiatric Association's Diagnostic and Statistical Manual of Mental Disorders, Fifth Edition (DSM-5), lists the following specific paraphilic disorders:

Voyeuristic disorder

Exhibitionistic disorder (including type I, the inhibited flaccid exposer, and type II, the sociopathic exposer who may have a history of other conduct)

Frotteuristic disorder

Sexual masochism disorder

Sexual sadism disorder

Pedophilic disorder

Fetishistic disorder

Transvestic disorder

(this is the current version.)

Yahoo. One is curious as to how dressing in clothes not conforming to social expectations based on your birth sex causes 'distress or impairment to the individual or personal harm (or the risk of such harm) to others'.

Getting twanged in the testicles by knicker-elastic, perhaps? Smacking someone in the eye when your bra pings loose?

I am reminded of when I took my ex, a lovely girl, zip-lining in Palawan. Basically this meant getting strapped into a parachute harness and then flying through the jungle. Shouting 'AAAAAIIIIEEEEEIIIIAAA' was optional.

Anyway, after we got back on terra firma and were heading for lunch, I was aware that my gorgeous companion was limping and leaning on my shoulder heavily.

'What on earth is wrong?' I asked her.

'Oh, my *balls*,' quoth my amour. It seems the harness was not well adapted to a tucked transwoman.

That sort of 'risk of harm'? Doctor?

Other paraphilias.

The DSM-V goes on to say:
'Other paraphilias, almost any of which could develop into a paraphilic disorder in certain circumstances, include (but are not limited to) the following:

- Telephone scatologia
- Necrophilia
- Partialism
- Zoophilia
- Coprophilia
- Klismaphilia
- Urophilia
- Autogynephilia
- Asphyxiophilia or hypoxyphilia
- Video voyeurism
- Infantophilia (a newer subcategory of paedophilia)

I'm having trouble not laughing here. Look, a significant proportion – possibly a majority – of Western autogynephiles are unqualified dickheads. There's no doubt that there are few classes of people more likely to be a complete pain in the neck, especially the late-transitioning gynephilic ones.

(Oh, and those guys who demonstrably are guys, with their nicely trimmed beards and business suits, but who 'identify' as women. Clever scheme to weasel your way into women's private spaces and ultimately their pants.)

But, returning to actual transwomen, is being attracted to the 'thought or image' of yourself as a woman really the same as getting off by shitting on a telephone (Telephone scatologia)? Or fantasising about sex with dead people? Eating shit? Suffocating or being suffocated? Well, I get that you might be a lil bit pissed off. I really do. I mean, come on.

And this could 'develop into a…disorder'. LIKE WHAT??!! Actually becoming a transwoman? Holy fuck the sky will fall on our heads, we can't have that!

Confusion.

Thankfully, Blanchard was aware that some confusion might arise from his concept of autogynephilia, which it clearly has, as you can see. So he explained:

> 'Autogynephilia denotes the propensity to be sexually aroused by the thought or image of oneself as female. The actual occurrence and extent will vary with time and circumstance. An autogynephile does not necessarily become sexually aroused every time he pictures himself as a female or engages in feminine behavior, any more than a heterosexual man automatically gets an erection whenever he sees an attractive woman. Thus, the concept of autogynephilia – like that of heterosexuality, homosexuality… refers to a potential for sexual excitation.' Blanchard 1991

Let's deconstruct all this, shall we? It's a propensity. A potential. OK. So, it only *might* happen. It's a possibility with some added probability. Somewhat more than an outside chance, somewhat less than a likelihood.

So let's think. Autogynephilia, as a sexualised reward-based concept, must be based in sexuality. And we are talking about people born male here, so it's male sexuality.

So far so good. I am male, and pretty sexually motivated. I like wearing suits and I think I look pretty fucking hot in an Italian three-piece, you know? Nothing makes a man look better than a good suit, except maybe full Highland. Does that make me want to crack one off when I look at myself in the mirror? No. Does it make me think, 'Hey, you sexy beast?' Well, yes, actually.

If I happen to meet a woman while looking like that and it becomes obvious that she's having difficulty focussing on anything other than what she's sitting on, is that a nice wee reward for me? YES! Yes of course it is. It's a sexualised reward, not a sexual reward. All men are attracted to the thought or image of themselves – it's just that for most of us, that image is a man.

The non-sexual sexualised reward is mental gratification, afforded by my male sex drive, that does not actually involve physical sex. Men do this ALL the time – and if they tell you different, they're lying. And we re-live the experience. I remember all the times a woman went dewy-eyed on me. I like remembering that. It feels good. It feels sexy. And ALL MEN DO THIS. That is why they are forever talking about the women they have had. It's partly status, partly a reliving of the sexual hit.

An autogynephilic transwoman has a MALE SEX DRIVE. She's doing exactly what I do. Precisely. She gets her gladrags on, whacks on the warpaint, looks at herself in the mirror and thinks 'Baaaaabe!'

It's just that her idealised sexy image of herself is AS A WOMAN while mine is of myself AS A MAN.

Which tells us that most men are – guess what? Autoandrophilic. They are rewarded by the thought or image of themselves as sexually active, powerful MEN.

Why Moser fucked up.

This is why Moser fucked up, by the way. Women may have an equivalent system, but it is unlikely to be exactly the same, since women have female sex drive.

The neurological studies show no evidence for shifted brain morphology in AGP transsexuals (while they do in HSTS). Trying to show autogynephilia in women misses the point.

Autogynephilia is not a function of female sex drive (though there may be equivalents) but of male sex drive. It is a variation on the propensity to be aroused at the thought or image of themselves, which all men show to a greater or lesser extent, but focussed on themselves as *women* rather than as men.

(By the way, if you want to see autogynephilia in serious action, assuming you are a man, try fucking a transwoman in front of a mirror. Trust me. Well, not one of the deranged homophobic Western Autogynephile profile. But any Asian who's up for it.)

So lets go back to Blanchard:

'An autogynephile does not necessarily become sexually aroused every time he pictures himself as a female or engages in feminine behavior any more than a heterosexual man automatically gets an erection whenever he sees an attractive woman.'

Check. I do not have a permanent erection from wearing, or imagining myself wearing, a nice suit and shoes. An AGP transwoman dressed in a miniskirt does not have a raging hard-on all the time.

'The concept of autogynephilia – refers to a potential for sexual excitation.'

Check also. Transwomen in Asia, who live all their lives as women, do not constantly untangle their engorgements, any more than I do while nicely dressed. Indeed, because of the hormones they take, they may well experience less physical arousal than a man does; but the psychological arousal, the 'feeling good about oneself as a sexual being'? They do. Just like everyone else.

Being autogynephilic is not the problem.

Both HSTS and AGP transwomen of the Asian profile (not the Western profile in Asia) are well-adjusted, generally happy, fulfilled people. Being autogynephilic doesn't make you an Andrea James. Growing up as a hostile, aggressive, thoroughly unpleasant man, will make you a hostile, aggressive, thoroughly unpleasant transwoman, if you transition.

You can't 'learn to be a woman' after 30 years as a man. Old dogs do not learn new tricks.

Asian transwomen, the Asian profiles anyway, don't do that. They learn to accept themselves and how to be happy and satisfied as transwomen, while they are still young enough for these lessons to stick.

The problems in the West are caused by Western, particularly USican culture, which ferociously denies sexuality as a motivation for anything. In the USA, baby boys' genitals are routinely surgically mutilated to prevent them fully enjoying sex, ever. US Government policy to reduce unwanted teenage pregnancy is 'preach abstinence'. Fathers ritually 'marry' their daughters to 'ensure' their sexual 'purity' without thinking that this is beyond creepy.

USican culture derives this nasty and wholly counter-productive attitude towards sex from the profoundly disturbed Anglo-Saxon culture it is based on.

Add to this rabid religious conservatism and a failed education system. Then, to put the icing on the cake, adopt the homophobic attitudes of religionards and make them social norms.

Make it so that anyone showing any sign of gender non-conformity will lose all their social status. Consider them a disgrace to their families and encourage those families to eject them from their homes. Then make sure they are beaten regularly if not killed.

I give you this, gleaned from LisaT on Reddit:

> 'As a late transitioner myself I don't believe there is such a thing as "late onset transsexuals". There may be late self-acknowledging transgender people, who have managed to hide/suppress their feelings for decades, but they are not late onset by any means.
>
> 'I have had some very interesting conversations with people and how they tried to cope/cure/deny/run away from/etc their gender feelings.
>
> '(They do things like) STEM work, military service, dangerous sports, periods of hyper masculinity and so many others.
>
> If you are in your 40s and 50s or older you grew up in very hostile anti GLBTI environment, so you hid. And those that managed to develop…coping skills lived long enough until there was a more accepting time (or those mechanisms broke down). Those that didn't manage (to do) that died…one way or another. I just made it…by skin of my teeth.'

In Asia today, Lisa might well have transitioned at 15 or younger. Her life might have been very different. She might have taken hormones and fought the masculinisation of her body. She might have grown up a normal, well adjusted, socially functioning and happy transwoman. Western culture denied her that.

It is Western culture that makes bitter, angry, late-transitioning transwomen, not autogynephilia. That should tell you something about Western culture.

The Warm Pink Jelly Express Train
ROD FLEMING
Sex.Sleaze.Trannies.Passion.Love against love itself.
A man caught between passion and reason,
a woman caught between herself and the world.
ISBN: 978-0-9565007-2-4

3. The history of buggery.

Caravaggio: Amor Vincit Omnia

The Greeks, whatever scholars might coyly say about 'intercrural' sex, where one partner rubs his penis between the thighs of another, were buggers on the grand scale.

The Romans, too, practised sodomy at every level of society. Even Emperors buggered and were buggered, in the swamp of fleshy decadence that the Empire became before Constantine introduced Christianity to instil some moral order.

Pederasty, the love of beautiful boys, was the foundation of the English Public School system and may still be, for who knows what goes on behind those closed doors?

Well, we do, because that queen buggeree, Quentin Crisp, described the night-time antics inside a typical English boarding school in her book, *The Naked Civil Servant*.

While buggery was part and parcel of monastic life in the Middle Ages, it was not permitted to the laity. Squads of inspectors roamed the streets of Renaissance Florence looking for 'broken arses'. Despite this, nearly every great Renaissance artist was well known for having his tool up boys' bottoms on a regular basis.

With the Renaissance and the beginning of the modern Western world, beautiful boys became a powerful sexual force once again. Donatello, Michelangelo, Da Vinci, Botticelli, all worshipped the beautiful boy both as a boy and as a transgender girl. Caravaggio famously made many paintings of androgynous boys in sexualised poses, most of whom he had openly buggered.

In England it got harsh after Henry VIII's enactment of the infamous Buggery Act, which was only repealed in 1967. It has been suggested that this law was brought in because of the widespread practice, amongst the outlawed Catholic clergy, of buggering choirboys. The King was not really against buggery, which he almost certainly indulged in, he just wanted to stop the Papists having any fun.

The consequences were less amusing: in the British Royal Navy there are recorded cases of seamen being hanged for buggery and Oscar Wilde, famously, was imprisoned and his life ruined for it. Alan Turing, the genius who did so much for the nascent science of computing, was forced to undergo 'chemical sterilisation' or face years in prison, under 70 years ago: he committed suicide.

Yet throughout the 17th and 18th centuries and into the 19th, London, like other British cities, was home to dozens of 'molly-houses' – where boys drssed up as girls and were buggered by men. They even organised 'weddings' which were consummated before the crowd. (The name 'molly' comes from the Latin 'mollis', a poof or queer; it gives us the verb 'to mollify'.)

Anal penetration

It was not the physical matter of anal penetration itself that offended; rather, that became taboo by association. After all, most of the men who crafted laws against 'buggery' were happily, themselves, buggering boys; and that includes King James the VI and I, who was notorious for it, as were many of his Stewart relatives.

No, the problem was that in an act of penetrative sex between two men, one of them becomes a 'woman'. This is because the difference is defined by who penetrates and who gets penetrated.

This goes back to Roman times and long before. It is all right to bugger boys, because, as boys, they don't have 'man' status; they are 'not-men'; they have no status to compromise. But woe betide any mature man who lets his rear cleft be punctured, for he is not only renouncing his own male 'honour', he is attacking every other man's. This is similar to the

'Roman distrust and fear of the galli, (who) not only deliberately made themselves unable to produce offspring, but…served as bad examples to others, tempting young men to join their ranks.' (My underscore for emphasis.)

The submissive partner was seen as having renounced his manhood and thus is no longer actually male; that person was now a 'not-man', of the same status as women.

'Pegging' is not a straight pastime

We know that many allegedly 'straight' men are far from being so, because of the prevalence of 'pegging'. For those who don't know, this involves a man being penetrated anally with a dildo, often a strap-on worn by a woman. Because of the daft notion that homosexuality is only about attraction, this is presented by the more terminally deluded as 'straight' behaviour.

Of course it's not. The desire to be anally penetrated is the definition of male homosexuality. It is the penetration that counts. Homosexual men are only attracted to other men because of their penises. As Mr Crisp says, 'a homosexual man will never tell you how kind his partner is, or how good looking. He'll just say "it's enormous".'

The only thing that stops these men doing the dirty with other men is their homophobia. But they will do it with a transsexual woman and many seek out HSTS transwomen and AGPs to just that end (and seeking out AGPs should give you an idea of how desperate they are.)

The result is that many so-called heterosexual men are walking time-bombs, constantly seeking a scapegoat for their own desire to be anally penetrated, which, by definition, makes them homosexual.

Feminine gay men are seen as a threat to the 'straight' man's most prized asset – a stiff member. After all, homosexual men are doing exactly what our 'straight' man would like to do – but which he believes will turn him into a woman.

It was Sigmund Freud, surprise, surprise, who first proposed that homosexuality was about attraction to the same gender rather than sexual practice. For him two males in a relationship are both homosexual irrespective of their sexual roles. One day we might write an article celebrating his remarkable achievement in being wrong about *absolutely everything*.

Femiphobia, sissyphobia or just plain homophobia?

The absurd idea that homosexuality is about 'male-to-male attraction' has been much vaunted by gay activists in America and elsewhere since the 1960s, because they think it will make society detest them less. In this they are just as misogynistic and homophobic as the straight men around them. They are desperate to hang on to that nice juicy privilege and white male status, while regularly having their anuses broadened, as Madame Crisp put it.

These homosexual men are notorious for their hatred of all expressions of femininity. Dr J. Michael Bailey calls this 'femiphobia'. Dr Alice Dreger prefers 'sissyphobia'. Well, I like calling spades spades, so I'll call it what it really is – homophobia. Yes folks, Western homosexual men hate nothing – nothing – more than homosexual men. It does cast light on their widely-noted self-loathing.

This is the reason for the absurd USican interpretation of homosexuality as an attraction between two Manly Manly (super strength extra Manly formula with added abs and maybe some sweaty sock aroma) men, no matter what role they may play.

'Queer Theory' – the ridiculous pile of unsupported pontification that has been spawned from the above deceit – insists that male homosexuality has nothing whatsoever to do with getting your arse in the air, munching pillows and screaming 'Daddy' while your clone retunes your colon. This, of ccourse, is an assertion that ten minutes watching gay porn will render ludicrous; which is why they really don't want to you to watch it *at all*.

Oh no, it's all about 'lerve'. Which just goes to show that if you begin a philosophical expedition from a false premise, all you end up with is gobbledygook.

There's a boy across the river, with an arse like two plums in a sock.

And they have a secret weapon: straight men think boys are sexy. Oh yes they do. Now we are not advocating, in any way at all, sexual relations between adult men and adolescent boys. This is taboo in Western civilisation because we recognise that children have rights. Nobody – I hope – would challenge this; children's rights are a fundamental part of modern secular democracy. It is one of the things that make our culture superior to, say, Islam, where children have no rights.

But that does not mean that heterosexual men don't find boys sexy. Evolution takes a tad longer than the 250-odd years since the Enlightenment. Consider this ditty, courtesy of one Peter Cook;

'Arseholes are cheap today,

Cheaper than yesterday,

Little boys are half a crown,

Standing up or lying down,

Bigger boys are three and six,

They can take bigger dicks,

Arseholes are cheap today.'

How can this be? Surely this notion cannot exist in a world where 'homosexuality' is all about 'man-to-man lerve'? Of course not; it's a blatant paean to raw lust. The whole point is that there's no love at all involved – just the pure delight of sexual pleasure. It's about lust, not love. (Does nobody ever wonder why the most popular 'gay' dating site is not called 'Friendly Pink Blokes' or 'Meet a Nice Fella'? Why that site is actually called 'Grindr'? I mean how literal do you have to be?)

So how can straight men be so obsessed with arse? Well, that delightful and very helpful old queen, Ms Crisp, explains it. 'Men,' she says, 'Are neither heterosexual nor homosexual. They're just sexual.'

And she's right. Men would fuck a decent-looking tree if that's all there were handy. We may deny it, but it's true. This has a great many consequences, not many of them good. But it's still a fact.

This author, for all his worn appearance and a jaded world-view that is what you get if you've been observing humanity for five decades, was once a young pretty boy himself.

I remember being on an oil-rig in the North Sea – now there's a macho environment. It was early summer and hot, so we roustabouts (deck hands) were all dressed in dungarees with no t-shirts to stay cool. A very large Texan 'company guy' approached me and absent-mindedly-began to twiddle my nipple. This definitely constituted an unwanted sexual approach and I made myself scarce; there's no doubt that had I not done so, he would have had me behind the cement silos and ruptured my virgin arse there and then.

But was he 'gay'? Don't be daft! No way would anybody get near his back passage. He was just a horny guy with a problem and the nearest woman was 400 miles away.

Technically this is called 'situational homosexuality' but actually it's just men being randy.

Think that was an isolated incident? One Texan too far from the nearest cute Palomino? Think again.

The next year, using the wodge of cash I earned plundering the Oil, I took a solo road trip to India, overland. Later I called it 'following the Silk Road' but actually I just kind of pointed myself towards the rising sun and found a bus going that general direction.

On the way to India, which took about four weeks of actual travel, I passed through Afghanistan; there was many a fine tale to regale you with from that den, but another time. Anyway, I have red-blond hair, which in those days went very red in the sun, and a ginger beard; and I have always looked younger than I am.

The first premonition that this might, ummm, cause me grief, I had in Istanbul when I met a guy called Mike from Upstate New York. He'd spent two years doing VSO in Kabul. He said, 'Afghanistan, huh? Watch it, they're all buggers there.'

He was right. And they thought nothing of copping a feel. After six weeks in the place my arse was black and blue – but my anal virginity remained intact. Not without effort on my part.

(It gave me a great sympathy for women who find themselves similarly on the receiving end of unwanted sexual attentions. It's the more horrifying when it's a toothless one-eyed Pashtun with major body odour doing it, believe me. The fact that they were all armed to the teeth added a certain frisson too.)

But this illustrates a simple fact: cute boys are attractive to adult men.

Technically, what men find attractive is called 'neoteny'. It means 'retention of youthful features'. In a way, however, it's a misnomer: it should be 'retention of non-masculine features'. Because, of course, masculinisation proceeds with age and the effects of testosterone, the two get conflated. But if we separate out the 'non-masculine' from the 'youthful' what do we get?

The author relaxing in Kashmir after evading the sexual advances of randy toothless Pashtun tribesmen

The Warm Pink Jelly Express Train
ROD FLEMING
Sex.Sleaze.Trannies.Passion.Love against love itself.
A man caught between passion and reason,
a woman caught between herself and the world.
ISBN: 978-0-9565007-2-4

4. Girly-boy beauty

Sexual transformation from boy to girl has always been hot. Enter the girly-boy: the transsexual or TS.

The oldest records we have prove the early existence of TS individuals, often priestesses or shamans. Their direct descendants are in the hijra of India, the kathoey of Thailand, the bakla of the Philippines, the travestis of the Americas, Blanchard HSTS and a host of transsexuals, trannies and shemales across the planet.

From the 'Dancing Boys' of Afghanistan to the trans girls of Asia, from down-town Sao Paulo to Paris, in every culture, all through history, boys become girls in order to attract men. The beautiful girly-boy has always been with us, and she is not going away.

Throughout Western culture, sexual transformation has been centre-stage, literally, since history began to be written. I remember, as a child no more than ten, falling desperately in love with Peter Pan, in a Christmas pantomime. But Peter was no ordinary boy, for like all his representations in theatre, he was played by a young woman. We are programmed to see sexual ambivalence as an object of desire in itself from very early ages.

Sexual Ambivalence in Art

Greek sculpture celebrated the beautiful girly-boy. This was a transgender passion, for the object of sexual attraction here was the youthful boy, the young male, who was regarded as so much more perfect than any woman, yet who played the woman in the act of sex. She was the recipient partner.

Consider Sparta, where warriors lived in barracks outside the city. Young boys beginning their life's journey would be partnered with older men, who were able to grow beards. This was believed to improve the efficiency of the Spartan army. Men would fight and die much harder for their lovers than for mere comrades. So they had sex with girly-boys, who would one day become men.

The Spartan system was so effective that men, old enough to take wife, often found it difficult to get aroused with women, which they had to, in order to sire more soldiers.

In Rome, girly-boy prostitutes were commonplace. The tradition of self-castration first recorded in the temple of Inanna at Uruk in Sumer continued there in the temples of Cybele, the Phrygian Great Mother. Young men called 'galli' ritually self-castrated and then 'adopted women's clothing and seemed to prefer the receptive role in anal intercourse'.

'The passion for transition and self-castration became so prevalent at its peak that the Emperor Domitian (81-96 CE) banned the practice'. These were the girly-boys.

Homosexuality is not only about attraction.

For a man to be in love with a beautiful girly-boy was not considered homosexual, because homosexuality was not defined by attraction. Boys were sexual beings and, as immature males, both subject to and responsive to the lust of older ones. In part, perhaps, this stemmed from the fact that sex with women was practically unavailable to the unmarried man and rare enough for the married one, in an era without contraception. Men either used prostitutes and risked the terrible diseases they might catch, or had sex with boys.

At the same time there is evidence, as we explored in '[Why Men Made God]', that human sexuality is not as cut and dried as Western culture, with its roots in the ghastly sexual repression and prescriptiveness of Christianity, might suggest. Sexuality is naturally fluid.

Situational Homosexuality.

Consider, for a moment, 'prison sex'. Homosexual relations between prisoners kept in same-sex institutions are well known. These are sometimes represented as symptoms of male dominance – the big, tough, mean men force weaker males to have sex with them. But this is not true. In many cases, if not most, the submissive partners become women, sexually at least, voluntarily. They seek out the beasts and offer themselves. Why? Partly for protection, but also for something else.

Quentin Crisp explains the desire that girly-boys have for men like this:

'(they see themselves as) young, frail, beautiful, and refined. Hence their predilection is for huge, violent, coarse brutes.'

This behaviour has been described as 'situational homosexuality' but that concept depends on the notion that heterosexual relationships between men and women are somehow more 'normal' than those between men and girly-boys. It is likely that the latter relationships are just as 'normal'. 'Situational homosexuality' therefore, would just be a normal part of male sexual expression.

Sex is not just about reproduction.

Put that another way: sex is not *principally* about reproduction, it's about sex. Men having sex are not trying to make babies, they're just trying to get off. If the recipient partner happens to lack a womb, who cares? An anus will do nicely in the dark.

(This, of course, would torpedo much of the biologically-determinist poppycock spouted on the one hand by pseudo-scientists like Steven Pinker, through to the Pope and the Ayatollah, on the other. For this reason such notions are unpopular.)

Consider the behaviour of soldiers in the days before women were in armies, where they had no access to real women. For example in POW camps, the men dressed up as women and put on shows.

'Military concert parties for the troops by the troops – featuring female impersonators – was a British military tradition that went as far back as the eighteenth century, if not earlier.'

Of one performer, a Dutch Eurasian, it was said,

> 'This fellow had dark brown eyes with long, curling eyelashes, and a smooth olive complexion. He was five feet, five inches tall and weighed about 150 pounds – the perfect size for a female impersonator – and when he was made up with a wig and what served as cosmetics, he was a dead ringer for the real thing.'

This performer was known as 'Sambal Sue' and it is clear that she was a girly-boy. Small, lightly-built and pretty, she was the classic HSTS as described by Bailey.

To understand all this you have to realise that contemporary Western notions of gender and sexual behaviour are somewhat particular, to say the least. In earlier cultures, and across the rest of the world today, society is grouped into 'men' and 'not-men'. The latter group includes women, girls and boys as yet unable to grow a beard. Girly-boys are those who remain in this latter group and indeed emphasis it through the use of hormones and other feminising techniques, as well as behaviours and dress.

In this milieu a sexual relationship in which a man (of age to grow a beard) penetrates a boy (not able to) is seen as heterosexual. It is 'man' penetrating a 'not-man' and so is the definition of heterosexual sex. It is permitted even in apparently homophobic cultures. This is why so many patriarchal religions have specific rules against men shaving their beards. To do so is to reject their own masculinity and so become not-men.

Denying the male cultural role.

In other words, it's fine for a man to have sex with someone who is a 'not-man'. But it is not allowed for a man to *become* a not-man. An adult male is supposed to adopt the cultural role appointed for him – of husband and masculine father.

For example, today, in Islamic culture, a boy is sexually equivalent to a woman; they share the lower status of 'not men'. As a result, boys remain, as they have always been, legitimate sexual targets throughout the Islamic world, while 'clone' homosexuals – two beard-growing men

– may be punished by 'being thrown off the highest tower in the town'.

What if you're a beautiful girly-boy who likes men?

The point, for girly-boys, was never to attract gay men: it was to attract *straight* men. They are sexually repulsed by gay men because they recognise that these are other 'not-men'. What they want is an actual man.

The way they went about that was not to develop their *faux* masculinity, as a New Gay Man would, but their femininity.

Of course the New Gay Men (extra manly manly man with added super pungent sock smell) tried to sweep girly-boys under the carpet and told them to grow a moustache and be a man about it. Girly-boys were shunned both by mainstream society and, today, by gay culture; the latter because it is desperate that nobody should ever learn the truth: gay 'men' are actually women.

A girly boy doesn't want to be a man.

She doesn't want to look like a man. She doesn't want to play the silly charade of the New Gay Man lifestyle. She just wants a nice hunky straight guy to cuddle up with after sex. She doesn't want to sport a moustache and be macho, she wants to wear hot pants and be girly.

This dilemma was highlighted and parodied by Freddie Mercury in the delicious video for Queen's 'I Want To Break Free' where he donned frock and apron while still wearing his famous facial hair.

These girly-boys know how beautiful they are, and how sexually intriguing they can be. They always knew that given the right mood and circumstances, they could seduce any man, not gays but *straight* men. They want to be taken like girls and they do not want to be asked to reciprocate.

They have no time for the foetid locker-room atmosphere of the clone gay scene, and the further they are from it the better. The solution is simple: from a dangerously alluring girly boy, become a beautiful, sexy transgirl. While the ancient priestesses of Cybele drank mare's urine and castrated themselves, today, a girly boy has a whole cosmetics industry that can help transform her in every way.

They get what they want – straight male dick – and their lovers get what they want – girls as sexy as only a girly-boy can be.

Let's put it this way: we take a girly-boy, attracted to men, enjoys being penetrated, and who understands that her inner psyche is feminine. We give her hormones that will reverse or arrest the effects of testosterone, then we have what we began with – the ladyboy, shemale, bakla, HSTS, whatever.

The perfect woman?

I wrote in 'The Warm Pink Jelly Express Train' (brilliant read by the way) that a TS is 'the perfect woman from a man's point of view' and I stand by that. No transsexual on the planet knows what it's 'like' to be a woman. They have no idea. So in 'becoming women' they are, in a sense, parodying them. There is no 'inner woman'; male-to-female transition is provoked by male sexuality. Blanchard proved it.

She wants to be girly because she likes to be fucked by hot guys – just like a straight girl would, but with the added pep that a turbocharged male libido gives you. She takes the hormones, maybe has a pair of bolt-on boobs installed; et voila.

I once wrote that these girly-boys 'drove a coach and horses through gay political thinking' and I stand by that. They destroy 'queer theory' just by their simple existence. They render it null; the vapid, meaningless chit-chat that it actually is.

Here were boys who wanted only to be submissive and who did not want to look or behave like men, but like girls; so they *became* girls.

A girly-boy is not the product of Politically Correct Western philosophy.

They are not 'genderqueer' or any of the other fucked-up products of Post-Modernist thinking, or the coffee-room twaddle of superfluous departments of Humanities. Girly-boys are girls and that's all they want to be.

They knew perfectly well that they were not women and still do; the object of their transformation was not to be women, but to be *more girly* in order to attract straight men. (Every girly-boy I know has literally dozens of gay male friends. They won't sleep with any of them.)

Their understanding of transsexualism is profoundly Dionysian. It is about the wildness of nature and lust and delight in sexual passion, earthy and untamed. It is about sex, not some weird notion of Platonic attachment, or your mental-patient 'inner woman'. It is about being fucked.

Dick crazy.

J. Michael Bailey quotes an AGP transgender person as saying that the girly boys (technically HSTS) were 'boy crazy'. Well, Dr Bailey was for once pulling his punches. They're not *boy* crazy, they're *dick* crazy. As Quentin Crisp said, they spend their lives looking at the front of men's trousers.

David Bonnie put it more directly: 'They're like men – they can't keep it in their pants'.

A girly-boy can love you like you have never known before, but her primary attraction to a man is what he has south of his navel.

It is also completely straightforward. It is totally honest. There is no lie, no cover-up. It's about sex, papa. Girly-boys feel love incredibly passionately and they actually understand it. They are walking, talking, living works of art, dedicated to love. They understand the foetid swamp of the Earth Mother that Camille Paglia described, the place of creation, of love, of death and of blinding lust, better than anyone else. It is their place; it is the world they inhabit, between penetration and orgasm.

I once said to a girly-boy just like this, on her hands and knees on the bed before me, that what was about to happen might possibly cause her some pain.

'I don't care if it hurts,' she moaned impatiently. 'I just want to *feel* it.'

What can a poor boy do?

5. Autogynephilia: Sex as a Woman

Autogynephilia is a self-reinforcing, sexualised self-reward system. It is stimulated by a man's desire to be, or appear to be, a woman. It is satisfied by achieving this. Although there are other rewards, the main one is by having sex as a woman.

Because it is self-reinforcing, the more often the satisfaction is achieved, the stronger it gets. It is narcissistic because it is focussed on the male self as a woman. Because sexualised reward is so strong, autogynephilia is extremely powerful and compelling. Sex as a woman turbo-charges it.

This reward is not always dependent on orgasm. It acts through other psychological reward systems too. So a person with it may receive sexualised reward from dressing as a woman, from going to the hairdresser, from being complimented by men, from being courted by men and having sex with them as a woman and so on.

Gender-typical norms.

When a woman puts on lacy lingerie or conforms to other gender-typical norms, she might feel sexy. She is receiving, through this culturally-contextualised idea of gender, affirmation that she is sexy and feminine. (This is absolutely not to suggest that all women take pleasure from satisfying cultural gender stereotypes, but most do, at least to some extent.) When an autogynephile does the same thing, that person is receiving affirmation that she is a woman.

This explains why Moser and others have observed what they suggested was autogynephilia in women. But it's not the same. A woman knows she is a woman. Her reward is to be affirmed as a sexy and desirable one, in the context of the culture and its gender roles.

For an autogynephile it is much more complex. Her first need, and as the condition progresses, this need becomes increasingly intense, is to 'be a woman'. The reward of being a sexy one is dependent on that initial one. First you must 'be a woman' in order to be affirmed as a desirable one.

Men do not normally find sexualised reward in wearing frilly panties or stockings and make-up. If they do, then they are expressing autogynephilia.

Now this presents an interesting conundrum: what in the first place makes the autogynephile desire to be a woman? Well, this again has to do with sex, and here Western 'queer theory' hits the buffers with a bang.

Sex as a woman: what binds all MtF transsexuals together

Transsexuals are divided into 'homosexual' and 'non-homosexual' variants. In Blanchard Theory, these are 'HSTS' and 'AGP' (for autogynephilic transsexual.)

HSTS tend to be, on average, light in build, small, have more feminine features and feminised speech patterns. All of these they have in common with feminine homosexual men and the link is easy to make. What makes them transsexual is their understanding that their desire for male sexual partners makes them women.

Remember, this is not about sex; it's about gender. That's largely a social concept. So HSTS naturally allow their femininity to become dominant over any vestige of masculinity they may have in order to be more affirmed as women, by appearing sexy and desirable to men.

They don't need these affirmations to become women: their sexual desire for men does that. So, like natal women, HSTS have a solid, realised understanding of their gender: they are women because they desire men. (And it is well known that by and large, women who desire women become more like men.)

This holes 'queer theory' and particularly its ridiculous assertion that 'gender identity' and 'sexual orientation' are separate, beneath the waterline. HSTS are women because they want to be penetrated by men. Sexual orientation – who you want to have sex with– and 'gender identity' – who you want to have sex as – are two sides of the same coin. Simple as that.

This makes HSTS really easy to identify and that is what Ray Blanchard did, along with virtually every other serious researcher before and since.

But what about dnon-homosexual transsexuals? We know that these tend not to look anything like as feminine as HSTS. They are, on average, taller, bigger, more heavily built, have more masculine voices, do not move in a feminine manner and so on.

Further, we know from their narratives that they are not initially attracted to men. Instead they are attracted to the *idea* of being women. They only become attracted to men as their gendered identities as a women develop. In other words, they are attracted to the idea of being women, but have no obvious means of affirmation.

Let's make a generalisation:

HSTS become women because they are attracted to men and AGPs become attracted to men because they want to be women. Both understand that having sex as women is the strongest and most rewarding affirmation of femininity that they can aspire to.

In the West and especially in Anglo-Saxon cultures, gender non-conformity has historically been suppressed with extreme violence both by the broader culture and the political authorities.

Further, homosexuality – which is understood badly in the West – is profoundly suppressed. On top of that, if it were not enough, anal sex is condemned such that in many jurisdictions it was illegal for a man to penetrate even his own wife anally.

So, appearing to be a woman – dressing in public as one – is banned. Being attracted to men, if you are male, is banned. Behaving like a woman sexually – having recipient sex with men – is banned.

What affirmation can the Western autogynephile have other than sexual fantasy and release through masturbation? None. Thus is born the idea that 'fetishistic masturbation' is a core reward in autogynephilia. It's not. It only becomes one if the other reward systems, like going out shopping with women, discussing crushes on boys, canoodling with boys and so on, are outlawed. It is a function therefore, of social intolerance.

It's easy for an AGP to play a male role in public. And this is what they do in the West: they live as men and satisfy themselves in private.

It's almost impossible for an HSTS to do this. She's just too feminine and her sexual desire is not to become a woman, but to have sex as a woman. She doesn't need to become anything: she's a woman. Her sexual need to be penetrated makes her that. She just needs some sex like any other woman.

Social intolerance.

Fetishistic masturbation may be useful, in the West particularly, as a diagnostic aid; but far too few who discuss this – and that includes the vast majority of Western autogynephiles – understand that this part of the condition is a consequence of social intolerance.

This doesn't mean that autogynephilia does not exist in Asia: it does. For many years I and others believed that if autogynephilia did exist there, it was very rare indeed. And it is true that the Western profile, with associated cross-dressed masturbation, wearing women's underwear under male clothes and so on, is rare. But that is not because autogynephilia is rare: it's because social intolerance is lower in Asia.

Although gender non-conforming behaviour is often discriminated against in Asia, the level of social intolerance is much lower than in the West. It's largely OK to be homosexual; Boy Abunda, a major star in Philippines television, has stated on air, 'I am gay', several times to my personal knowledge. It doesn't damage his ratings at all. The highly gender non-conforming Vice Ganda (Vice means what you think, 'ganda' means beautiful) is one of the biggest stars in the country.

No big deal.

In the Philippines and Thailand homosexuality is a big 'so what?' It's OK to grow your hair long and wear hot pants to show off your legs – which, if you're 5'11" are probably pretty amazing. Across south-east Asia, finding yourself standing next to a tall transsexual with big feet is not even remarkable. It happens every day. The insertion of penis into rectum is not considered a criminal offence and never has been.

What this means is that while the Western autogynephile is desperately trying to make sure nobody finds out and is reduced to masturbating in panty-hose, the Asian one is out and proud, dressed as a woman, socialising as a woman, and probably having sex as a woman – with men. She doesn't 'transition' at age 65. She transitions perhaps at 13.

Western autogynephiles are fond of saying that the differences between them and HSTS are to do with age of transition. This is partly true. The effects of testosterone on appearance are drastic and may make it impossible for an AGP in the West ever to be convincing as a woman. Her Asian counterpart is scoffing birth-control pills from puberty. Yes, it makes a difference.

Masculinity.

Add to this that Asian men are markedly less masculine in appearance than Western males. They tend to be smaller, have finer features and so on, even if they are completely straight men. You take one of these guys, do a feminising make-over and he could walk down the street in Paris or New York, as a woman, and nobody would have a clue. That means that for a person so inclined, dressing as a woman and behaving socially as one, is much easier. Even autogynephilic transvestites – who don't take hormones or desire sex change and wear women's clothes only part time – pass easily in Asia, which they rarely do in the West.

Further, in all Asian cultures, it is bad form, to put it mildly, to offend another person. So people are inclined to go along. It is unusual to hear anyone misgender a transperson, even in the highly religious Philippines. You want to present as a woman, it's fine. Nearly everyone you meet will call you 'maam' and treat you as one, even if you're six foot with size 10 feet. This extends to social courtesies; men will give up their seats for a transsexual, just as they would for a woman, even if they know that she's TS. (Of course, often they don't.) This is because, even if the person does not really approve of your behaviour, in Asia, it is deeply impolite – and may result in violence – to compromise anyone's assertions about themselves. To do so would cause loss of face, and there is no greater insult.

Academic lie.

This, by the way, gives the lie to Western academics' attempt to explain the differences between the West and Asia on the ground that the West has more 'respect for the individual'. It doesn't. Yes, Asian culture is in many ways more conservative, but attacking someone's identity is one of the biggest taboos that exist. It's simply not allowed. If you disapprove of transsexuals, culture, in Asia, tells you to just play bonny anyway.

So we have sympathy here for the Western non-homosexual transsexual. They frequently assert that they have, all their lives, struggled to hide their condition – whereas their Asian sisters were busy flaunting it, mama.

Once you know what you are looking for, it's quite easy to distinguish HSTS and AGP transsexuals in Asia. The former tend to be smaller, lighter and cuter, to have more naturally feminine voices and to be more like women in their comportment. Further, HSTS are more sexually motivated than AGPs.

In essence, an Asian HSTS is motivated by sex and a powerful desire for men. She knows that her need to be penetrated makes her a woman. The AGP desires to be a woman and she knows that being penetrated by men will make her so. It's really very simple.

Transition.

There is no compelling reason for an AGP to have sex with women. Remember, her passionate desire is *to be* a woman.

Sex is a powerful reward: you can learn to like sex with just about anything, if you're a man. That is the foundation of 'situational homosexuality' as found in prisons, navies and all-male boarding schools. Asian AGPs are conditioned by their childhood support network – the other gender non-conforming children they grow up with – to see sex with men as affirmative. While it is be possible that primary homosexuality in men – with its concomitant physical attributes – may be innate, it is a simple fact that anyone can learn to like anal sex. If such sex makes you what your dream says you are, then of course it's attractive. Asian AGPs like sex with men because of its affirmative power.

Attraction to women.

Why then, in the West, are so many AGPs attracted to women? Well to begin with, that is how they start off in life: they are attracted to the whole idea 'woman', especially as a role they can invest themselves in.

AGPs do enjoy sex with women although such sex may not be affirmative. In addition, all AGPs, everywhere, prefer the company of women to that of men. (HSTS generally do not; they prefer men's company to either women's or gay men's – though their best friends might be gay men.) This might be why Western AGPs are so strident in insisting that they are 'real' women; involved as they so often are in sexual relationships with women, they do not have the powerful affirmation that comes from sex with men. (Asian transwomen tend to be much less afflicted by this delusion.)

This explains the almost Platonic relationships evident between Western AGPs and their wives: they have actually become sisters. In many cases the relationship will lose its sexual component, or it will have been of low importance ever since the beginning. The AGP would be penetrating her best friend and in a culture where to be penetrated incurs a reduction of status, this causes problems.

Homophobia.

Unfortunately however, the main reason appears to be simple homophobia. Western autogynephiles often, like Bruce 'Caitlyn' Jenner, express a level that is truly shocking. Of course, this represents a conflict that could hardly do other than cause neurosis. The AGP wants to have sex with men, because she knows it will affirm her as a woman, but she knows she is actually a man. So to be penetrated would be a homosexual act, which she has been conditioned to think is something completely unforgivable.

For a man to become a woman is the greatest contumely possible in Western society. It destroys, entirely, a man's being. What makes men so special? They can penetrate. A man can penetrate and be penetrated, a woman cannot. Just as giving birth is unique to women, penetration is unique to men. Men are conditioned to reject the fact that they can indeed be penetrated and enjoy it, because to do so destroys their patriarchal status. If men start playing women in sexsociety itself might collapse.

Nearly all AGPs in Asia are either attracted to men (pseudo-bisexual) or analloerotic (asexual). The latter derive their sexual reward from such things as winning beauty pageants, becoming models or entertainers and so on. This is a specific substitute for affirmative sex. Others may take jobs as women – result the same. Only a few seek relationships with natal women. They often form them with other transsexuals – usually transmen. Of course, they desire the underlying femininity, wrapped up in an affirming appearance.

Something unexpected.

Finally, for now, the Asian example shows something that might be unexpected in the West: once we take out of the equation the 'fetishistic cross-dressing' masturbatory element, there is practically no difference in the rewards sought by homosexual and non-homosexual transsexuals. In other words, they are both motivated by autogynephilia, if we define that as 'a male's propensity to be attracted to the idea of himself as a woman'.

It begins to look as if autogynephilia is the stimulus for all male-to-female transsexualism. The difference between the profiles appears to be about sexual orientation rather than underlying cause. HSTS are the way they are because underneath, they are classic homosexual males; AGPs are heterosexual males. But they both desire sex as a woman, though in the case of AGPs, this may be overlaid with a form of pseudo-lesbianism.

In other words, all transsexuals are to some extent autogynephilic (using my definition) and the differences between the types is a result of orientation, which itself has been shown to be associated with different physical profiles, and of cultural pressures.

6. Not Men: bekis in the Philippines

Social division into 'men' and 'not men' groups, together with a domestic matriarchy, explain why transsexual expressions in Asia differ from the West.

Male to Female (MtF) transsexuals are normally scientifically categorised as homosexual or nonhomosexual with regard to their birth sex. I'll use the term HSTS for the former. Blanchard explained the latter in terms of autogynephilia, love of oneself as a woman. These we term autogynephiles or AGPs. There is a discrepancy, between the West and Asia, however. Whereas in the West, most AGPs are older and about 60% seek relationships with women, most AGPs in Asia transition much younger and are almost exclusively attracted to men. Why is this happening?

(There are some classic Western AGPs but they are rare and tend not to occur in traditional Asian culture but amongst more Westernised families.)

I'll use the Philippines example, but Don Kulick, in his book 'Travesti', reports very similar phenomena in Brazil and it is, to my knowledge, current throughout southeast Asia and India.

Men and Not men: Two Groups

Traditional Filipino society is divided into two social groups: men, and every one else. Borrowing from Kulick, I call the latter 'not men'. This group is formed of women, children, female and gender non-conforming adolescents, and older 'not men' including gay males and transsexuals. Kulick goes as far as to define gender in Brazil as 'men' and 'not men' and, again, I agree with him.

Gender conforming adolescent males form a 'proto-men' group, where they learn the social skills needed to join the 'men' group. Typically these include playing basketball, football and similar sports (but not volleyball); learning how to chase girls; learning how to talk about girls as sexual objects; often, learning to smoke and crucially, learning to drink. As they grow into adulthood, boys like this will be accepted into the 'men' group. So the 'proto-men' group is an extension of the 'men' group, not distinct from it.

A gender non-conforming (GNC) boy, teenage or adult male is automatically placed in the 'not men' group. The reasons for this are complex but devolve to showing 'unmasculine' character traits. These include things like being somewhat nervous; being a pretty boy; having crushes on men and boys, liking to dance; liking flowers; liking to wear feminine clothes; the desire to be a woman and feeling 'like a woman inside'.

Harsh.

This may sound harsh, but it is not as bad as it seems, because while traditional Filipino culture is outwardly very patriarchal, it is in fact a domestic matriarchy. Within the home, women are in charge, and the practical head of the family is Lola – the grandmother. It is common for several generations to live in the same household, and while Lola's mother may still be alive, she will have been retired. Lola's daughters are her captains, maintaining control and order in the house, assisted by their lieutenants, their own elder daughters.

Men do not socialise in this milieu, in fact they avoid it. While Lolo – grandpa – will be a much loved figure, his focus, if he is still earning, is outside the house. Within it, nobody gainsays Lola.

It is true that a GNC male or beki (the name for Philippine TS/TG) will lose status by not being able to join the 'men' group, through the 'proto-men' group. However in the 'not men' group she will find himself in the middle of a supportive and powerful cohort of women and other GNC individuals. And while, even in the 'not men' group, bekis are lower status than women, they are still given a social space. Within the 'not men' group they develop the circle of GNC and natal women friends who will be with them all their lives.

Learning to be women.

Just as, within the 'proto-men' group of gender-conforming boys, adolescents are learning how to be adults, so it is in the 'not men' group. Here, bekis are not learning how to be men but how to be women.

Young transpinays or bekis, learn, within the 'not men' group, the behaviours and social roles that they need to, in order to survive as adults.

Bekis form a subset of the 'not men' group. Their social identity is completely defined by it. In socialisation, therefore, they are first 'not men' and second bekis, so they adopt all the mores of the not men group.

Amongst the most important of these is that women are penetrated by male sexual partners. So although in the West, AGP transsexuals (who form part of the beki group in Asia) may express sexual desire for women, in part because of their socialisation as men, in beki culture that is a 'not match' and so instead, young AGP TS/TG seek sexual and romantic relationships with men. This means that nearly all bekis, with very few exceptions, appear as androphilic.

Gay = GNC male.

GNC males who are primarily attracted to men and those who are attracted to *being women* both consider themselves to be 'gay'.

Note here that the word 'gay' in the Philippines just means 'gender non-conforming male'. By the same token, 'lesbian' means 'gender non-conforming female'. The Western sense of 'gay' meaning 'attracted to masculinity' is only a part of its meaning here. As well as this, there are other GNC expressions that fall under the heading 'gay' and are also therefore, bekis. These are homosexual and bisexual males who retain a masculine or intermediate gender expression: they may not transition.

On the other hand, they might; many bekis are somewhat 'gender fluid' and will move from one expression to another as social pressures require. But at all times, and no matter how they are presenting, they understand that they are 'women inside' and this is what makes them bekis. Do not run away with the idea that bekis are in any way ashamed of what they are. This is a powerful and supportive sub-culture which even has its own language. Being beki is a social identity worn with pride.

The primary androphilic group, the equivalent of Blanchard HSTS in the West, will have crushes on boys and older men. They have desired male partners since childhood. Since women have male partners, they therefore understand that their desire makes them 'women inside'.

Those attracted to the idea of themselves as women already are 'women inside' and, since women are attracted to men, they start havining crushes on them

To put that another way, HSTS learn that they are women because of their powerful sexual desire for men, and AGPs learn that they should desire men because of their feeling – their gender identity if you like – of being 'women inside'.

The two statuses are, as you can see, very similar. Essentially, both groups see themselves as 'women inside'. It's just that their reasons are subtly different. These two developmental pathways are united in beki culture.

Confusion.

It is not at all unusual for transpinays to be confused by the Western division of 'homosexual' and 'non-homosexual' transsexuals, because of the above. Since they all identify as bekis, they place less value on how they came to be so. An individual beki may never have even considered whether her attraction to being a woman (AGP) or her attraction to men (HSTS) came first.

However, the truth can be teased out in a number of ways. We know from studies done in the West that HSTS tend to be, on average, smaller, more lightly built, lighter in weight and more feminine in appearance than AGPs and this holds true in Asia too.

In the West, most AGPs transition much later than HSTS, in their late 30s or above. In Asia they may still appear a little later than HSTS, but usually still in their teens or twenties. On the other hand, many do transition soon after puberty and begin hormones then.

An AGP may relate how she liked to wear her mother's clothes, or her sister's; how she liked to be to be with girls and felt comfortable with them; how she 'knew she was a girl'. For her, being beki is internal; it's about how she feels about herself. It's introspective. Outward not inward.

An HSTS will tell you about her first crushes on boys, or her first sexual encounter, if she has had one. She might remark that her mother's friends had commented that she 'looked like a girl'. Almost certainly, she will equate her early desire for men with being a woman inside.

She may actually have preferred to play with masculine boys – except this was her rehearsal for womanhood, in which she would become the focus of the male attention she desires. Her pleasure came from the nascent erotic thrill that the close company of her sexual targets gave her. Her vision is outward, not inward. She was turned on by men, more than by her self-image as a girl.

It should be easy to see how the close relationship of these two types as 'women inside' blur the distinctions that are so obvious in the Western profile.

As they grow up in the 'not-men' group and develop their own circle of GNC friends, both HSTS and AGP transsexuals may begin dating men. However, by no means all do.

Sex and virginity.

Westerners, used to the prominence of transwomen sex-workers in places like Pattaya, often assume that all transwomen do this. That is not true.

Many transwoman, probably a majority even in Thailand, where there is much less of a taboo than the Philippines, have never worked as prostitutes. In the Phils, although it has one of the highest rates of prostitution in the world, the vast majority do not work as prostitutes. Indeed, a substantial number in both countries, but probably more in the Philippines, have never had sex at all.

Naturally this fits very well with one type of AGP, the analloerotic. She is happy just 'being a woman' and living her life as one. Others, an increasingly large number today, spend their lives on the internet chatting up men. They may make this a business and milk men for support: these they call 'sponsors'. These women see nothing at all immoral about having ten or more men in various parts of the world, sending them money in return for sexy chats.

They have no intention of ever meeting these men. If one threatens to appear, they will vanish. They have to, because they know that if they spend three or four weeks with one man, they will lose all their other sponsors.

Some work as 'cam girls' in which they put on sexy shows for paying customers, over the internet. Naturally, for AGPs, this is rather a satisfying way to make money, but at least as many HSTS do it.

Sexualised, non-sexual reward.

Others get their sexualised reward, or affirmation, from their professions. Many Thai transwomen work as primary school teachers. This is seen as a woman's job, and doing it provides affirmation. In the Phils, every third girl I meet seems to have done or be doing a course in Hotel and Restaurant Management. Many are nurses or hairdressers – again, all seen as women's professions.

They may be performers in cabaret, or work the many trans beauty pageants. There are thousands of these and efforts in the Philippines, mainly by conservative church leaders, to close them, have clearly failed. Most of these are performed in the street or the baranggay or village hall, but the big ones are lush, professional events with prizes that could be over a year's salary in many jobs.

Both HSTS and this profile of AGPs seek work like this. Where the Western AGP profile appears, such as in the recent public transition of racing driver Ian King, they may, as he did, pursue masculine careers. But these individuals tend to have been much more exposed to Western culture. In the Phils, they may come from 'Fil-Am' families or may have grown up in the USA.

Once again, the two traditional profiles in Asia are very close and differ from the Western AGP profile as described by Blanchard. This indicates that there are cultural influences affecting the Western, late-onset AGP profile that differ from those I have described above.

Situational Homosexuality

Blanchard described the phenomenon of AGP transwomen (who are attracted to femininity) having male lovers as 'pseudo bisexualism'. But we could also describe it as situational homosexuality.

This is what we see in prisons, in navies, in boarding schools and other places where men are enclosed with no access to women. To take the prison example, it was often thought that the big, tough, aggressive men forced weaker men to be their sexual consorts. This may well happen, but studies show that in many cases the opposite is true. The submissive males *offer themselves* as sexual partners.

Now in outside life these are not 'gay' men. So why are they doing this? The answer is twofold: protection and status. They gain status by being the lover of a powerful prison mogul and nobody, but nobody is going to pick on them when they have someone that mean on their side. Everyone from other prisoners to the wardens, will treat them with respect.

So this is not about lust, but business. It is an exchange of sexual favour for reward.

In certain tribes in Borneo, people believe that boys are turned into men by the ingestion of semen. Boys and adolescent males will arrange trysts with older men and offer themselves sexually. Once they are old enough to grow a beard, they begin 'donating' semen to younger males in turn. Once again, this is an exchange for reward: the boy is getting the semen that will make him into a man.

Nevertheless, in interview, these men claim to have 'enjoyed' their years as the recipient lovers of older men. As Quentin Crisp put it, 'men are neither heterosexual nor homosexual; they're just sexual'. He meant that in the right circumstances, men can enjoy any kind of sex. This certainly seems to be the case here.

In Honduras and other Central American locations, there are classes of male sex workers who dress as women to attract clients. During the day they are ordinary men, usually with ordinary jobs; at night they cross-dress to supplement their income and, once again, engage in homosexual sex (these are definitely not transwomen) for reward – money.

Affirmation.

For an AGP transwoman, the reward is affirmation. The act of sex with a man affirms her as a woman. In Asia, she is conditioned by her inclusion in the 'not men' group and her adoption of its values – particularly, that a woman desires men, and to desire men makes one a woman. This makes her open to the idea of sex with men, even if that is not her primary orientation.

Remember that autogynephiles are attracted to themselves as women; so they have to be attracted to femininity. (And they are, very much so.) Their conditioning in the 'not men' group, however, teaches them that the single most powerful affirmation they can have, that they are women, is to have male partners. It also teaches them that to have female partners would compromise their identity as women.

An HSTS will see her partner very much in the same way as a woman of the same age does – in romantic and erotic terms, as a physical lover. AGPs tend to see their partners in idealised terms and talk about their 'eventual life partners'. They are looking to replicate the lives

My ex, who is Asian-profile AGP. Despite her beauty she is not passable because she is 5'11".

of their natal sisters.

This is to conform to the mores of traditional Asian culture, where they get to be respected members of their own domestic matriarchy. Of course, this is complicated because they can't have children. However, a beki who does well and contributes to the family finances will find her status elevated. She may become one of Lola's trusted captains.

This should not be taken to suggest that AGPs in Asia do not like sex. They may be less directly sexually driven than their HSTS sisters, at least in their attraction to men, but they certainly do, if they are sexually active, enjoy it.

Now I recognise that this will get up many noses, but the disingenuous political lie of SOGIE, that gender and sexual orientation are not intimately linked, cuts but little mustard outside the West. Being penetrated by a man makes you a woman. This is good news for both forms of Asian MtF transsexual.

The Warm Pink Jelly Express Train.

I wrote about this in my book *The Warm Pink Jelly Express Train*. Here the narrator, Brian, is talking about the first time he had sex with the heroine, Rafy, a Brazilian TS:

> 'for Rafy that first union between us must have been a moment of truly inspirational power. Look: a man, exactly the type of man she believed she should love…a man she had chosen but who had courted her, finally took her as the woman she was…It was the final kiss that brought Pygmalion's beautiful creation to life. When I made love to Rafy in that chalet, I made Rafy. The more I thought about it the more humbled I felt.'

So the reward is being made into the woman she feels herself to be. Harry Benjamin commented on how powerful this was for transsexuals, and nothing has changed.

The affirmative sexual hit that a transwoman gets from sex with a man – or sex as a woman as I have previously described it, meaning being penetrated – is huge. It is so powerful that girls can get addicted to it.

The affirmative power of sex work.

It is often, mistakenly, thought that the myriad MtF trans sex workers in places like Pattaya are all congruent with the Western HSTS profile. This is not true. Many of them are AGP, again in conflict with the Western model.

It is the power of gender affirmation that sex provides – and especially the fact of being paid for it – that these transwomen are responding to. This is why they so enjoy the life of a sex worker. (In Brazil, this lifestyle is actually called 'La Vida' – The Life.)

So although they do present as androphilic and, if asked, will normally say they are not attracted to women, they are not necessarily HSTS. (This is why I dislike the term 'androphilic TS' as a substitute for HSTS. They are not the same at all.)

While some Asian AGPs do have female partners, these are often transmen, or, in Thailand, 'Toms'. A small number do involve themselves romantically with women. So why are so many Western AGPs gynephilic?

The answer is homophobia. These individuals, in the West, grew up in a society with crushing levels of homophobia. They are conditioned from childhood to be homophobic themselves. They identify 'feeling like a girl' with 'being homosexual' and that is bad enough. It leads to the feelings of self-loathing that are so often clear in the characters of late-transitioning Western autogynephiles. They literally hate themselves because they are afraid that they might be homosexual men.

This is why these individuals are so strident in their insistence on the absurd – that they are 'real women'. Of course they're not. But the only way that they can assuage the guilt that their homophobic conditioning has cursed them with, is through that untruth.

It's even worse, however. Having sex with a man is the one thing they are not allowed to do; yet it is, by far, the most powerful affirmation they might have. Without it, their very existence as women remains unproven. They are only women because they say so.

Gay sex.

'Kristine' a presumably AGP transsexual commenting on Yahoo, said this:

> 'Many transsexual women consider (recipient anal sex) to be too close to their perceptions of "gay sex". (They) are desperately trying to fight stereotype concepts of who they are, even within themselves...A great many transsexual women avoid sexual activities and relationships altogether.'

Clearly, homophobia is acting on the minds of the transsexuals Kristine is discussing. There could be no reason to deny oneself sex with men 'because it would be gay' otherwise. Sex is just sex. Even if it were 'gay' for a transwoman to have sex with a man – and it would not be, anyway – the only thing that could make that bad is homophobia.

Although transphobia does, unfortunately, exist in Asia, homophobia in the Philippines is practically non-existent. The place is a gay paradise and Thailand even more so.

Late-transitioning AGPs appearing in the West now and over the last two decades, grew up at a time when homophobia was even more stiflingly repressive than it is today. Because of it, they learned to hate the form of sex that can most affirm them. Instead they harp 'I'm a real woman' and bully anyone who disagrees.

Tough guys.

They did not grow up surrounded by supportive girls and other GNC children, learning how to be women. They grew up as tough, masculine men, determined to prove that even though they knew there was something unusual about then, the one thing they were not was homosexual. So they became fighter pilots, engineers, CEOs; professions as distant as possible from anything feminine.

Worse, they learned how to be men, and all straight men see women as sexual targets. Growing up as a man means learning to identify women that might be persuaded to give you sex, and the techniques needed to make them do it. What was the 'Cotton Ceiling' scandal other than rape culture with a frock on? It was a blatant attempt to coerce a lesbian – who doesn't have sex with people who have, or used to have, penises – into agreeing to sex by shaming her into thinking she is being transphobic for exercising her legitimate right of choice.

Western AGPs are fond of saying how the difference between themselves and HSTS is 'just one of age of transition'. The distinctly creepy Jack Molay, an autogynephilic transvestite in full denial, has posted screeds on this. And yes, age at which hormones are started is important. But while trumpeting this hardship, AGP mouthpieces are careful to avoid the concomitant fact – not only did they start hormones too late to prevent their bodies masculinising, they socialised as men. They have no clue whatsoever about being a woman.

Isolated, alone and full of loathing for themselves, they became twisted and bitter. Western AGPs hate women for being that which they desire to be but cannot; they hate HSTS for just being so darn cute; and they detest gays because all their lives they have been trying to hide their autogynephilia for fear that it was homosexuality.

This created the typical angry, bitter, deceitful, misogynistic, homophobic, late-transitioning Western autogynephile.

Her Asian sister could not be more different. She didn't grow up learning to be a homophobic man, she grew up learning how to be a GAY! Homophobia could not be further from her mind. But what she shows us is important. She shows us that it is not necessary to be as disturbed as so many Western late-transitioning AGPs are. She shows us that it is not autogynephilia that makes them so, it is homophobia, and what society does to them.

There will never be a return to the domestic matriarchy that works so well in Asia, in the West. Nor will there be the support network of beki culture that sustains GNC youth of all kinds. There will never be the supportive personal networks that give young bekis a start in life and allow them to face the slings and arrows of homophobia and discrimination, resolute in the knowledge that somebody really loves them for all their faults.

But in the West, as in Asia, a new phenomenon has risen – the internet and social media. Through this, young Western GNC people are coming together. This is why referral rates for transition are going through the roof.

In 2010, Dr Larry Nuttbrock suggested that autogynephilia appeared to be on the decrease. But what he meant was traditional, late onset AGP of the classic Blanchard model. One reason why this might be happening is that over the last two decades, since the arrival of the internet, AGPs have been transitioning younger. (Meanwhile, more HSTS have avoided being bullied into being 'gay men' by the likes of Jim Fourrat, which we can only be thankful for.)

We can expect this to accelerate. The arrival of the smartphone a few short years ago put the support network in every GNC child's pocket. We may, in the not too distant future, even see the disappearance of the Western late-onset Blanchard autogynephile.

In all honesty, I can't say I'll miss her.

7. Autogynephilia Explained

Autogynephilia was defined by Dr Ray Blanchard. His studies focussed on patients born male who desired Genital Reconstruction Surgery (GRS) to change their male genitalia into cosmetic facsimiles of female ones.

Blanchard's work is the definitive basis of the science on the subject of male-to-female transsexualism.

He defined, in the first place, a group he called 'Homosexual Transsexual' (HSTS). The most important factors that link the individuals together is that they are uniquely sexually attracted to men, in exactly the same way as women are, and that they are remarkably feminine in manners, comportment and appearance. Their parents and siblings would have noticed from an early age that they were 'like girls'.

Perhaps more importantly, however, Blanchard identified another group that was presenting in significant numbers. This group he found puzzling. The people in it were older. They were not in any way feminine or effeminate and they had extreme difficulty 'passing' as women. They were overwhelmingly white, with middle-class, professional backgrounds who had been successful in their careers. In addition, they were nearly always married and usually had children. Frequently these last were at the point of becoming independent. Most importantly, however, these individuals were never attracted to men, at least prior to transition.

Dichotomy.

This dichotomy had been observed before, since the time of Magnus Hirschfield, but nobody had been able to explain what was going on. Blanchard HSTS were easy to understand: they are socially, sexually, romantically and behaviourally women. It really is that simple. They may not be women in a biological sense but in every other way, that is what they are.

The second group was not like that and their profile was much more difficult to describe. These individuals were sexually, socially, romantically and behaviourally men as well as being biological males. They could not have been more different from the HSTS profile. Blanchard argued that the root cause of their condition must reside in their male sexuality, since they clearly could not have a female one.

This observation, backed up by statistical surveys and questionnaires, led Blanchard to the discovery that the most important such factor in this second group's profile was their attraction to themselves, as women. This allowed him to formulate a testable hypothesis:

> 'Autogynephilia is a man's propensity to be sexually aroused by the thought or image of himself, as a woman.'

Unchallenged.

Fundamentally, this remains unchallenged science. However, other researchers have highlighted differences in the profiles of the AGPs they studied, from the Blanchard model. This probably means that there is significant cultural overlay on the basic condition, which is already complex.

Looking at the situation in Asia, where most AGPs present with markedly different profiles from the West, tends to confirm this. So while the attraction of the subject to the idea of being a woman remains the underlying motivation, the precise manner in which this may be satisfied is remarkably varied.

Most people, including HSTS, are attracted to personalities outside the self: other people. AGPs are different: their primary objects of sexual attraction are themselves, but as women. Blanchard called this misdirection of sexual attraction an 'Erotic Target Location Error'.

In the West, many men with this condition remain secret fetishistic cross dressers all their lives. Their visibility is directly related to social factors: the less acceptable it is for a man to wear women's clothing, the more likely that they will keep their behaviour a secret. A great many go to their graves without their wives or children ever knowing the truth.

Autogynephilia in Childhood.

Psychologically, the development of the condition follows a defined path. Usually, either at or at some time after puberty, the subject becomes sexually aroused by the thought of himself in women's clothing or, more rarely, just by conceiving of himself, in fantasy, as a woman.

Increasingly, however, evidence is appearing that some people do experience autogynephilia in childhood, before puberty. What may be happening is that the subject is having early crushes on the idea of being a woman.

This appears to be consistent with the way that people with other orientations show early crushes on the target that will become their adult sexual desire. This suggests that autogynephilia is a distinct orientation which may sit alongside a more conventional one.

Sexual reward.

Although many AGPs masturbate while dressed as women, not all do. However, Blanchard was able to show that there were other activities which, while not specifically sexual, could still provide sexual reward. Put that another way: could still make the person feel sexy.

Ask yourself this, if you are a heterosexual man: would putting on lingerie and stockings make you feel sexy? Would wearing lip-gloss and eye-liner get you hot and bothered? What about a pair of hot pants or a push-up bra? A nice new hair-do and a manicure?

If you are a heterosexual woman, ask yourself: would wearing a three-piece suit make you feel sexy? What about some nice brogues? Or what about growing a beard – would that make you feel sexy?

These feelings are sexual rewards, even though they are not actually sexual acts. And this is the basis of autogynephilia. It is an orientation in which appearing as a woman provides a range of sexual reward, *to a man*.

Because sexual reward is so powerful a confirming agent for behaviour, this practice leads to an intensification of the condition. Sexual reward, after all, is the basis of human bonding. However the bond being formed here is not between two separate individuals, but within the mind of a single, male individual.

This means that a second personality must be created by the subject, to fall in love with. Typically this appears soon after the onset of the condition.

This second personality grows within the mind of the subject. It was created as an object of desire and has been nourished through rewarding behaviour, often for decades. It may become so powerful that it overwhelms the male personality that invented it. At this point the subject becomes intensely uncomfortable with being a man and feels a need to transition.

In the West this typically happens in middle age; it was overwhelmingly the case when Blanchard was researching autogynephilia. The results can be catastrophic. The wife of such an individual may be told she must 'become a lesbian' by the man she married. However he is not really the man she married but a secret personality he has been developing for decades. The man she married is effectively dead, his personality swamped.

The classic, late-transitioning Western AGP remains a man in every sense except that of appearance. His attraction to women remains exactly the same as a hetero-normative male's.

Two other forms.

This 'classic' profile accounts for some 60% or more of Western AGPs. However, Blanchard identified two other sexual desires.

The first he termed 'analloerotic'. Sometimes these individuals are misrepresented as 'asexual;' but this is simplistic. Analloerotics are unable to derive sexual pleasure from sex with other people. Instead they get it from such things as using women's toilets, from 'dressing parties', which are frequently advertised in the media targeting AGPs; and from knitting and other stereotypically 'women's' roles. Here the reward that feeds the autogynephilia is social acceptance as women.

However, since this article was published, correspondents have stated that at these parties, group masturbation sessions are common. So while analloerotics may not be interested in having sex with other people in a conventional, penetrative sense, it appears that sexual release as part of group activities, although self-stimulated, is rewarding for them.

The other group of AGPs identified by Blanchard he called 'bisexual'. Like the others, prior to transition, these men have no sexual interest in other men. However, once they begin hormone therapy and begin to feminise, these individuals explore being women in a more challenging environment. For them, going out in public dressed in women's clothes is not enough. They need to be sexually desired by men.

This is an extension of their autogynephilia, in which the person they have created must be taken, not just socially but also sexually, *as a woman:* to be 'fucked like a girl'. Blanchard called this phenomenon 'pseudo-bisexuality'. In this, the AGP will identify her anus as a vagina, as commented on by Blanchard and others. The individuals in this group often elect to have GRS, but not always.

There is a significant number of sex workers in the West who conform to this type. Many of their male clients are also AGP.

Competition reward.

Another path that AGPs may follow to assuage their autogynephilia is through competition against natal women. Mianne Bagger, for example was the first transwoman golfer.

More concerning is Fallon Fox, who became an MMA fighter after transitioning. Success in these fields satisfies the autogynephilia through the fantasy of being 'accepted' as women – though quite how using a man's physique to beat the pulp out of natal women can be tolerated is unimaginable; well, if you're not persuaded by the Post-Modernist bunk of 'Identity Politics'.

A more civilised form of competition – or at least one less likely to cause physical harm – is in beauty pageants and modelling. This is hugely popular across Asia and elsewhere and HSTS and AGP transsexuals compete with each other on all fours– and the AGPs often win. Competing in the sex market.

Even more interestingly, perhaps, is a phenomenon seen in Italy and

Spain. Both are well known destinations of South American travesti, or transsexual prostitutes. Many of these advertise through websites like Arcaton or Distintas, which categorise escorts as 'travestis' or 'women'. Only a minority have GRS but if they do, they will immediately remove all trace of their former selves and re-appear, as women prostitutes. They then compete directly with women for male clientele.

Such avenues are closed to the majority of Western AGPs because they transition so late. By the time they do, they are thoroughly masculinised physically; they can never hope to pass as women, far less compete with them in physical beauty. Furthermore, their youthful socialisation has given them no training in how to act like a woman, so not only do they look like men, they act like them.

However, in the decades since Blanchard defined autogynephilia, much has changed. Even in the West, autogynephiles are presenting much younger and can be extremely attractive (if tall.) Dutch model Kelly van der Veer and Canadian Jenna Talakova come to mind.

The fact is that autogynephilia is an enormously complicated and disparate phenomenon which science still has much to learn about. What is not in doubt is that it is real and it is the stimulus for an unknown percentage, possibly a majority, of male-to-feminine transitions.

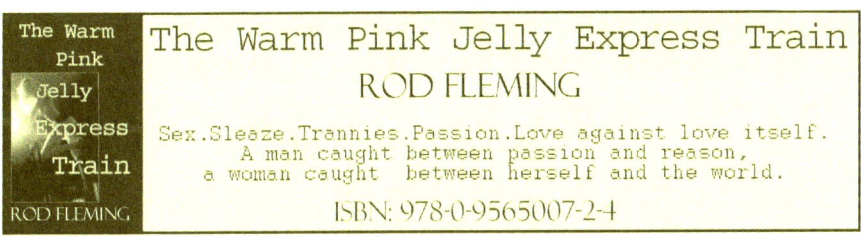

8 Brain Sex?

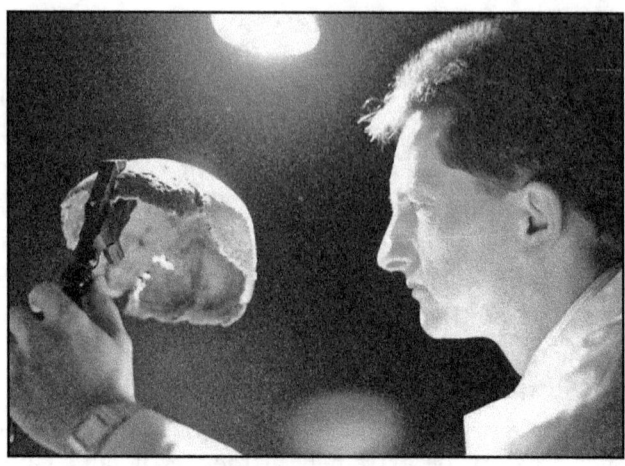

Brain Sex? What is that? Some sort of cyber-intercourse?

No. 'Brain sex' is how many transsexual activists explain how their condition came about. They specifically say that

> 'Transsexualism occurs when an individual of one sex has certain sex-related structures in the brain that are typical of the opposite sex.'

In other words, according to this notion, transsexualism is a physical condition and not a psychological one. Putting that more technically, what is being claimed is that transsexualism is caused by a form of intersexuality that is localised in the brain. This is 'brain sex'. However, physical heteromorphism of this type should be observable. So is it?

Intersex – what is it?

To understand that you need to know a little bit more about what intersex is. In it, individuals of one chromosomal karotype – XX or XY – may be born with sex-related structures typical of the other. In a condition called Complete Androgen Insensitivity Syndrome, the individual, as birth, looks like a perfectly normal girl child.

She grows up to appear to be a typical, healthy women. Then, when she is unable to get pregnant, testing is done and at this point it is discovered that she is actually XY – she has male-typical chromosomes. What has happened is that her body is insensitive to the masculinising effects of testosterone.

There are many intersex conditions, like Partial Androgen Insensitivity, for example. There's Klinefelter's Syndrome, where the individual has three sex chromosomes, XXY, 'mosaic' (XYXY), congenital adrenal hyperplasia (CAH) and a host of others.

While these intersex conditions are relatively rare, there is still a large number of people with them. They are found all over the world in all populations. In some cases, their genitalia differ greatly from the 'normative' and this led, in the past, to many unnecessary surgical interventions to 'correct' it. (Thankfully this is much less the case now, but if you have a child you think might be intersex, then please find out as much as you can before agreeing to surgeries.)

Most importantly, perhaps, we can directly observe the effects of these conditions, although in some, like CAIS, this might not be at all obvious till much later in life.

Trapped in the wrong body?

Transsexual activists, through the brain sex hypothesis, are suggesting that something similar causes transsexualism, but the site of the heteromorphism is in the brain.

This has been linked to another idea popular with some transsexuals and many transgender people, that they are 'trapped in' the wrong body. 'Look,' they say (if they are male-to-female) 'I may have a man's body but I have a woman's brain.'

They are claiming that transsexualism is caused by a physical condition. Specifically, a brain-restricted form of intersex.

It's not clear when exactly this claim was first made, but it was certainly current by the 1980s.

Ray Blanchard.

During that decade, Blanchard was working at the Clarke Institute in Toronto, Canada. One of his roles was to provide letters of recommendation, for individuals seeking Genital Reconstruction Surgery (GRS) or a 'sex change'.[1]

At that time, it had been broadly assumed that 'True' transsexuals were very like extremely feminine homosexual men. They were certainly physically attractive and very 'passable' as women. They tended to present while they were very young, often in their teens. But their most noticeable characteristic was a powerful sexual desire for men.

Blanchard had no difficulty with this group, but he soon realised he was seeing another group too. These were older, very masculine, didn't look or act like women at all and – critically – were not primarily attracted to men.

However, they were in distress. So Blanchard began to develop an explanation that would allow him, ethically, to give them a letter of recommendation for GRS.

This difference had previously been noted by researchers and the types had been classified as 'True' and 'Pseudo' transsexual. In most cases 'Pseudo' transsexuals were refused recommendation for GRS, because they were considered to be fetishistic transvestites.

Blanchard's Typology.

Blanchard is a realist and he was not interested in the kind of pejorative thinking that would deny these people relief from their distress. So he carried our systematic statistical surveys over a period of years.

This allowed him to show that the 'Pseudo' transsexuals were actually exhibiting a condition he called 'autogynephilia' (AGP). This he described as 'a man's propensity to aroused by the thought of himself as a woman'.

The old 'True' classification he renamed 'HomoSexual Transsexual (HSTS) and the old 'Pseudo' transsexual as AGP. The result was Blanchard's Typology. Now, both types could legitimately be recommended for surgery.

Unfortunately, rather than being thankful for this intervention, the proponents of the 'brain sex' hypothesis were upset. They attacked Blanchard for calling HSTS 'homosexual'. That was a ridiculous attack; they were males who were attracted to other males. However, they were

---

1 The term 'sex change' is misleading. The surgery is purely cosmetic. The subject's sex does not change in anyway. Strictly, the genitalia are reconstructed to look like those of a person of the opposite sex – sometimes very convincingly. Hence 'GRS'.

not gay men, they were transsexuals. Hence, HSTS. (All the HSTS whom I have explained this to have agreed that it is accurate; and in any case, this is science, not some touchy-feely humanities woo. There is such a thing as objective reality and taxonomy matters.)

Misreading Blanchard, and misleading the world.

However, in a blatant misreading of Blanchard, they also accused him of saying that AGPs were just closet fetishists who put on women's clothes to masturbate.

In fact, Blanchard defined three discrete orientations within AGP (bisexual, analloerotic or asexual, and gynephilic, attracted to women.) He also defined several different forms that AGP could take. So it's a very broad description and the only thing that holds it together is the core notion of being stimulated by the idea of being a woman.

This cuts right across the 'brain sex' hypothesis, which claims that inside their brains, these individuals are *actually* women.

Before we look at neurology, which is clearly the only science that might resolve this, we have to know a few things about the brain. It is the most adaptive organ in the body. Just thinking about something changes it. The brain makes new connections all the time, in response to new thoughts and things learned. It's changing as we change.

For example, musicians have measurably different brains from non-musicians. But do their brains make them musicians or does being a musician change their brains?

Nature and nurture.

This is sometimes, colloquially, called the 'nature-nurture debate'. More scientifically, the idea that certain brains lead to certain behaviours is called 'biological determinism'. It is a contentious proposition, to put it mildly.

What that means is that even if we were able to show that there were differences in brain morphology between transsexuals and other males, we could not just assume – as the 'brain sex' hypothesis does – that this *makes* them transsexual.

Establishing this would be next to impossible. Since changes in brain connections happen hand in hand with behavioural changes, we would have to test a random sample of children. We would have to note whether they had these heteromorphisms, then observe them and see if they became transsexual, later. And all the while we would have to control for and exclude any influence that the experimental procedure itself might cause.

Good luck with designing that experiment and getting permission and funding to do it.

Brain sex in individuals.

Blanchard, aware of this, suggested that when it became possible to observe inside the brains of transsexuals, his HSTS type would be found to have brains more like women's, whereas the AGPs would have men's brains. Bear that in mind.

The 'brain sex' hypothesis got a major boost in 1996 when Zhou et al published results of autopsies on the brains of 6 MtF transsexuals. These were not controlled for HSTS/AGP. Zhou found heteromorphism in the BST corpus, which is a part of the amygdala.

'Lo!' claimed the 'brain sex' apologists, 'We are vindicated! Transsexuals have women's brains.'

They then argued that since the amygdala forms early in the embryo, this must be a precursor to transsexualism.

The problems were manifold. Firstly, just because an area of the brain forms early, does not mean it can't change later. The BSTc is particularly subject to change under the stimulus of sex hormones.

Six subjects is not enough to 'prove' anything; it's an observation, that's all. The notion of causation was moot and to be fair, Zhou never claimed that the BSTc anomaly 'caused' transsexualism. Others did that, for political reasons.

Unfortunately, these obvious problems didn't stop the 'brain sex' enthusiasts from seizing on Zhou and putting it centre-stage. They even got the legendary Bob Sapolsky, he of the huge beard, to go along with this.

MRI Testing.

However, in the first decade of the 21st century, MRI testing became available. In 2010 two teams set out to see if they could find out a bit more. Both these teams were experienced in using MRI testing in areas of sexuality, with proven track records.

One team, (Rametti et al) screened out AGPs using the Blanchard instrument, and the other (Savic and Arver) screened out HSTS. So Rametti only scanned HSTS and Savic and Arver only scanned AGPs. These were large-scale studies with many controls built in. They were conducted on individuals who had not yet commenced hormone treatment. The results were compelling.

Rametti found that HSTS have brains shifted toward the typical for women on 'all tested parameters'. Savic and Arver found that AGP brains are 'no different' from men's. This suggests two things.

As Guillamon's review paper put it, this, along with a welter of neurological evidence from other brains scans and autopsies, suggests two things. The first is that there *is* evidence for a localised form of brain intersexuality, but only in HSTS and not in AGPs. Secondly, Blanchard was right: there are two distinct forms of MtF transsexualism – but only one of them has what might be called 'brain sex'.

So where does that leave the 'brain sex' hypothesis? Well, in the first place, none of the testing, or Guillamon's review, establishes causation. Brains are as likely to have been changed by behaviour as the other way around. As well as this, the principal advocates of the 'brain sex' hypothesis are identifiable as AGP. They have no such brain intersexuality, either as a result of their transsexualism or as a stimulus for it. They just have men's brains.

So, maybe HSTS is caused by a form of brain intersexuality, or maybe being HSTS changes your brain; but if you're AGP, it doesn't matter, because you have a standard man's brain anyway. Oh what a surprise.

The principal arguments of AGPs, which they have ruthlessly pushed, consistently bullying and 'no-platforming' anyone who dared challenge them with science, have been shot to tatters.

There are indeed two types of MtF transsexual; and only one of them has a brain like a woman's. That type is not the AGP. As far as they are concerned the 'brain sex' hypothesis – and they are the ones who have been pushing it – is dead in the water.

9. The Man Who Would Be Queen

Dr J Michael Bailey's seminal book *The Man Who Would Be Queen* (TMWWBQ) sparked huge controversy when it was published in 2003. The furore it caused, while small in focus, was spectacular in its incandescent rage at the author.

This was categorically different from the conservative reaction to works of other controversial authors like D H Lawrence, or even Vladimir Nabokov's deeply unsettling study of male attraction to pubescent girls. In those, the hostility was principally against the work; not so here. It was J Michael Bailey in person who was vilified.

And to cap that, TMWWBQ is not a work of fiction, but of popular science. It is well written, in non-scientific language, is easy to read and deeply sympathetic to its subject. So what on earth happened, to provoke such a furious backlash? It included entirely spurious attempts to end Bailey's career, personal slurs and threats of violence against him. His attackers even accused him of sexually molesting his children.

The campaign against Bailey, coordinated by a small group of internet bullies, amounted to nothing more or less than a blatant attempt at censorship associated with a virulent personal attack on the author. It's time, now, to revisit this book and see why it caused such a storm in a latte cup.

Homosexuality and Transsexualism

The book begins with a general overview of the scientific understanding of male homosexuality, firstly by describing the life of a young, highly feminine cross-dressing boy called 'Danny' (not his real name.) Danny began to show feminine behaviour and to cross-dress when he was three years old; his mother came to Bailey for help.

In Part Two it progresses to describe femininity in adult male homosexuals and contrasts this with masculinity in the same group. At the end of this section, Bailey briefly discusses the known history of male homosexuality.

He introduces the ideas of 'transgender homosexuality' on one hand, in which although both partners are born male, one plays a woman in all manners including appearance, comportment and in sexual intercourse. On the other hand there is 'egalitarian' homosexuality, where both parties are masculine in appearance and comportment.

The former is the norm across the world and was the only model until the 20th century. The latter appeared in Western culture, specifically the USA, in the 1960s and has been spread by contact since. Bailey makes the important point that in the former, only one partner is actually homosexual, since she is born male but desires masculine men, while her partner desires women and plays a masculine sexual role. In the latter, both are homosexual because both desire men and appear to be men.

Assessing Transgender and Egalitarian Homosexuality.

He makes the accurate assessment that transgender homosexuals, since they are attracted to straight men, who are therefore attracted to femininity, are naturally driven to appear to be as feminine as possible. On the other hand, egalitarian homosexuals, themselves attracted to masculinity, appear to be masculine themselves. This is sometimes called 'clone' homosexuality. The author then poses questions about how Danny's adult life might proceed in view of all of this.

In Part Three, the book discusses persons born male who desire to become women, in the light of the preceding parts. Bailey calls these individuals 'transsexuals'. He makes it clear that this is a broad church that is not limited to those persons who wish to undergo or have undergone Genital Reconstruction Surgery.

He discusses the popular 'brain sex' idea, which posits that male-to-female (mtf) transsexuals are 'women trapped in men's bodies' and notes that there is no evidence to support this. In any case, he asks, how does anyone know what it feels like to be someone else?

Bailey explains that there are actually two different types of male-to-female (mtf) transsexual. This had been noted almost a hundred years earlier by the German psychologist Magnus Hirschfield and repeatedly confirmed by later scientists. None, however, had been able to explain this difference.

Ray Blanchard

He then describes the research carried out by Dr Ray Blanchard, which explains these differences by showing that there are two distinct profiles of people born male who wish to become women. These profiles have nothing in common save that the subjects are born male and become women. The differences are enormous, and Blanchard's research, for the first time, explained these in proper scientific studies. This is the foundation of the modern science of transsexualism.

This section is illustrated by descriptions, again sensitively handled, of the lives of several transsexuals of both types. It is quite clear from the writing that these examples are meant to serve only as examples.

The two types, Bailey explains, are 'homosexual transsexual' or HSTS, and 'autogynephilic transsexual' or AGP. Bailey explains that HSTS are uniquely attracted to masculine men, whereas AGPs, at least before transitioning, are attracted to women.

What motivates HSTS?

The core motivation for HSTS is a powerful desire for straight, masculine lovers. They may have numerous gay friends but they are not attracted to them.

This, Bailey explains, is a relatively easy orientation to understand. HSTS transsexuals are naturally feminine boys who desire men. If they think they can be successful as women, they are likely to at least try to follow this path. Everything they do from the point they decide to transition is in order to make themselves more attractive. This, after all, whether feminists approve or not, is what most young women do.

(HSTS do not take hormones and have surgeries in order to become more 'like women' but to become *more beautiful* women.)

On the other hand, the core motivation for autogynephilic transsexualism is 'a man's propensity to be aroused by the thought or image of himself as a woman'. While it is complex, autogynephilia, like HSTS, is rooted in male sexuality. It could hardly be rooted in any other type.

Three sexualities.

Blanchard identified three distinct sexualities of autogynephilic men. These were heterosexual, the majority, who retained their normative male attraction to women and never or rarely had sex with men. Bisexuals begin experimenting with sex with men after transition or while 'dressed'. Finally 'analloerotics' need no other person for romantic or sexual satisfaction. (These last are sometimes called 'asexual' but this is wrong; just 'being women' is a sexual release for them.)

To complicate matters even more, autogynephilia may manifest in four different manners. In transvestic AGP, the subject is stimulated by cross-dressing. In behavioural, the stimulus comes from doing 'womanly' things such as knitting. In physiological the attraction is to female bodily functions like menstruation (AGP men may wear sanitary pads and urinate in them, for example). And in anatomic, the subject is aroused by the thought of having a woman's body parts such as a vagina.

These four manners may occur individually or in conjunction with each other and they affect the three types of autogynephiliac. The complexity of this condition, and the incisiveness that Blanchard showed in identifying the cause of them all, autogynephilia, are obvious.

So what causes autogynephilia? Put simply, this is an 'Erotic Target Location Error'. Instead of the subject being romantically attached to a person outside of themselves, they are attracted to a pseudo-personality created within their own minds. This is a facsimile of a woman. (She has to be since they are gynephilic, or attracted to women.) As the condition advances, this pseudo-personality is strengthened through sexual reward until it overwhelms the male host. At this point the subject experiences feelings of great psychological unease as the created pseudo-woman now in control rejects her male body.

(This is so different from the 'gender dysphoria' that HSTS experience that some HSTS reject the term.)

Typically young.

HSTS typically present while still young, often in their teens and rarely over the age of thirty, while AGPs, on average, present much later, with a median age of 43. This has allowed some AGPs to claim that the only difference is one of age at presentation; but Blanchard debunks this.

At the same time, thanks to the internet and social media, there is significantly more overlap in age now than when Blanchard was researching. It is possible to compare the types side by side now; they are completely different. HSTS are extremely feminine and have no difficulty 'passing' as women. They often, themselves, claim they are 'useless at being men'. AGPs (in the West), even when younger, find it difficult to be feminine at all, and those who transition later in life may really struggle.

Bailey observes

> 'There is the rare exception, but for the most part, autogynephilic transsexuals aspire (with some success) to be presentable, while homosexual transsexuals aspire (with equivalent success) to be objects of desire.'

(Note, however, that HSTS are interested in attracting straight male lovers and are in direct competition with natal women for them; AGPs, in the main, are not.)

Bailey, as a clinician, is equally sympathetic to both types and makes it clear that both should be treated fairly.

Having presented the case that male homosexuality may be genetic Bailey then suggests that autogynephilia may also be so and run in families. If that's true it would therefore be a discrete, genetically-dependent orientation in itself.

'Gender dysphoria' is a deeply-felt discomfort with their male physical attributes, associated with both types of mtf transsexual. Indeed it is the clinical diagnosis upon which a referral for surgery must be based, and this has caused some considerable confusion.

In talking to many HSTS transwomen both online and in person, it is quite clear that they do not suffer gender dysphoria in the way that AGPs do. For the latter, this is a deep and unsupportable loathing of their male organs. It is triggered by the collapse of their male persona under onslaught from their pseudo-feminine one.

Most HSTS have no such issue with their organs; they have an issue with *being beautiful*. This is so that they may compete with natal women and be accepted as sexual partners by straight men – who are the only men they are interested in. If winning such a man means losing the penis, so be it.

(Bailey is pessimistic about the extent to which GRS improves a transwoman's chances of winning and keeping a straight male partner.)

Throughout, Bailey avoids inflammatory language and, while this is not a science textbook, writes in a very neutral manner. He presents the evidence and explains the scientific theories, but leaves the reader to draw conclusions.

The book is not perfect and this in part is because it was published over a decade ago. Where it falls down most is where there was least scientific research. In addition, the author tends to extrapolate from the US experience to the global one, which is unsupported. He somewhat assumes that the US milieu can be regarded as a 'standard of normativity' when in fact, many observers would regard it as a very peculiar one indeed, informed by some deeply unpleasant Anglo-Saxon prejudices.

For example, the author clearly regards the idea that 'Danny' should grow up to be a gay man, rather than a transsexual woman, as a good outcome. He acknowledges that this must mean Danny suppressing his femininity, and does remark that if he grew up in a milieu less prejudiced than the US, he would probably be transsexual. But he makes no attempt to argue that US culture should be changed, meaning that boys like 'Danny' must continue to suppress their true natures, however hard that might be. (Today, social change means that there would be a much greater chance that 'Danny' would indeed grow up to be transsexual, even in the USA.)

Notwithstanding these points, which Bailey might well view differently today anyway, *The Man Who Would Be Queen* is, overall, an excellent book. It lays out the science of transsexualism in a clear and easily understood manner and thus provides an accurate and factually correct lay person's guide. I would say this book is a very useful primer and explains a great deal that would otherwise be mysterious.

All in all, it is well written, contains much insight and treats its subjects with great respect. It preserves their dignity, even when describing practices that most people would be surprised by. It is not at all prurient or lascivious and maintains a consistent good humour throughout: so why on Earth did it cause so much trouble?

Storm in a Latte Cup

While *The Man Who Would Be Queen* discussed several different types of sexuality and the individuals who have them, only one of these groups showed any negative reaction to the book. Gay men and HSTS transwomen were largely silent. (I have explained Blanchard to many HSTS transwomen; all were suspicious at first but very quickly recognised themselves in his description.) The only group that objected to the book at all was a small number of AGP activists, most of whom were themselves academics.

This is surprising because academics, while frequently scathing about each other's conclusions, are usually very careful to avoid any kind of *ad hominem* attack; but the very opposite happened here.

While some AGP activists did try to debunk Blanchard, whose research informed much of the book, they were unsuccessful.

In any case, Blanchard did not write the book that caused the anger; J. Michael Bailey wrote it. He, rather than Blanchard, was the target of what his colleague Dr Alice Dreger called a 'narcissistic rage attack'. A classic case of 'shoot the messenger'.

A shocking attack.

The attack on Bailey was shocking for its intensity and its personal nature. An investigation by Northwestern University, where Bailey is a professor, fully vindicated him and an excellent rebuttal of the attacks was written by Dreger. However there is no doubt that a small group of people in positions of responsibility, including senior academics, colluded to ruin Bailey's career and destroy his private life. Thankfully they failed but this reflects no credit on the perpetrators whatsoever.

The attempt to discredit both Ray Blanchard and Michael Bailey was not on scientific grounds, but on personal ones. There is no credible evidence to refute Blanchard. Yet, to this day, many autogynephile activists and even a few HSTS ones (who should know better) claim that his typology is 'out of date' or 'debunked'.

Nothing could be further from the truth. While some of the terminology has been modified in certain publications, the core ideas have become the *de facto* scientific consensus. These are that there are two distinct types of male-to-female transsexualism, both rooted in male sexuality. Individuals in one group are strongly attracted to men, while the others are attracted to the idea of themselves as women.

Blanchard's typology remains the basis of the APA's understanding of transsexualism, along with that of the WHO and other psychological and psychiatric bodies across the globe.

Confirming Blanchard.

MRI tests on separate and controlled groups of HSTS by Rametti *et al.* on one hand and on AGPs by Savic and Arver on the other, results published in 2011, clearly demonstrated major differences between HSTS and AGP brains. This directly confirmed Blanchard.

Today, the principal researcher into autogynephilia is Dr Anne Lawrence, herself AGP. She has amassed many narratives from other autogynephiles that fully support Blanchard, which she also does. This, of course, has also made her a target for attack, despite the thorough and painstaking nature of her research.

Academically disgraceful.

The attacks on Bailey were academically disgraceful. It is worse because senior academics prosecuted them. They attempted to force the acceptance of an explanation that lacked any independent support. They rejected properly designed, supported, peer-reviewed scientific research, as Blanchard's was.

When it became impossible to break the science, they used the tactics of politicians, rather than scientists. They attempted to shout down a perfectly well developed and executed piece of research and to destroy the lives of those who proposed it. When all else failed they resorted to simple defamation, character assassination, accusations of child abuse, personal insult and innuendo and even death threats. Nobody could be in any doubt that this was an atrocious way to behave. Why did they do it? Because they had no evidence to refute Blanchard.

This is no different from the anti-science mindset of Flat-Earthers. It is no different from the preaching of extremist religious fundamentalists who deny evolution or how the universe came to be. It is the wilfully ignorant point of view that because one believes something, it must be so, irrespective of whether it is true or not.

Well, the Earth is not 6,000 years old and Darwin was right. Science is the only credible means we have to explain natural phenomena. To deny it because it might harm the interests, or hurt the feelings, of some people, is unacceptable. That such a position is held by some claiming to be scientists themselves is egregiously so. For those people to then collude in a pack attack on others with whose ideas they disagreed with is beyond the pale.

Vindication

In the thirteen years since this celebrated storm in the latte cup, further research has vindicated Blanchard. No serious scientist now subscribes to the 'brain sex' notion, at least as regards non-homosexual MtF. The consensus is firmly that there are two distinct conditions that lead to male-to-female transsexualism, both rooted in male sexuality. The politically-correct myth that non-homosexual MtF transsexuals are 'women born in men's bodies' has been debunked, not once, but time and again.

This has not prevented autogynephile activists from continuing to promote it, to the detriment of HSTS transsexuals and of course, women. So persuasive have they been that many lay persons apparently believe that the only way to be a 'real' woman is to have been born with a penis. To this end they continue to use the same tactics as they used against Bailey: misrepresentation, traduction, quote-mining, bullying, character assassination, defamation and flat lying.

Blanchard and Bailey today.

Blanchard himself no longer researches in the area of transsexualism. He was on the editorial board for the most recent revision of the Diagnostic and Statistical Manual. J Michael Bailey has returned to an earlier fascination. He recently collaborated in research which re-examined, using pairs of identical twins, the idea that homosexuality might be genetic and innate. His contribution to studies in the field of human sexuality remains important. Lawrence continues to publish and contribute to the actual science of transsexualism – rather than the socio-political nonsense that is all too prevalent.

Conclusion

The Man Who Would Be Queen, in summation, then, is a well-written and enjoyable book that explains the science of transsexualism in everyday language, citing real examples of real people. It is a must-read for anyone interested in this subject. The book makes it possible to understand the phenomenon of people like Bruce 'Caitlyn' Jenner.

While not itself a scientific textbook it is an accurate and readable primer that points the reader in the direction of the peer-reviewed research, on which it is based, with an excellent bibliography.

It would be of especial interest and help to those who have, in their families, autogynephilic transsexuals, particularly women whose hus-

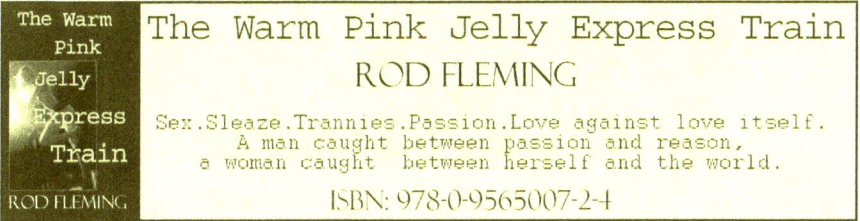

The Warm Pink Jelly Express Train
ROD FLEMING
Sex.Sleaze.Trannies.Passion.Love against love itself.
A man caught between passion and reason,
a woman caught between herself and the world.
ISBN: 978-0-9565007-2-4

bands have announced that they intend to transition, as well as the sons and daughters of such men.

10. Jennifer Laude, Victim of Hate

On the 11th of October 2014, a young woman went to a cheap hotel in Olongapo City in the Philippines, with a man later identified as a US marine, and one of her friends. The woman's name was Jennifer Laude. She was 26 years old.

Later that night, Jennifer's body was discovered by hotel staff. She had bruises all over her and had been the victim of a sustained and savage beating. She had been strangled. But the actual cause of death, according to the coroner's report, was asphyxiation through drowning. Jennifer's murderer beat her half to death, then strangled her half to death and finished off by forcing her head into a toilet bowl and drowning her. Despite being a US Marine and well-educated in the means of ending human life, Jennifer's killer wanted to be sure she was dead.

Jennifer had her whole life before her. Yet that life was ended in obscene savagery. She must have been utterly terrified, until the beating she received at the hands of a trained killer caused shock to blur her consciousness.

Why would anyone want to kill someone in this way? Could it have been theft? Did Jennifer try to steal this man's wallet? His watch? No. No reasonable person surgically beats a person senseless, strangles them and then, when they are absolutely incapable of defence, drowns them in a toilet bowl, because they have tried to steal a wallet. Even the most brain-dead grunt would have measured the consequences, realised that his career and possibly life would be over, and simply overpowered the girl and thrown her out or called the police.

Newspaper reports say that two used condoms were found at the scene. We may safely assume that Jennifer's murderer used at least one of them. But this was not rape; Jennifer willingly went to the hotel room with her killer, and even sent her friend away.

So the act of sex was consummated, by two consenting partners, and only then did the killer unleash a frenzied attack of staggering savagery.

Criminologists know how to read the signs that tell the tale of a murder. The brutal, sustained and excessive beating, the strangulation and finally, holding the victim's head in the toilet bowl while flushing the toilet all say the same thing: Jennifer's murder was deeply personal and provoked by visceral hatred.

What could make a man – someone with a good career in the military, which he must have known all along would be ended – murder someone he hardly knew with such anger and hatred? The answer is simple: Jennifer Laude was beaten, strangled and drowned to death for being transgender.

For those who do not know, that means that the gender she had been assigned at birth, on examination of her genitalia, did not match her understanding of herself. As far as Jennifer was concerned, she was a woman, and the picture of her above, which has circulated the web, shows how beautiful she was.

Jennifer, attractive, stylish and seductive, was a 'target woman' – the kind of woman that men try to have sex with in order to enhance their standing amongst their peers. Only Jennifer's body did not correspond to the standards that were required for her murderer's conquest of her to count as a trophy.

Instead of a vagina, Jennifer had a penis. In the patriarchal mindset, there is no grey area; there is no rainbow curve. There are only men, who are expected to dominate, and women, who are expected to meekly become their sexual trophies. Sexually possessing Jennifer was what her killer wanted. It matters not whether money changed hands; the intent remained the same.

But then, after the killer had sex with Jennifer (as is proven by the used condoms), what irony: there was no vagina to be taken possession of and instead, he had made love with a woman who had a penis.

For his conquest to have been complete, Jennifer had to have a vagina, one that her attacker penetrated. Instead, Jennifer's penis destroyed every concept of honour or belonging that her murderer had ever known. His reputation was ruined and his crew-mates would all, from now on, condemn him.

Yet it's not just his crew-mates, or the NCOs and officers who use psychological abuse and codes of 'honour' to pervert young men into killers, who are culpable. A glance through the comments section of media all over the world reveals the truth: there are people out there prepared to justify beating, strangling and drowning another person just because of her genitalia.

Every one of these people is in part guilty of Jennifer's murder.

Jennifer was engaged to a German, Marc Sueselbeck. The couple met online two years before the murder and had spent three months together.

One can only imagine the pain and grief that Mr Sueselbeck is now suffering, especially in view of the tone of the media reports that consistently have misrepresented his fiancée. He is angry and I support his anger. I am angry and I did not even know Jennifer. Sueselbeck had invested his love in her, made plans to spend his life with her, shared a dream with her – and then an immature, testosterone-fuelled bigot who had been trained to kill robbed him of everything.

Jennifer's death is not unique. Twelve years ago an American girl, Gwen Araujo, was beaten and burned to death and then buried in the desert for the same reasons as Jennifer: her murderers were conditioned to believe they had a right to expect certain features to be present on the body of a woman who had sex with them.

Every year, in Brazil, around 100 transwomen are murdered, often in similar circumstances, and globally the number is much higher. And this does not count the innumerable beatings, insults and discrimination transpeople have to suffer just for being true to themselves.

American attorneys have invented the entirely bogus defence of 'gay panic' which suggests that seeing a penis is terrifying enough for a man that he may be excused for killing its possessor in the most savage manner imaginable.

Well it will not do. I have since my teens been opposed to the death sentence, but if it will stop one more poor, terrified girl being beaten to death by a man, then so be it. Hang them high.

Jennifer Laude, in part thanks to the tragedy of her death, will be remembered as a beautiful young woman who meant no harm and just wanted to be herself.

Her killer will be remembered for what he is: a hate-filled, brutal, evil man who beat, strangled and drowned a weaker, vulnerable person for not living up to his expectations.

The name of the accused, currently in custody, is Private First Class Joseph Scott Pemberton of the 2nd Battalion Ninth US Marines. We hope his unit, corps and country are proud of him and what he has done.

The Warm Pink Jelly Express Train
ROD FLEMING
Sex.Sleaze.Trannies.Passion.Love against love itself.
A man caught between passion and reason,
a woman caught between herself and the world.
ISBN: 978-0-9565007-2-4

11. Pansexual: the human norm

When we did the research for *Why Men Made God* we spent a lot of time looking at how societies might have been structured in the era before the development of agriculture and the establishment of the patriarchy (I will be calling these 'traditional' societies.) Clearly, we can't directly study the human groups that existed outside Africa between 50,000 and 5,000 years ago, because they no longer exist.

They left very little evidence. Although they did use stone and bone, a great deal of their artefacts were made of wood or leather and were perishable. The few that we do have are somewhat mysterious.

To try to shed light on this, we reviewed a wide range of anthropological literature. We especially concentrated on extant traditional societies, of which there are a surprising number, despite the attempts by the patriarchy, especially the Christian and Muslim ones, to eradicate them. (As a matter of fact, Islam has been less damaging to many traditional societies than Christianity, as we see from the number of traditional groups still living, and respected, in Indonesia. Sadly, this is changing as more intolerant forms of Islam gain ground.)

We reviewed the mythology that was recorded soon after the invention of writing in the culture that leads to the Western Patriarchy, which appeared in Sumer in the 5th Millennium BCE. We then compared this to modern mythologies which form part of traditional cultures.

We also looked at close relatives of humans, particularly our closest, the Dwarf Chimpanzee or bonobo, Pan paniscus.

Bonobos have a fascinating social model. They are pansexual and gender-fluid. Males are not dominant and rape has never been observed in bonobo society, either in the wild or in captivity. Generally speaking, they have very relaxed, cool societies with notably low levels of aggression and stress.

In fact, bonobos use sex as the antidote to aggression and stress. Instead of fighting, they love each other, to be blunt. What is interesting is that when they do this, there is no dominance imperative: partners in bonobo sexual relations are equals. Females and males are equally likely to initiate sex. Furthermore, they have no defined preferences – they will as happily have sex with same-sex partners as with opposite.

Sex is a powerful bonding agent in bonobo society. It holds groups together and prevents division. This protects the group from falling apart and thus the individuals within it are more likely to survive. So sex has an evolutionary imperative alongside the reproductive one. In fact, bonobos don't have sex to make babies, they have sex with their friends and for fun, because they like it. However, they have so much sex that there is no shortage of bonobo babies. Bonobos are evolved to be pansexual and gender-fluid, and we argue that this is the case for humans too.

It should be clear how this torpedoes the 'homosexuality is an evolutionary dead-end' argument. It might be, as far as individuals are concerned, but when everyone is having sex with everyone else, this is not the case. Being exclusively homosexual does mean an end to the individual's genetic line, but this is not how same-sex sex works in either bonobo or traditional societies. The individual male only has to impregnate one female to reproduce his genes; and given the amount of sex in bonobo society, and the variety of it, this is easily achieved. The same, of course, holds true for females – if they give up having sex with each other occasionally to have it with a male, job done. Bonobos are naturally pansexual, to accommodate this, and we argue that the same is true of humans, and back it up with examples.

Further, bonobos are gender-fluid. This does not mean what some people think it does; it is not about wearing a miniskirt and sporting a beard. It means being happy to play either the penetrating or receiving role in sex. Bonobo males are routinely observed having sex, in which one penetrates and the other receives, and immediately after, having sex again and swapping roles. Then they will go off and have sex with females, who probably were having sex with each other in the meantime. Bonobo children are brought up by the group.

We share over 98% of our DNA with bonobos and our traditional social models are almost identical. We wondered if we would find something in traditional societies that pointed to similar behaviours in humans and we found it.

All over the world, traditional societies exist. In many, same-sex activity is normal; frequently this is observed between adult men and boys. (Unfortunately, and probably due to the fact that the anthropologists doing the research were men, there is far less information about the women's sexuality.) The adult men in these relations have women partners too.

We know of the Spartans that not only the men but the women had normalised same-sex relations.

However, bonobos have had to do without the curse of organised religions, so are still happily having sex with anyone they like, while we invented a whole raft of ridiculous rules and conventions about it.

With that in mind, it is disappointing to see how the modern gay 'accommodationist' movement imposes rules of behaviourm such as the outlawing of effeminicy, or that 'once gay, always gay'. These rules have been invented by white gay male academics and activists and do not stand up to scrutiny

The Warm Pink Jelly Express Train
ROD FLEMING
Sex.Sleaze.Trannies.Passion.Love against love itself.
A man caught between passion and reason,
a woman caught between herself and the world.
ISBN: 978-0-9565007-2-4

Politics

1. We Live in Interesting Times

We live in interesting times, as the proverb says, politically speaking at least. The 'United' Kingdom's lack of unity is being demonstrated once again and the whole beast now seems to be in the throes of a terminal case of dyspepsia.

For decades the right-leaning south of England got its way; it elected Margaret Thatcher, a puppet of the patriarchal hegemony, and the decline has gathered pace ever since. Even when a government calling itself 'Labour' and playing the socialist card was elected, under the repulsive Tony Blair, it was soon shown to be Tory Party Lite.

The result of decades of rightist government has been the almost complete abandonment of any controls on the behaviour of business and in turn the consequence of this has been a string of boom-bust cycles each worse than the previous.

The most catastrophic came in 2008 and is still, seven years later, being paid for. Remember, that was a right-wing financial collapse brought about by right-wing economic policies.

The right's response has been so-called 'austerity' – for certain parts of society. It is an absurd and deeply offensive policy that has seen soup-kitchens once again operating in the country and millions more people thrown into abject poverty – and all while the rich and their poodles in the right-wing parties continue to get richer.

There can never be an objection to managing budgets with care; yet that is specifically not what the current administration in the disUnited Kingdom is doing. Theirs is a 'silk purse and no knickers' policy that starves, dispossesses and disenfranchises the very poorest while 'investing' in completely unnecessary trinkets like a replacement for Trident – which will never, ever be used. It is exactly like the father who spends all his money on a new car and has not the wherewithal to feed and clothe his children. The 'financial probity' of the right is no more than the dietary awareness of pigs at their trough.

And for decades this continued, with the two major 'UK' parties vying with each other to be the more oppressive on the most oppressed.

Something has changed and the patriarchal hegemony of the English establishment do not like it. Oh no sirree they do not, and their horror is clear to see.

Last week a televised debate was held in which the leaders of seven

'UK' parties took part. These were the Tories, the Liberals, Labour, the SNP, Plaid Cymru, the Greens and UKIP. These parties were represented by three women and four men. What was interesting – and deeply satisfying – was that the four men had their collective backsides well and truly kicked by said three women, most especially by SNP leader Nicola Sturgeon, whose approval rating was the highest amongst viewers – including the English, who cannot vote for her. After the broadcast a Twitter storm broke out that again confirmed this.

We have to admit to being proud that a Scottish woman did so well, but the fact is that we should all be glad that women were able to give a coterie of some of the nastiest products of a vile patriarchal hegemony such a hiding. It is, unreservedly, a very good thing and it is not before time. Furthermore, it is something the British State is determined to prevent, and that makes it all the more pleasant a turn of events.

Democracy itself, for the patriarchal hegemony, is an annoyance that it tolerates as long as it does not interfere with its ability to get on with running everything in its own interests.

Even when women are allowed to 'rise up' it is because they have so successfully adopted the patriarchal model of behaviour that they are better at playing men than the men are. Margaret Thatcher would be a classic example of this, and one that makes us believe that 'transgender' should have a much wider meaning – were it not for the fact that the transgender people we know are all such thoroughly nice folks.

On top of this, within the disUnited Kingdom, 'democracy' has been tailored to ensure not only the preservation of the patriarchal hegemony, but also the continued primacy of the south-east of England over all other parts, and indeed the whole, of the disUnited Kingdom.

As such, all the 'major' parties have concentrated their efforts there, which is one reason why Labour has abandoned all of its founding principles and become just another party of the right.

Yet now, there is a very real prospect that what the English like to call 'the regions' – but are in fact, at least in Scotland's case, national partners – might actually be more important than the whim of the bloated and gluttonous south-east of England. Horrors! And how can this be?

In fact, the Tory and Labour parties have become so entrenched in their desire to please the voters of the Home Counties that they are indistinguishable– the Blue Tories and the Red Tories. Lacking any substantial differences, they have become irrelevant to most people and the result of this, as well as other demographic changes, has been that the old 'first past the post' system of 'UK' voting, which is expressly designed to ensure that a party lacking an overall majority of the vote might nevertheless command an unassailable majority in the House of Parliament, has broken down.

In the last General Election, the Tories were only able to form a government with the assistance of the Liberals, in order to achieve which, as we expected, the Liberals threw out whatever vestiges of principle they were still clinging on to. (One must not forget that the Liberals are actually the party of the landed gentry, once known as the Whigs. Political connivance has ever been their stock-in-trade.)

The direct result of that opportunism– every cloud has a silver lining – looks likely to be the virtual eradication of the Liberals as a political force; yet the two major parties are unable to make up the ground and stalemate – in the form of a hung parliament – looms.

Enter the SNP, Plaid Cymru, and the Greens. In Scotland, the SNP looks set to hammer the Labour Party at the polls. If they do as predicted they will send a phalanx of perhaps 40 MPs to Westminster. They would therefore be cast as kingmakers, able to support one of the major parties so that it could form a stable government.

However, the SNP has made its position clear: it will not support a Tory government, even if the Tories have more seats than Labour. That means that even if the English vote Tory, they might well still get Labour. Even more galling– for them – would be that because the SNP is significantly more progressive than the current version of the Labour Party, it would oblige Labour to implement socially-inclusive and egalitarian policies, and, perhaps, even put an end to the obscene profligacy of Trident's replacement.

This has the mouthpieces of the English Establishment foaming.

Scottish voters are not meant to count; only English, and particularly, southern English voters are. Scottish MPs are expected to do as the leaders of their London-based, English parties decide. That is why Winston Churchill described the Scottish MPs as 'cannon-fodder'. They were makeweights and that is all; all they would ever be allowed to be too.

While Scottish politicians have been from time to time honoured with positions of power by their London masters (notably in the Labour Party over the decades of the rise of the SNP – we wonder why) the corollary has always been that they must not rock the boat; London and the southeast rules and must always do so.

So the prospect, of a democratically elected force that does not obey the 'London First' rule, having a pivotal role in governance, is deeply objectionable to – well, London and the southeast in general and to the Tories in particular.

It's quite all right for a minority Tory group to form a government with the acquiescence of the Liberals – but for shame! Decent humanitarian policies to be put in place because voters outside the southeast of England desire it? An end to the outright deceit of 'austerity' because other people see that it is only a way of making London richer at the expense of everyone else? That would never do.

Those very English politicians and pundits who only last year fought tooth and claw to prevent Scotland leaving the disUnion– thus depriving the British Exchequer of its assets – and who promised with tearful eyes how they would never again take Scotland for granted, how, if only Scotland would stay, they would be better people in the future and not lie, deceive and chisel at every opportunity, are now up on their hind legs baying for blood.

How dare the uppity Scots attempt to rise above their station? How dare Scotland influence how England shall be governed? How dare a woman (who is not one of those creatures who have already sold their souls and principles) presume to tell men how things should be run? (And this last in terms reflecting the outright misogyny of the writers, lest they should think we might not have noticed.)

Which leads us to reflect that these commentators might be well advised to consider that for decades, Scotland has had the will of English voters imposed upon it willy-nilly, and that women, an overall majority, have had to do as men decide, not for decades, but millennia.

An impartial observer might think that what is sauce for the goose should also be sauce for the gander.

So in the disUnited Kingdom last week, momentous events took place. Three articulate, intelligent, educated women gave a public dressing-down to four of the most repellent examples of the privilege-assuming patriarchal hegemony that is 'meant' to run things; once again, the Scottish National Party, far from being crushed by the manoeuvring of London and its agents, has returned stronger, bigger and more powerful; and for perhaps the very first time, the southern English may have to recognise that democracy is a tool that does not exist to serve them alone.

It is all deeply gratifying and frankly, we can't wait for more.

2. Swivelly-eyed Brexit panic.

The first signs of widespread panic amongst the UK's hard-right, swivelly-eyed Brexiteers have begun to appear. In our last Politics we pointed out that Brexit, as promised by the triumvirate of swivelly-eyed-ness, Johnson, Gove and Farage, is dead. It can't happen. Now that realisation has got through to those whose eyes are usually so swivelly they can't read a Daily Mail headline.

They've figured out that they were blindsided (it's the swivelly eyes) and they're livid. Beside themselves. Last Friday, probably after he had read my piece, Bill Cash, a person whose eyes are so swivelly we wonder how he drives to work, broke the ranks. 'Brexit must happen,' quoth he.

B-b-b-but Bill, is there any doubt? Surely…..I mean it's only been a month since the Phony Referendum…

See, here's a thing about Bill. He's a loony, yes, we give you that. Especially when he's not taking his lithium. But you don't get to be a backbencher as long as he's been without learning a thing or two about duplicity in Government. (Well, some do. But not Wull.)

He watched with narrow swivelly eyes as Theresa May, a Europhile, was handed the reins of power. He's a lifelong Tory and he knew what the runes were saying: 'If you think Brexit is going to mean "leaving Europe" think again.'

Now Bill is so passionate a wee thing that he can't stand to see his precious flagship – the one that he thinks will tow England across the Atlantic and make it a part of New York State – sunk.

So he was the first to bawl out, with a wailing, pitiful diatribe about how the Brexit referendum had to be 'respected'. It was the will of the people.

Oh really Bill? And if the Scots had voted to leave your precious

'UK' would you have honoured that? Don't bother answering, I know you'll lie anyway.

Enter John Redwood in a lizard suit.

With the literally frothing at the mouth Cash having broken purdah, others followed suit. John Redwood's eyes don't swivel. But that's because he's a reptilian. If you watch carefully you'll see his inner eyelid swipe across now and then. Redwood has a stare as fixed and unblinking as well, a thing so reptilian it must be a reptile.

This is what he had to say on the 26th:'I want the full Brexit and I would get straight on with it…...'

Now why did John-boy feel the need to say that? If the EU referendum called for Brexit, and governments always respect the will of the people, then surely he could just go on back to the Cat and Two Pigeons and enjoy another pint of warm flat Bass.

Ah, but he goes on, repressed swivelly-eyedness getting the better of him: '(But) some people absolutely want to water it (Brexit) down.'

Really, John? That would be people who actually have the job of managing the UK responsibly, not backbench lobby-fodder like you?

Swivelly-eyed backbench revolt. Kinda.

Within hours, the Daily Mail had multiplied Redwood's comment into a full backbench revolution – for which, since it's the Mail and not constrained by honesty, we should read 'a couple of swivelly-eyed rent-a-quotes'.

It couldn't be that maybe, just somehow, there's a sniff in the air that Brexit won't happen? That these interventions are a swivelly-eyed attempt to steel Theresa May's resolve?

Well, these mutts are barking at the wrong cat if they think that's gonna work. I've watched May for a long time now and she is ferociously smart with a hide made of buffalo-leather. Good luck intimidating that one.

The evident panic was perhaps explained by a statement by Jean-Claude Juncker, the distinctly non-swivelly President of the European Commission, on the 26th. He was sanguine – which really should have the alarm bells sounding. Oh, he said, those crazy Brits. Of course they need time to 'establish their position'. I give the job to negotiate to a guy. He can handle it. But he don' need even to start till October. Nice holiday.

Umm, I thought the UK position was, 'We're leaving, fuck you'. Oh wait. Maybe Juncker figured it out too.

The meaning is in the message. Britain can do a 'Hard Brexit' and close down its economy. And of course, Juncker and Europe's other two Presidents, Donald Tusk and Martin Schulz, will then facilitate Scotland's entry into the EU as the 'successor state' of the by then defunct and absent without leave, 'UK'.

So, Hard Brexit = a Depression the likes of which few today have ever lived through, and the final collapse, after all these years, of the 'British Project' – make the world England. Which will then be an international laughing-stock. Well, it is already, but we try to be nice.

Of course the government that does that will be out of power for, what, 20 years? 50? The Liberals were out of power for nearly 90 after they dropped the ball and Ireland told England where to shove it. And they were only brought back as a makeweight for a disastrous Tory government led by David 'Tweedledum' Cameron and George 'Tweedledee' Osborne, the most obnoxiously incompetent UK politicians in recent history.

You know, try as I might, I can't see a bunch of shameless power-junkies like the Tories signing up for that.

On the other hand we could have a 'Soft Brexit'. In which we get to do everything Brussels says but we have no power to influence what they say. We still have to pay a membership fee, but there will be no rebate. And oh boy, whoopee-de-doopee, we can have a seven-year moratorium on immigration. Kinda. But only new immigration, the ones here already have to stay. And after the seven years? Well, back to normal. Except, no rebate. And no voice.

And you know, the thing is that they already offered Tweedledum a four year moratorium. So all that for three extra years in which no new European citizens can take up residence in the UK. Three years. That's all that this pain and misery will 'gain'.

By which time the UK, by the way, will have ceased to exist.

So in this case, the Tory Gummint gets to give the opposition bucket loads of ammunition. 'Look' May will cry, 'I respected the will of the people!'

'Yes,' they will counter, 'And you left us with no voice at all in Europe, worse off and STILL with free immigration! What exactly was the point? Just to satisfy a bunch of rabid, reprehensible, racist, semi-educated Little Englanders?'

To which, of course, there would be no credible response. That is why Auntie Tess will not be doing it.

Juncker has every reason to be satisfied. At last, if only the Anglais are stupid enough to actually depart the EU, he gets to be rid of the most annoying, selfish pest in it, while retaining all the advantages of access to the UK market. (You think this free market thing just works one way? Duuuh.)

Yes, the swivelly eyed's eyes are swivelling so hard they'll spin right out of their heads, while Juncker and the hated Eurocrats calmly put their feet up on the desk and say, 'Yeah, whenever. No problem. I have some meditation to get on with while you lot stab each other in the back. Call me when the last bodies have been swept out the door and dumped with Gove's.'

The point being, they all know Brexit is finished. Auntie Tess was put in to clean up the mess, not to make it worse.

3. The British Project: the sun goes down

The British Project was – and is – simply this: to make the world England. To profit from it and get rich on the military colonisation of other, weaker people, yes, that was its stimulus. But its philosophical motivation was to make the world England.

When I was at school, we had maps on the walls that showed a world covered in 'pink bits'. Those, it was said, were ours. They had been 'our' Empire; now they were our 'Commonwealth'. This was another way of saying that all of these countries were still 'ours' but we were nice chaps and we let the darkies play unsupervised these days. The whole concept was about as offensive as it gets.

So what was this 'Empire' that had turned so much of the planet a most unlikely salmon-pink?

The British Empire

The British Project was launched at the time of the Enlightenment, when Classical ideas were most fashionable. Rome – a barbarous and genocidal empire on one hand – was also the vehicle of Greek ideas. Those were and still are regarded, in many ways rightly, as the finest expression of human thought and aspiration imaginable. (Our teachers avoided mentioning that the Athenians, for example, were the most preposterous misogynists, or that Spartan men preferred boys to women, which might have explained a few things. One learns early that educators are not entirely trustworthy.)

Of course, the Greeks had an Empire too, thanks to Alexander, but it was significantly gentler than its successors. The Greeks did not go in for genocide and they appear to have been rather well-liked; the Ptolemies, for example, were accepted as true Egyptian Pharaohs.

The British Project had the conceited notion that it was akin to the Greek Alexandrian Empire. It was a means of civilising the uncivilised. Of bringing better ideas to the ignorant. And in a way, it did do that; after all, Britain gave India its bureaucracy. But its velvet glove always concealed an iron fist.

The truth is that the British Empire was much more like Rome's. Take what you can, convert the natives and if they won't come quietly, kill them.

The British Project, of which the Empire was but one artefact, sought to turn the whole world into a clone of England. Everyone would speak English; they would all doff their caps to the English sahibs and mem-sahibs; they would never argue with an Englishman. And they would all eat their bananas with a knife and fork.

What was the justification for this? It was that being English is the best thing possible. It was the highest expression of human culture. This was self-evident; how could it be argued with? Except of course, it *was* argued with, principally by the French, who thought much the same thing about themselves and were engaged in a French Project designed to make the world France.

The End

When I was still in primary school, the news was filled with the face of a man called Ian Smith, who was the Prime Minister of 'Rhodesia' (Zimbabwe.) Smith had done the unthinkable. He had said that Rhodesia would declare independence from the Empire whether the British liked it or not. My God, the outrage was so thick it positively leaked from the television.

Nobody gave a damn about the condition of the Africans – whose country, lest we forget, it actually was; no, not at all. The rage was because Smith was defying Britain. He was defying England. He was wrong – oh, he was wrong all right, he was a dyed-in-the-wool racist. But that wasn't why the British media loathed him. They hated him because he was holding two fingers up to England and saying 'You can go and fuck yourselves, Queen, country and Empire.'

And that would never do, would it?

Now look at the demographic of last Thursday's vote in England. Overwhelmingly, people aged over 60 voted to leave the EU. That is, English people over 60. English people, therefore, older than I am, who grew up believing what they were told in school: that the sun never set on England's Empire. That it was the finest expression of civilisation that had ever been. That being colonised by the sahibs and mem-sahibs was positively an honour.

Non-English people of all descriptions had to gasp in awe at the passing of that most luminary of humanity; an English gentleman. The natives had to kneel before him, as his shining light of cultural purity washed over them. They had to accept the trinkets he gave them in return for their servitude. The individuals upon whom the English conferred their limitless largesse had to be thankful they were not tied to the wheel of a gun and trailed before the massed ranks of other natives until they were smashed into a literal pulp of bone and meat. (You didn't know what 'breaking on the wheel' was? I hope you are suitably sickened.)

And the natives could not say one word against it – otherwise, Amritsar. In 1919 Brigadier-General Reginald Dyer was charged with calming riots in that city, which had begun when Imperial authorities had arrested several nationalist leaders. Dyer's tactic was to line up his troops and open fire into the crowds. 379 people were killed and over 1000 were wounded. Dyer was later censured, but he still enjoyed huge support in the media and in public, for his actions.

That was what the British Empire really was; a place where the people had to accept English supremacy or die.

The fact is – and the demographics prove it – that a huge number of people who voted 'Leave' last Thursday, were brought up believing in the British Project – make the world England. These people are, underneath their skin, profound racists. They hate everyone and everything that is not English.

It is not however, just the aged, who have this sad condition.

Young people are infected too

I remember, a couple of years ago, waiting for my daughter at Lyon St-Exupery Airport. Outside the terminal was a woman with a tribe of children. She was clearly not a wealthy person, nor was she educated. I'd say she was around thirty. In the few minutes that I observed her – in stealth mode, appearing French – she must have used the words 'England' or 'English' a dozen times, and every time she did so, she raised her voice. 'Come on children, we'll soon be back in ENGLAND.'

I wondered about that for a long time. Clearly, she was insecure. She was struggling with unruly children. Her body-language made it obvious that she felt intimidated, though by what I had no idea. How did yelling 'ENGLAND' at the top of her voice help?

Now I know. Last Thursday, I learned. What intimidates English people is 'foreigners'. And the mantra, the talismanic magic word that keeps an Englishperson safe while surrounded by all these terrifying foreigners, is 'ENGLAND', shouted at the top of one's voice.

That was what we saw on Thursday. A collective cry of 'ENGLAND! Save us from the foreigners!'

The Empire died 50 years ago and the UK has been a part of the EU for 40; but the rot of English supremacy is still there, corrupting a nation's soul. The myth of the all-powerful white sahib and his gracious mem-sahib to whom the world must bend the knee. The comfort of Queen and Country, and a world made England; the promise of the British Project.

Well, it's done. England is a laughing-stock. Today, it tears itself apart politically, as an Opposition, that should have come together in the face of a crisis, instead stages a bungled palace coup while the government itself has no leader. Like a child smashing up the doctor's surgery because she has a cold, the English have shamed themselves.

There were, and are, good arguments against the EU as presently constituted. Many of us think it should be a looser confederation, with far less centralised power. The Euro has been a disaster for many of its members and they should pull out of it now. But the UK is not in the Euro. It never was. And when the English voted as they did, they were not voting for a rational critique of the EU, or to transform it into something better; they were the collective Alf Garnett screaming, 'Bloody wogs!'

Now I know not all English people are shits. But you need to look at yourselves. You need to recognise that the horrible clinging-on to the badges of Englishism from Enid Blyton to Harry Potter, from the Queen to Big Ben, are not signs of your greatness, but of your sickness.

You have never even been able to accept your Britishness, although you expect your partners to; you will always be ENGLISH, yet you are offended when I tell you I am Scottish, not British. Your home will always be ENGLAND and not the United Kingdom; and you most certainly never could be a European. I mean they don't even speak ENGLISH there.

We know all that now. The polite mask is off. Fool me once, shame on you; fool me twice, shame on me.

For the Scots, there remains only one credible course of action: to sever the ties with England at once and re-establish our nation as proud to be European.

4. Cameron's Phony Referendum

When is a referendum not a referendum? Answer – when it is a politically convenient device used by a slippery Prime Minister in trouble with half his MPs.

The EU Referendum held on the 23rd of June was phony. It has no legal consequences. That in turn means that it has no effect. Whoever becomes leader of the Tory Party and thus Prime Minister of Great Britain, will, if she or he wishes to cause the UK to leave the EU, have to follow the normal Parliamentary procedure for the making of law. It could take years for legislation to pass, if it is not blocked from the start by the majority of pro-EU MPs.

Let me explain.

First let's look at how laws are made in the UK.[1]

First, a Draft Bill is published. This would usually be called a White Paper or a Green Paper. The former is a Paper that proposes the Government's specific intention and the latter is a broader consultation document.

Once the Draft Bill is agreed, it is presented to Parliament as a Bill for 'examination, discussion and amendment'.

Commons and Lords

The Bill then goes through its First and Second Readings in the House of Commons. Amendments may be made as a consequence of the debates on these Readings. It then goes to the Committee Stage, for technical and legal revision. After that, the Report is published and the Bill has a Third Reading in the Commons.

We're not done yet. Once the Commons has approved the Bill it goes to the House of Lords, where it goes through exactly the same process: two Readings, Committee and Report, and Third Reading. A Bill 'must be approved in the same form by both Houses before becoming an Act (law).'

---

[1] Source: http://www.parliament.uk/about/how/laws/

The House of Lords is not obliged to approve the Bill at all and may send it back to the Commons for revision. Today, thanks to the Parliament Acts, Her Majesty's House of Lords cannot indefinitely block legislation:

'Bills can be held up by the Lords if they disagree with them for about a year but ultimately the elected House of Commons can reintroduce them in the following session and pass them without the consent of the Lords.'[2]

In order to change the Law, proposed legislation must pass the whole of the above procedure.

In the following example, the consequences of the vote were clearly stated. This is because this referendum was held only after the relevant legislation had passed all its Parliamentary stages. In other words the consequences of the result had already been approved by both Houses of Parliament and had received Royal Assent prior to the referendum.

Alternative Vote Referendum 2012.

So let's look at Section 8 of the Parliamentary Voting System and Constituencies Act 2011, which triggered the referendum on the Alternative Vote in 2012.[3]

'(1)The Minister must make an order bringing into force section 9, Schedule 10 and Part 1 of Schedule 12 ("the alternative vote provisions") if–

(a)more votes are cast in the referendum in favour of the answer "Yes" than in favour of the answer "No",' and '(2)If more votes are not cast in the referendum in favour of the answer "Yes" than in favour of the answer "No", the Minister must make an order repealing the alternative vote provisions.'

The consequences of the referendum here are clearly stated. The legislation contains an instruction as to what the Government had to do after the vote was held. The Minister concerned was directed on one hand to enable the law if the result was a majority 'Yes'. On the other, to repeal it if the result favoured 'No'. The provisions under which he or she

---

2 Source: http://www.parliament.uk/about/how/laws/parliamentacts/
3 Source: http://www.legislation.gov.uk/ukpga/2011/1/contents/enacted/data.htm

was to do so were likewise framed in the Act. (This referendum voted against.)

In other words, the relevant legislation had passed through all the debates, stages and approvals required for a Bill to become an Act (Law). Furthermore the consequences of either a favourable or otherwise result had also been discussed and written into law.

The 1973 EEC Referendum.

Now let's look at another referendum, the 1973 referendum regarding the UK's accession to the EEC.

Like the one above, the relevant Act, the European Communities Act of 1972, had already gone through all its stages in Parliament and had received Royal Assent. It was the law.[4]

Indeed, the UK had already signed the Treaty of Accession which made it a part of the EEC. It was only because of protest that a referendum was held, but that referendum had no authority over Parliament. This was not made immediately obvious because the votes in the 1973 EEC referendum and also the 1975 one, preserved the status quo.

In other words, the legal stature of these referendums was never tested. In fact they were technically 'consultations'. They had no effect in law at all. But this was never made obvious, because the result of the votes was to leave things as they were. Parliament had already made the law by the proper constitutional process.

The Phony Referendum.

Now look at the enabling legislation for the 2016 European Referendum. This is the European Referendum Act of 2015, and the title alone should be making you wonder.[5]

Here is what it says:

'(1)A referendum is to be held on whether the United Kingdom should remain a member of the European Union.

---

4 Source http://www.legislation.gov.uk/ukpga/1972/68/section/1
5 Source http://www.legislation.gov.uk/ukpga/2015/36/contents/enacted/data.htm

(2)The Secretary of State must, by regulations, appoint the day on which the referendum is to be held.

(3)The day appointed under subsection (2)–

(a)must be no later than 31 December 2017,

(b)must not be 5 May 2016, and

(c)must not be 4 May 2017.

(4)The question that is to appear on the ballot papers is–

"Should the United Kingdom remain a member of the European Union or leave the European Union?"

(5)The alternative answers to that question that are to appear on the ballot papers are–

"Remain a member of the European Union

Leave the European Union".'

That is it. It then gives the official wording in Welsh. There is no more substantive detail, the rest of the Act is all about procedure. It is the shortest Act of Parliament I have ever seen – and the most meaningless.

There is not one word about what happens after the referendum. Not one.

Not Worth the Paper it's Printed On.

This Act, which went through all its Parliamentary stages easily, ONLY sets up a referendum. Its substantive section, above, does not refer to any other legislation. It does not place any burden upon Government to do anything at all, dependent on the result. It has no consequences.

Let me be quite blunt: constitutionally, this document is not worth the paper it is printed on. Its sole purpose was to hold a phony referendum with no constitutional force.

The phony referendum has been held in accordance with the Act and that, my friends, is that. Done and dusted. Time to move on. The 'Brexit' vote was meaningless. We can – and we should – forget about it.

Parliament is Sovereign.

Only Parliament can decide to leave the EU. And before it did so, an appropriate Bill would have to be drafted and go through the procedure described above of Readings, Committee Stages and Reports in both

Houses.

In fact, Parliament has not discussed one line of any Bill that might be enacted and its consequences realised, as a result of the phony EU referendum.

Parliament could have debated and enacted a Bill that did provide for legislative change after a referendum. It is sovereign. But it did not. And I do not think that any such legislation would have sailed through. This is almost certainly why there are no legislative consequences in the 2015 Act. The people who framed the Draft Bill it must have known that to actually debate leaving Europe would have caused the most unholy row.

Cameron only wanted to defuse the Eurosceptic Tory MPs. So he gave them a phony referendum with no powers, probably hoping that it, like the previous two on Europe, would preserve the status quo and so its lack of legal substance would never be exposed.

You may well wonder about a man who would play fast and loose with the futures of his own country and people in such a way. No wonder he left in a hurry. We sincerely hope that his reputation never recovers.

I am shocked that we have politicians so ignorant of their own constitutional responsibilities that they have not already challenged the current mass hysteria provoked by the verdict of this most spurious of referendums. It is a phony; it is literally inconsequential.

I am gravely disappointed by my colleagues in the Media, that they have not gone through the simple exercise of downloading and reading the relevant legislation, which would prove, for once and for all, that the phony EU referendum was nothing more than a slick political device.

For shame.

5. Super-emasculated men and autogynephilia

Over the last few decades, particularly in schools and academia, strong masculine role models have been suppressed in favour of emasculated ones. This, today, has led to a situation where the majority of teachers, outside the hard sciences, engineering and maths, are either women or emasculated, effete men.

When I returned to university in 2010 to complete my Master's I was shocked to see the extent to which this corrosion had progressed — and that was in Scotland. Not only were a majority of teachers either women or emasculated males, the few remaining masculine males were marginalised. There were, literally, no straight male role models. (I became one.)

In other parts of the world, this is a hundred times worse. It is obvious that academia in the US and, increasingly, elsewhere, has been infected by an anti-male social cancer which insists that everything male is bad and everything female is not just better, but so much better that maleness itself must be destroyed.

Emasculated transvestites

One result of this is that we see far more males appearing as autogynephilic transvestites. While Blanchard related the classic autogynephile to the closeted, narcissistic cross-dresser who puts on feminine clothes to masturbate, this modern type is most closely related to the super-emasculated beta-male who first began to appear 20 years ago in 'emo' culture.

These men's desire for emasculation has been stimulated by a culture that hates maleness. This culture has oozed out of institutions of learning and has infected business, government and industry, no more so than in the soft technologies of social media, where men are reviled and emasculated beta-males are vaunted. It has leached into politics, where masculine men are detested — just look at the reaction Donald Trump has suffered from its adherents. They are not particularly troubled about his policies, but by the fact that he is an alpha-male who is proud to be masculine and rejects the emasculation of Political Correctness and Identity Politics.

This is also why there are now so many females 'transitioning' into men: if being male is no longer a requirement to be a man, (as 'gender theory' teaches) but masculinity is still seen as a badge of social dominance (as 'Political Correctness' does), the logical conclusion is that females should become masculine to assert authority. This creates an ersatz form of matriarchy, a bastardised succubus that totally disregards the huge amounts of evidence we have of how true matriarchies work. In those, men are revered as brothers, sons, fathers and lovers, while women are revered as sisters, daughters, mothers and lovers. Men are loved in matriarchies, not hated.

Political Correctness

In the ersatz matriarchy of Political Correctness, all things male must be emasculated and the roles of men assumed by females. The more they shout about 'ending the patriarchy', the more they promote it -- as long as they are in charge. Now women act out the regressive, hierarchical roles that once were played only by men.

Just look at the Left's counter to Donald Trump in last year's US Presidential Election. A person born female who had fully adopted a masculine role, to the point that we might reasonably call her a 'transman'. And consider the President that Trump will replace: the antithesis of masculinity, a weak, cavilling fool who pandered to the worst in the society that he 'represented' to the point that his party, the 'Democrats' might never see power again — one should hope.

In that election result we saw the first real challenge to the ghastly culture of feminazis and their emasculated beta-male poodles, the first strike back against the culture of male-hatred.

The consequence of this culture is on one hand, to see females adopting male roles and being every bit as unpleasant as men can be — how easily some gender roles are copied — and on the other, males becoming so traumatised by the constant derision of their masculinity that they 'fall in love' with the idea of being women. These are betamales par excellence, the symbol of the eradication of masculinity; for if the regressive-left feminazis cannot kill all male babies — which they would do if they could — what better than to turn them into facsimiles of women?

Sympathy

I suppose one must even have sympathy with the sad products of this diseased culture, the men-become-women who are still rejected by the women they desire. 'Look,' they say, 'We destroyed our masculinity to supplicate you! Why then will you not be our lovers?' The absurdity of such a person becoming totally emasculated in order to so delight women that they would allow him to fuck them is positively hilarious — or would be were it not so tragic.

No transsexual (Blanchard HSTS) is confused in this way. She does not desire to emasculate anyone. She loves masculinity, delights in it, adores hairy chests, big muscles, strong men and being fucked. It is her raison d'etre, the deep-seated powerhouse that drives her life: her sheer adoration of and lust for masculinity. She can never be masculine herself but loving men, indeed, that is well within her gift. To her, the autogynephile, with his fake femininity and desire, nevertheless, for sex with women, is pathetic.

Transmasculine feminazis

Of course, autogynephiles and transmasculine feminazis — the opposite sides of the same ghastly coin — know this and that is why they attempt, at every turn, to erase transsexuals. Consider: if my enemy's friend is, by definition, my enemy, then what is my enemy's lover? She who will wait on him, pursue sex with him, clean house for him and be the best of lovers, giving her body unreservedly to him? She who will nurse his wounds and soothe his hurts? Who will fall asleep in his arms, happy in the protection and security that her man gives her?

The hatred of feminazis and autogynephilic transvestites knows no bounds. Why? Because transsexuals are the very women that feminazis wish did not exist. They take every 'gender stereotype' and wear it like a badge of honour. And every autogynephile, no matter where he comes from, knows this reality: he can never compete with a transsexual. If one appears in the same room as he, the laughable pretence of his pseodo-femininity is at once exposed for the tissue of lies that it is.

These are the real reasons why emasculated autogynephiles and the harpies of supremacist feminazism hate transsexuals. They desire to erase them and those men who love them. They desire a world without men, women who love men and most of all, males who become women in order to love the Enemy — the powerful, dominant alpha male.

'Gender Neutral' Parenting

To this end they advocate 'gender neutral' parenting — in other words, the deliberate mental abuse of children in order to satisfy their supremacist anti-masculine agenda. How is punishing a male child for acting like a boy more acceptable than it would be to punish him for being a girl? The sheer hypocrisy of these people sticks in any right-thinking person's craw.

Hell, they even loathe gays like Milo Yiannopoulous — why? Because he loves real men. The very men they loathe and have spent so many years plotting to destroy.

Well, I have news. Last November we struck a blow. It was a battle; we won it. Now we must win the war. To do so we need, now, to capitalise on the disarray of the feminazi and race-supremacist Left.

Gender pay gap myth

There is no 'gender pay gap'. The 'race pay gap' is a myth. There is no 'institutionalised racism'. A coloured person today finds it easier to go to college or find work than a better-qualified white person. Everyone has the vote and is equal under the law. In marital law, women are favoured over men. Everyone's life is equally valid. There are no white slave-owners and we the descendants are not responsible for the sins of people who died a century and a half ago. There are no 'reparations' to pay. Egalitarianism is over; its ends have been achieved.

Today, the only slave-owners are those who have long profited from this ghastly trade and whose evil creed legitimises it — Muslims. They currently hold at least 23 million black people as slaves — 46 times as many as were held in the southern states of the US at the outbreak of the Civil War. 46 times as many.

There is no 'rape culture' in the West; rape culture, today, is a function of Islam. It is the principal means by which that cult maintains social control. This we see in the wave of Muslim rape-terrorism sweeping Europe today.

White male privilege is a chimera

There is no such thing as 'white male privilege'. It is a chimera invented by the Regressive Left to attempt to emasculate that which they hate most — white men. They can no longer hide behind the mask of egalitarianism and have been exposed for what they are — supremacists who hate straight white men and the women who love them.

The only enemies of freedom of speech in the West today are the feminazis and race-supremacists of the Regressive Left. They know that silencing dissent is the keystone in their arch of darkness. In a chilling Orwellian fantasy, thoughts themselves are policed; voicing a legitimate opinion about 'oppressed' people — those who bask most unashamedly in their false, assumed, victim status — will get you a visit from the agents of the state, even in such 'bastions of free speech' as the UK.

Lies are the core of the Regressive Left's assault on humanity, but we have struck a blow for freedom. The war, my dears, has only just begun.

The Warm Pink Jelly Express Train
ROD FLEMING
Sex.Sleaze.Trannies.Passion.Love against love itself.
A man caught between passion and reason,
a woman caught between herself and the world.
ISBN: 978-0-9565007-2-4

6. Scene from an Imaginary Western

In the little white-painted town of Santa Westminstera, havoc had broken out. The town was ruled by two gangs of ruthless bandits. But both of these had begun fighting amongst themselves. The rule of the bosses had collapsed and anarchy reigned.

In an adobe house in the main street huddled one of the last remaining families.

Little Angelina was cuddling into her grandfather's chest.

'Oh papacito, what will become of us?' she sobbed.

Another shot rang out. A bullet crashed through the last intact pane in the window and shattered the Madonna on the wall

'Oh, no,' cried Angelina, going to collect the shards. 'Not the Mama Maria!'

As she did so, a man staggered out of the pulqueria opposite. It was called the Worker's Arms, but it was many a long year since any worker had dared enter. The man puked onto the street, fired his gun into the air, and then collapsed, dead drunk.

Miss Theresa's.

Meanwhile, on the other side of the road, the saloon, recently renamed Miss Theresa's, was doing roaring trade. Flashily dressed gamblers and ladies all in sequins and brocade filled it, their hair piled high and their eyes hard. But there was no order, and several groups huddled together, casting their eyes around, their hands on the silver-plated pistols at their waists.

Suddenly an altercation broke out; a big, burly man with tousled blond hair staggered out into the street, and fell forwards, a huge dagger in his back.

'Oh!' cried Angelina. 'Miguel la Rana has killed Boris el Oso! Caramba!'

'What is to become of us, indeed?' murmured the old man. 'Our money is worth nothing now, and neither is our house. And there is no work any more. Even your mother and father have lost their jobs and have had to take zero-hours contracts. Meanwhile all the politicians do is get drunk and fight.

'El Barboso sits in his room over the pulqueria with a shotgun on his knees, chanting mantras that nobody understands, while his own people try to break his door down.

'Snake Cameroono has locked himself in the cellar of the saloon and gets drunk while his people kill each other. Mama mia!'

Suddenly, Pepito, Angelina's brother, who was looking out the window, exclaimed, 'What is that? It looks like a cloud.'

The distant riders.

'It's too low to be a cloud,' answered Angelina. 'It's horsemen. Many horsemen.'

'Oh, Mama Maria, what now?' wailed the old man. 'Who comes to terrorise us now?'

The children watched. Sure enough, they could soon make out the figures of the horsemen, under the cloud of dust their horses' hooves raised. As they entered the village's only street they unholstered their guns. All had gold-plated Colts with grips of ivory encrusted in diamonds.

All save two, who rode a little behind. These carried long Winchesters, magnificently ornamented.

The men rode at canter, neck-reining, their faces set and grim and their long black cloaks waving behind. As they passed long the street, two by two they peeled off and, dismounting, took up station on either side of the road.

To her considerable astonishment, Angelina saw, as they turned, that they all had what looked very much like triangular fins on their backs.

Unable to help herself, for children are curious, Angelina ran out of the house and approached the leader.

'Senor, senor,' she cried. 'Who are you? And why have you come here?'

Triangular teeth.

The man looked down at her and then, removing his hat, smiled. Angelina was somewhat surprised by his perfectly white, triangular teeth, but she was too polite to say anything.

'I am Miguel de los Reyes,' said the man, leaning down towards her. 'And this is my Company. We have brought the Federales – the Federal Marshals.' He indicated the two men with the long guns who were now standing outside the little church.

He patted Angelina's head kindly. 'Here is our message, mamacita. We have come to bring the law back to your town. Tell all the people.'

Angelina clapped her hands in delight and ran into the house to give him the message. 'Papacito, papacito! We are saved! We're saved!'

It wasn't quite like that, when I read that Mishcon de Reya had mounted a legal challenge to an early – and unconstitutional – Brexit; but it was close.

I was reminded of when, a long time ago, the newspaper I was on proposed to publish a story about a certain gentleman who had allegedly been having naughty soirées with a couple of working girls. Apparently – and I quote one of the ladies – he 'liked to have his nipples sucked while the other one wanked him off.' Which, by the way, is very damn good fun. Don't knock it if you haven't tried it.

Anyway, as always when you're about to publish a story as juicy as that, this had to be checked by a lawyer. We call this 'legalling'.

We couldn't use the firm we usually did, because it was Scottish and, um, we were writing about the President of the Scottish Law Society. We could feel the sharks circling already.

'So who's legalling us?' I asked at Editor's conference.

'Mishcon de Reya,' was the answer.

'Ouch,' I said, 'That's gonna cost.'

'Yes,' came the reply, 'But if you want to send a message, you get Mishcon de Reya.'

The New First Estate?

I thought a lot about Mishcon de Reya's surprise entrance into the post-Brexit fray, yesterday, delivering a stern message that the law would not stand by and allow itself to be mocked by politicians. Senior law firms – and they don't come more senior – don't do things like that, usually.

We used to say that the First Estate was the clergy, but they're largely irrelevant today. We should pass that honour to the legal establishment.

I imagine that it went something like this: members of the legal establishment have been watching with horror as the political class in Westminster went out to lunch after the EU referendum on 23 June.

To call the situation a shambles would be the understatement of the decade. The pound tumbled. So did the UK's credit rating. There was a truly egregious outpouring of xenophobic hatred by the English. The UK – and particularly England – became an international laughing stock. Possibly more to the point, huge and lucrative accounts began discussing a move to Amsterdam.

And meanwhile the party of Government was leaderless, with the lame-duck Prime Minister, David Cameron, apparently in hiding. At the same time Her Majesty's Opposition chose the very moment when it should have come together, to provide a voice of calm and reason, to launch a palace coup which is not done yet. The nation was drifting, with no-one at the helm, towards the Maelstrom. Nobody – least of all the Brexiters – had a clue what to do next.

Pro-Brexit Tories showed a lack of morality and plain decency that was truly sickening, while the antis drank their fill of hemlock. One might reluctantly excuse Nigel Farage; after all, being an arse is a professional calling for him.

The only UK politician with a plan, as Faisal Islam of Sky News said, was Nicola Sturgeon, the First Minister of Scotland. But she was off doing her best not to look like a cat who'd been at the cream, while glad-handing EU leaders delighted to find somebody British who wasn't a complete jerk.

And the legal eagles would have feared that if a Brexiter got elected to lead the Tory Party, that person might just go and say to the EU that the UK was leaving. That would really put the cat in with the pigeons.

I suspect that there were many little meetings of men and women in not too flamboyant but very well tailored suits, in wine bars and clubs, all over London, last week. Discreet phone calls may have been made.

'What the hell are we going to do about this bloody mess?'

'We need to send a message. Something they'll understand.'

'What about we get somebody to, er, deliver a package of fish? You know what I mean?'

'Hmmmm, I like that. Behave or you sleep with the fishes. Okay….. so who do we get to deliver the message?'

Mishcon de Reya is who you get, when you want to send a message.

7. Socially aware, libertarian, scientific, secularist

I was asked today if I was a 'liberal'. Now in all honesty, until quite recently, I would just have said 'yes' and moved on. Simple, easy, checks the right boxes. But the world is not as it was; liberalism has become infected with some appallingly bad ideas that we have to stand up to and defeat. So when I analysed 'what I am' I came up with this: a socially aware, libertarian, scientific, secularist.

So what does being a socially aware, libertarian, scientific, secularist, mean and why is it not the same as being a 'liberal'?

Well, in some areas there is overlap. I am socially aware. I believe in universal free education. That societies which do not have free universal health care are sick. I think there should be a social safety-net for those who fall out of the system. That everyone has a right to a decent home, with security and tenure, without having to starve to afford it. I think we should all have clean water, access to electricity, internet, that stuff. That wealth should be redistributed, by taxation, from the richest to the poorest.

A socially aware, libertarian, scientific, secularist is obviously libertarian. I believe in absolute freedom of speech, about everything. Nobody has a right 'not to be offended.' If you hold ideas that I find offensive, then I reserve the right to offend you, personally, by challenging them.

I believe we all have the absolute right to 'blaspheme' and that all anti-blasphemy laws should be repealed.

If you're saying things people find offensive on social media, so what? It should not have the consequence of the police coming to your door or the suspension of your account privileges.

There is no such thing as 'hate speech'. There is speech and there is assault. It is not 'hate speech' to tell a Muslim that his religion is misogynistic and that this is unacceptable in a secular, egalitarian state. It is not 'hate speech' to tell Muslim women that they must uncover their faces in a secular public space. Breaking a Muslim's head would be assault, and that carries penalties – as it should.

The same applies, of course, to Christians and everyone else. You may not prevent a woman from controlling her fertility because of things it says in a book written thousands of years ago by men determined to oppress women, or in the name of a totally fictional 'god' that, despite hundreds of years trying, science cannot find the slightest trace of.

A socially aware, libertarian, scientific, secularist believes absolutely in freedom of thought. You have the right to believe and to think what you want. You have the right to express those in your speech and writings. However, that is as far as it goes. You do not have the right to force your beliefs on others. Nor do you have the right to harm or discriminate against others on the basis of your beliefs.

You have the right to live as you will, as long as that does not damage or impinge on anyone else's right to do the same. So if you were born male and want to live as a woman, that's fine. However, you do not have the right to oblige anyone else to use specific language that you pre-approve, even when talking about you.

Being a part of an 'oppressed minority' – which should not exist in a truly secular state anyway – should afford you protection. You should not be attacked, beaten, discriminated against – in any way – because of the colour of your skin or the nature of your body, your gender or the language you grew up speaking.

On the other hand, these protections do not extend to the notion that you can somehow prevent others from adopting the fashions you espouse. 'Cultural appropriation' does not exist; it's a political illusion. I speak French but I am not French. That is not 'cultural appropriation'. It's speaking French.

If a person of white skin wants to wear dreadlocks, people of black skin cannot complain because this was first popularised amongst black Africans. You can't stop me playing the Blues any more than I can stop you playing bagpipes. No more can you prevent a novelist from imagining herself in the role of a person from a different background, or creating characters that are not of her own, on the grounds that she is not one of them. You have the right to hold her critically to account for her success in doing so but you may not deny her right to do so.

(And if you think you might, and you are a writer yourself, then you should be ashamed. You just torpedoed freedom of speech, the most important freedom that writers have. Well done. Thanks.)

Being a socially aware, libertarian, scientific secularist, I believe in the right of self-defence. I therefore believe that all citizens have the right to keep and bear weapons. They have the right to learn to use them in self defence. These rights include the right to keep and bear firearms.

I believe that the State is the enemy of the people and the only good State is one that fears the people. That they should be armed is therefore axiomatic.

As a socially aware, libertarian, scientific, secularist, I recognise that science is the only reliable means by which we may come to understand and know the physical universe that we live in. Religion and philosophy were earlier attempts to understand reality, which are less reliable and indeed, entirely inaccurate in many ways. I believe, furthermore, that there is a hierarchy applicant here, with religion at the bottom and science at the top. The least reliable way to know about reality is religion and the most reliable is science. No philosophical argument may be countered by a religious one and no scientific argument by a philosophical one.

A socially aware, libertarian, scientific, secularist must believe in absolute equality before the law. That there should be one law for everyone, and that all law should be secular and voted for democratically. So, no Sharia, ever. But equally, no religious law of any kind. Secularism has teeth. That means no churchmen in legislatures, unless they were duly elected. So the late Reverend Ian Paisley is in and the Arhbishop of Canterbury is out.

I believe that legislators have a legal responsibility to tell the truth and that we should prosecute those who do not. They should further be disbarred from ever seeking election again. If legislators make laws, on the basis of untruth, that harm others, then they should be personally liable. We should be able to sue the pips out of them, or throw them in jail.

All workings of the State, save a very few areas directly connected to immediate security, should be public. Julian Assange and Wikileaks are doing what States should be doing themselves.

Because a socially aware, libertarian, scientific, secularist accepts science as the 'gold standard' then, excepting rules to protect the weakest, the best contemporary science should be the basis of law.

Had this been the case, then the imminent threat of Climate Change could have been avoided. Legislators would have been obliged to ignore vested interests like the fossil fuel industry and listen to the real science.

It follows therefore, that we have some requirements of our politicians and legislators. The first is that they be scientifically competent. You don't have to have a BSc, but not understanding and accepting fundamental scientific truths like evolution, climate change or the big bang should be a disqualification from ever holding high office.

We live in a time when the very nature of not merely Western but also global human culture is at risk. Religious totalitarians hate us. So do the intellectual Fascists of 'Political Correctness' and its ill-formed spawn, 'Identity Politics' and 'Cultural Appropriation'.

Anti-human death-cults that are totally incompatible with our society, like Islam and fundamentalist Christianity, threaten our basic freedoms.

We live at a time when, outside of the USA at least, States have taken increasingly stringent measures to prevent us from defending ourselves. Our freedom of speech is curtailed increasingly, by social media companies seeking concessions from the very States that we are trying to hold to account. We are facing a global climatic catastrophe that will cause the deaths of billions and in all likelihood, eradicate our culture.

There was never a greater need for socially aware, libertarian, scientific, secularist thinking. We never needed cool heads more. We have the capability to avert the impending disaster. Yet we do all we can to avoid addressing it.

The conservative right hates me because I believe that the State has a duty to ensure a fair society, and that science and not religion is the gold standard. Regressive 'liberals' hate me because I believe in freedom of speech and thought and that we have the right to defend ourselves.

Yet, ask yourselves, what are the two models that have led us to the brink of catastrophe and potential extermination? Conservatism and liberalism. Hidebound with their ideas of religion and race and both determined to deny science for short-term political or financial gain.

We have the power, today, to ensure the destruction of our species. We just have to keep doing as we have been. That's all.

I am against both of these horrors, the conservative religionards and the liberal 'social justice warriors'. A plague on both their houses. That's why I am a socially aware, libertarian, scientific, secularist. We need more like me, fast.

8. The first of our 3 Ps is Pot; marijuana

Pot – marijuana, cannabis, grass, weed, call it what you like, has been used by humans since the beginning of recorded history. It is likely that we have been using it for tens of thousands of years.

While there are risks associated with the use of pot, these are vastly overstated and much less than those of using alcohol or tobacco, both of which cause huge numbers of deaths and human suffering and by the way, cost society a vast amount of money. Marijuana prohibition is one of the greatest misuses of state resources and taxpayers' money in the world today.

Until the 1930s pot use was legal and largely unremarked. William Randolph Hearst, the American media tycoon, changed that. Hearst was the inventor of 'yellow journalism' the sensationalising of factually incorrect and often invented stories for political purposes. He was a fanatical right-winger and a friend of Adolph Hitler. Up until the engagement of the United Sates in World War II, Hearst remained in close contact with Nazi authorities in Germany and regularly had his newspapers run anti-Russian, anti-Communist and pro-German articles, which were provided by the Gestapo's propaganda services.

Hearst was anti-British and a fervent 'isolationist' who used his media to discourage American entry into the European war. He repeatedly attacked Roosevelt's attempts to help European states, especially the UK, against the Nazis, through schemes like lend-lease. He severely restricted the President's ability to assist in the disaster. Amongst his other crimes, therefore, Hearst may be indicted for being accessory to the murders of millions of Europeans, especially Jews and other minorities like homosexuals. It was only at the point of the Japanese attack on Pearl Harbor that he was forced to backtrack.

At home, Hearst had invested hugely in forestry and other resources to produce wood-based paper. However, making wood-based paper is very damaging to the environment and relatively expensive. Paper made from hemp (the male pot plant) is cheaper, a better product and less damaging. Hearst risked being undercut.

Hearst, as well as being a Nazi and fascist sympathiser and more, was a virulent racist who particularly detested Mexicans. Marijuana use was popular amongst them and, never being one to waste an effort, Hearst saw a way to make sure his investment in wood-based paper production paid off, and to make as many Mexicans as miserable as he could: he used his media to persuade the US government to make hemp illegal either for paper production or for consumption.

He was greatly assisted in this by Henry J. Anslinger, a career civil servant in the recently-formed Bureau of Narcotics, who was also a white supremacist racist. Like Hearst, Anslinger despised blacks, Mexicans, Asians and Filipinos. He also hated Jazz and Blues music, which, here revealing his profound misogyny, he thought caused white women to become 'immoral'. Since marijuana was popular amongst Jazz and Blues musicians, Anslinger was presented with another easy target, which Hearst lost no time in demonising.

The sick mentality at the heart of the American right was revealed in the attitudes of these two evil men: racism, white supremacy, misogyny and the appropriation of women's bodies.

Using its usual combination of threats and bullying, the US, again motivated by Hearst's media empire, 'persuaded' its trading partners to do the same.

So the fact is, ladies and gentlemen, that smoking pot is illegal because it suited the business ends of a Nazi-sympathising media tycoon with no respect for truth, and the career of a bureaucrat. That is why countless billions have been wasted and innumerable lives lost and ruined in the entirely specious 'War on Drugs'. There is no other reason.

Smoking pot is a victimless crime. Even if it were proven that it were as damaging as other, legal, recreational drugs, the only person being harmed is the person consuming it. Any other harm comes simply from the fact of its prohibition. As country star Willie Nelson said, 'The most dangerous thing you can do with marijuana is get caught with it.'

A little personal history. I began smoking pot when I was 15, while I was a young musician playing in bands. I loved it. I didn't drink alcohol. I smoked pretty much every day for the next six years, and then toned it down, only because my life changed a bit. When I did so, I had no difficulty. I didn't become an addict. I took my degree and entered journalism as a photographer. I was headhunted for the launch of Scotland on Sunday, and soon became the youngest, ever, Executive Picture Editor in Scotland. I ran a very successful photography business for decades, I have beautiful children who all took or are taking degrees, I took my Master's degree and I own my home outright. Does it sound like pot ruined my life? Don't be a blithering idiot. And I still enjoy a blast, believe me.

And it's not just me. I know countless people who would say the same – who run good little businesses, some good big businesses, who, for years, every time you saw them, had smoke coming out of their ears. Doctors, lawyers, university professors (a lot of them, actually) journalists, you name it. Reeking for years and you're telling me it hurt them? Away, what utter garbage.

Did any of us succumb to the draw of stronger drugs? No. We just looked at that and said, 'That shit ain't for me bud, don't bogart that joint.'

And while I was smoking a lot I hardly ever drank. My friends and I would go weeks at a time without even a pint. Can you believe that?

Which should tell you why pot is still illegal, so long after Hearst's death. Yes folks, it has nothing to do with the paltry harm it can do. It has nothing to do with the (now discredited) suggestion that it can cause mental instability. It has nothing to do with utter nonsense about 'gateway drugs' or non-existent 'social consequences.'

The main reason pot is still so widely illegal is that the alcohol producing companies spend fortunes hiring sharp-suited little shits to persuade politicians to keep it so, because they think that way, we'll buy more alcohol. They are aided and abetted by career bean-pushers like Anslinger who populate police and regulatory bureaux across the globe, whose only interest is their next pay cheque.

A wise man once told me, 'When you see people doing something there's no reasonable explanation for, the answer is always money.' Case in point.

Pot is important and it's the first of the 3Ps because in the first place, its use is a crime that is in itself utterly victimless. Its victims stem from a specious attempt to prohibit it, either through lives and livelihoods lost to government agencies like the American DEA, or amongst the criminals to whom the business has been ceded by politicians. The persecution of consumers has ruined the lives of countless otherwise hardworking, ordinary people. They were victimised for smoking a plant that will happily grow in your garden. Is that a fair use of the power of the state?

Criminalising the use of pot criminalises pot consumers. Even if you are never caught, criminalising a relatively harmless natural substance makes consumers reconsider the relationship of individual to state. Now while most pot consumers are probably by nature non-conformists, knowing that the state holds you to be criminal, for doing something that does you no harm, makes you rethink your perspective on the law. It makes you ask, 'How many other laws are as absurd as this one?'

It tells you that obeying the law is a matter of choice, because if the law is wrong about pot, then what else is it wrong about? It means we have to look at each and every law and decide, one by one, whether or not we think it should be obeyed.

In the absence of moral authority, which law abandons the instance it criminalises people for doing something that harms no-one else, why should we obey *any* law? Only out of fear. Is that the relationship we want to have between state and people, one of obedience enforced by fear? I don't want a society like that.

I do not think it is helpful for the law to be considered an ass, but for the law not to be considered so, all the ass-like laws – and this is one – have to be repealed.

Prohibition didn't work with alcohol in the 1920s in America, and it hasn't worked with pot. The so-called 'war on drugs' has been an unmitigated disaster. It has destabilised large parts of the world and led to untold death and suffering; yet it has not impacted one iota on the availability of pot.

Face it, that war is lost. It's over. If you want to do some good, maybe – just maybe – you could divert resources from the failed attempt to prohibit a substance that dos no harm to really working on one that does, like meth – and not through prohibition, but rehabilitation. Hell, give them pot instead – it might work.

Prohibition of pot has poured billions directly into the pockets of organised crime families all over the world. Not only is that money then used to fund far more nefarious operations, it has other consequences. Today, in the UK, thousands of Vietnamese have been smuggled in to work in marijuana-growing factories – as SLAVES. That is right, prohibition of marijuana has *directly* led to the re-establishment of a slave economy actually inside the UK. And the same is true across Europe.

Does anyone imagine for one second that this atrocity would be permitted in a legal business? Are you nuts? There would be inspections, Health and Safety, minimum wage, working hours... the people who now are working as slaves would actually be making a living. And they would be PAYING TAX. Just as the business owners would.

The alcohol business generates huge amounts of tax revenue that goes to the exchequers of the countries where it exists. This comes through duty, through point of sale taxes, through income tax paid by workers and corporation tax paid by the companies.

Not ONE PENNY of a potential fortune goes to any government

where marijuana is prohibited and instead ALL of it goes into the pockets of the crime bosses and, further back the chain, is used to fund terrorism, killing, extortion, people trafficking, smuggling and the panoply of criminal activities.

The only way to stop this is to legalise the consumption, trade and sale of marijuana and control its production – which is exactly what we do with alcohol, so we have the mechanisms and the personnel already in place.

In the UK, according to a 2014 survey, 29% of the population had used an illegal substance – and so are criminalised under this absurd law – while 52% of voters favour legalisation. In the light of that, is continuing with a failed attempt to outlaw something that almost a third of the population has used – with no ill effect – an intelligent use of the power of the state? Is that a reasonable use of taxpayers' money? Yet the politicians, ever in the pockets of business, continue to throw taxpayers money at prohibition, when simple legalisation would save all that, put an end to the crime barons and their slave trade and raise huge amounts of revenue for the Exchequer.

In recent years, chinks of light have begun to appear. At time of writing, just under half (24) of all American states have either decriminalised or fully legalised pot, with absolutely no ill effects to public health and, in some case, considerable benefit to their exchequers. Colorado, with a population the size of Scotland, 5 million, raised $76m (£48m) in marijuana tax revenues during its first year of legalisation.

In Europe, improvement is slow but only today we read that several English police forces have decided to stop prosecuting for growing or consuming the plant. In Spain, you can both grow and smoke in your own home. The Czech Republic has legalised cannabis, one more reason to go there. And despite pressure from France and Germany, the Dutch capital, Amsterdam, remains a toker's refuge.

Nevertheless we would have to consider that, on this measure of our freedom, we are not doing well. Government authority is being used in an unreasonable way, damaging the lives of huge numbers of otherwise law-abiding, taxpaying citizens and turning them into criminals. Doing so debases both the notion of criminality and the justice system itself. It makes legislatures a laughing-stock and plays into the hands of crime barons. On this 'P' we need to do much better.

I think imma smoke me a spliff now.

Gratuitous picture of a pretty little girl because like kittens

9. Je suis Paris

I was out on my Ducati on Friday; you know, Friday the 13th. It was a beautiful morning, sunny and mild, and I was thinking how nice it was for what would probably be the last time I venture out on a motorcycle this year. The sun struck low across the landscape and the trees, which are already mostly bare of leaves, filtered its rays. But they were still strong and sometimes it was hard to see, even though I had cleaned my visor before venturing out.

The contrast in light between the sunny parts of the road and those under the trees, especially those grouped together where they still have their leaves, was huge. It was like switching the lights off as I passed onto the shade.

I've been riding motorcycles for four decades now and you don't do that without learning a thing or two. I was reminded of one on Friday: watch it! It may be beautiful and sunny with perfect dry tarmac out in the open, but under the trees the road will be wet.

This happens because the dew that forms overnight does not evaporate as it would where there are no trees to insulate it from the sun's warmth. And Friday was a very good example of the case in point; under the trees it was not only so dark it was difficult for my eyes to adjust, but also it was lethally slippery with damp and, to make matters worse, there were many fallen leaves on the road, just waiting to catch a careless back tyre and flip me over.

I reflected on this and thought it might make a nice philosophical post, you know, Reverend Rod, the atheist minister, droning on somewhere forgotten in cyberspace. But I just noted the headline idea and got on with the day's work.

The next morning, Saturday, I was wakened by a stack of messages on my phone from my girlfriend, Crissy. It's quite usual to find one or two, which is sweet, but this time there were many and they were urgent.

'Are you all right?' Half asleep, I wondered what she was on about, and messaged back a generic 'What up?' To which she responded. 'Paris. Have you seen the news?'

Well I don't do television, so no, but I was quickly enough apprised of the situation through Reuters and AP. A terrible black horror born of hatred and intolerance had reached out and stabbed at the heart of this great country. Over a hundred already confirmed killed; now we know it's many more.

There will be time later to talk about the evil that caused this to happen; how relentless Western interference in the Middle East has turned it into a poisoned sore; how our ambivalence has sent the wrong signals and made us appear weak; how our continuing to do business with the appalling state of Saudi Arabia allows them to fund terrorists whose only desire it to kill all non-Muslims; and how our own policy of bombing, then walking away to let the locals repair the damage, time and again, has provided recruits by the tens of thousands for a Dark Age cult of killing and revenge.

But we shall come to that; meantime I wanted to think about the aftermath for those who have lost loved ones. My own son's 25th birthday is today and I think of all the other young people, those who were there, gathered to watch a metal band thrash.

Sunny days, sunny days, warm dry roads…yet so so slippery under the trees.

Could we have foreseen the tragedy of Paris? Yes, of course. We have, once again, been guilty of that favourite European pastime, fence-sitting. We have seen how the streams of immigrants coming from the Middle East are mostly men and we know that amongst them are large numbers of fighters. Are they all now peaceful? We know that as well as a group of radical Islamists who came to Europe specifically to carry out this outrage, there were sleeper cells already here who supported them. We should have known. We should have acted. Instead we did nothing.

As a result we have this. And there will be more violence. And more.

There is an old Thai saying: you are responsible for that which you tame. Our policy of hit and run, of avoiding entanglement, has been a disaster and it is this that caused Friday the 13th in Paris. When we meddled in Afghanistan and then walked away, we turned it into a running sore. When we invaded Iraq, left hundreds of thousands dead and displaced, and then walked away, we left the devastated nation open for the evil ones.

Why did we do this? Because the United States had had enough of Saddam Hussein. How had he become so powerful? Because the United States armed him to fight Iran. But rather than be responsible for the untold mess his country had created, Obama walked away, and the rest of us did too.

The West, led by the United States, did not like Bashar al-Assad of Syria. So when the opportunity came, we armed those who rebelled against him. And the most powerful amongst them was Daesh, otherwise known as ISIS or ISIL. Its unalloyed evil is the direct result of Western political intervention. The United States, through the CIA, funded, armed and trained Daesh, and now sits back, happily distant, while Europe bears the fury of the war that America began.

People – many Muslims – who point to Western hypocrisy – are right. We are responsible for killings on an unimaginable sale and, like cowards, we have run away from the mess we created. The Middle East and the Arab world are rich – yet have hardly a functioning state left. Afghanistan, Iran, Iraq, Syria, Egypt, Libya – all failed states and the cause of this failure is not Islam – appalling though it may be – it is US-led Western policy. We have relentlessly and remorselessly interfered in these states, killing an untold number of people, since before World War Two and we continue, in cowardice and irresponsibility, to refuse to stay behind and clean up the mess that we ourselves created.

From the very first day we began to interfere – as long ago as Suez, or when we propped up the Pahlavi dynasty in Iran, through to vaporised babies under retaliatory French bombs today, we have been running up an account of misery that we have simply not paid. Well, now comes the bill.

Enjoy the carefree times as you ride along in sun and warmth; under the trees it is dark and slippery.

Croutons and Cheese!
Rod Fleming
Continuing the hilarious, madcap adventures of a family 'Lost in France'.
ISBN: 978-0-9572612-4-2

Islam.

1. Qandeel Baloch: killed by Islam.

A prominent Pakistani Facebook personality, Qandeel Baloch, was murdered by her own family. She was 26. To be an independent woman in an Islamic place is to invite your own close relatives to kill you.

Not only was Qandeel killed by her own brother, her parents, who were present, did nothing to stop him. They have been arrested.

Horrifying as Qandeel's killing is, such murders are commonplace in the failed state of Pakistan. And why is Pakistan a failed state? Because Islam.

Nobody should be under any illusions now: we are at war already.

Qandeel is a victim of Islam. If you are a woman, Islam will enslave you, and kill you if you refuse to comply. Qandeel's death proves that. Dare to show your bare head in public, and your own brother will strangle you to death for 'offending' Islam.

Refuse to marry the man your male relatives choose for you and they will kill you. Marry a man they don't want you to and they will burn you to death. Allow yourself to be raped and you will be flogged and perhaps judicially murdered as an adulterer. This is Islam and we are at war with it.

If you are a Christian or a Jew, Islam may permit you to live, as long as you pay the dhimmi tax and defer to Muslims at all times. Otherwise it will kill you.

If you are of any other religion and refuse to convert, Islam will kill you.

If you are gay or homosexual or gender non-conforming, Islam will kill you.

If you ever express a doubt that Allah exists or that Mohammed was hardly the 'perfect man', Islam will kill you.

But its most potent hatred is for women. In Islam they are not fully human; they are objects, chattels of their male relatives, who can do as they like with them: Qandeel's death proves that.

Islam, as it is presently constituted, is the most violent and dangerous death-cult on Earth. It fully intends to totally destroy the West. When it has succeeded, women in the West will be slaves of men.

It is doing so by a process of infiltration and colonisation. Its aim is to impose a global Islamic Caliphate, governed by Sharia, its depraved 'Law'. Its preferred method for doing so is by Stealth War – the slow infiltration, colonisation and ultimately overtaking of democratic nations.

Islam intends to destroy democracy, though it will exploit it to gain power. The erasure of democracy and its replacement by an Islamic theocracy is the purpose of Islamic Stealth War. If you get in its way, it will kill you.

Islam intends to re-establish slavery as normal. Wife-beating as normal. Paedophilia as normal. Killing adulterers as normal.

At the same time, it intends – fully – to kill all homosexual and 'gender non-conforming people'. Although Islam has a long tradition of both homosexual practices and transsexualism, the modern, Wahhabist form will kill every single one.

The list just goes on and on.

From now on, the only question we should be asking our politicians is, 'What are you going to do about Islam?' And if the answer is 'nothing', then we know what to do with them.

When you are at war with a ruthless enemy whose sole aim is to destroy everything you have and kill you, you must accept strange bedfellows. And we are at war now, with just such an enemy. We may not like the politicians who are strong enough to fight, but we need them now.

I know. You have nice Muslim friends and they would never harm anyone. Islam is a religion of peace, isn't it?

No, it's not. It is a religion of war and killing. Its disguise of peacefulness is just taqqiya – the lying and dissembly that all Muslims must practise until Islam is strong enough to take over. Then countless other women like Qandeel will die.

'Peaceful' Muslims?

The only peaceful Muslims are those who are not actually practising Islam. We have to support people like Maajid Nawaz – but he is loathed by huge numbers of practising Muslims who know, as he does, that the reforms he proposes are actually the abandonment of Qur'anic authority. This brave man's life is in constant danger and the chances of him succeeding alone are practically nil.

When politician Humza Yousaf of the SNP swore loyalty to the British Queen wearing a kilt and sporran, people were quick to say how this was the true face of Islam: an urbane, polite, educated man adopting and respecting the traditions of the nation that had welcomed him.

I have no reason to doubt that he is an intelligent and courteous man; indeed I fervently hope he is. We desperately need many more like him.

However, though he is of Pakistani descent, he does not practise Islam. If he did, he would know that Sharia specifically interdicts a man from wearing clothing below the ankle. His is not the true face of Islam. His is the face of an apostate, or perhaps something more dangerous.

Is Yousaf a decent secularist who has abandoned any literal interpretation of Islam for a moderate, cultural 'identity' that is not really a religion at all? Would he have stood between Qandeel and her killer, or would he have refused to interfere, as her parents did?

Or might he be a Stealth Warrior practising taqqiya, appearing in disguise before his enemies to gain their trust, before he attacks? If he is, how do we know? When our own and our children's lives are in danger, can we take the chance?

Some questions.

Ask your peaceful Muslim friends these questions – which I would also ask of Yousaf:

Do you think a Muslim is permitted to refuse to sell alcohol to the public, even when that is why they have been employed?

Do you think a Muslim taxi-driver has a right to refuse to carry a blind person, because that person is accompanied by a guide dog?

Do you think a man may beat his wife?

Do you think a woman should cover her head in public?

Do you think homosexuality should be illegal?

Do you think those who leave Islam should be killed?

Do you think those who 'insult' Islam should be killed?

Are there any circumstances under which you would approve a terrorist attack, anywhere?

If you knew of an extremist cell with in your community, would you conceal that information from the police?

Do you think it would be a good idea if Islam were to take over the world completely?[1]

If the answer to any of these is 'yes', then the person you are talking

1 These are all questions that have been asked by Pew research. A depressingly large number of respondents, even in the West, answered in the affirmative.

to is not your friend. You are looking at the enemy who may one day murder you – and not think twice about it.

We have seen enough, now. The reason for the killing and the murders perpetrated by Muslims is not poverty or hardship. Nor is it grievance, real or imagined, over the Middle East. The reason is Islam. It is not Muslims; they are just people. But Islam is the most corrosive and dangerous death cult that exists and it remorselessly corrupts those it infects.

This week we have seen a brutal terror attack in France, with responsibility claimed by Daesh. We have seen a coup in Turkey fail. In its aftermath we see the brutality that only Islam knows. Turkey has fallen; it is well on the way to becoming a failed state like Pakistan. Its last chance to stem the tide of Islam has gone.

Poor Qandeel Baloch's brutal killing was just the most recent in a list of murders carried out in the name of Islam. It will not be the last, by a long way.

2. Dar al-Harb: The Islamic stimulus for war.

Central to Islam is the notion that the entire world not under its control is Dar al-Harb.

(This is the second chapter of the book World War Three.)

The Quran is the codification of messages believed by Muslims to have been received by Mohammed from the Angel Gabriel. It says a territory may exist under two conditions: Dar al-Islam and Dar al-Harb. These mean, roughly, 'Land of Submission'. and 'Land of War'.

Dar al-Islam is territory whose inhabitants have accepted or submitted to Islamic Law, Sharia, or which has been occupied by Muslim armies who then enforced Sharia.

Dar al-Harb is all those lands and territories which are not under Islamic control and where Sharia is not in sway.

A Muslim's sacred duty, expressed in the Quran, is to do everything in his power (women have no say in Islam) to turn Dar al-Harb into Dar al-Islam. 'Holy' War to conquer non-Islamic territory is the purpose and meaning of jihad. Although the word can mean 'struggle' in a spiritual sense, this is a secondary meaning. The principal one is that Muslims must wage a war of conquest over the world.

Freeing land from Islam returns it to Dar al-Harb.

Bad as this is, there is a worse injunction: no land that was ever under Sharia may be permitted to escape from it. If it does so, it becomes a special form of Dar al-Harb. In this, the occupants are not seen only as enemies but also as traitors.

Just as the punishment for a Muslim who converts to another faith is death, so the punishment for a population that breaks free of Sharia is to have the most savage and brutal war rained down upon it.

It is the duty of all Muslims everywhere to establish the entire world as Dar al-Islam. The front line in the war to destroy Dar al-Harb is those territories that once endured Islam and have rejected it. It is here that the most vicious attacks of jihadists are seen.

This is why, as an aside, the stated objectives of Daesh today, also known as 'Islamic State', include the conquest and Islamification of Sicily,

Corsica, Spain and parts of France, as a first step towards global domination. Europeans would do well to take this menace seriously.

Occupation of the Holy Land.

The Christian liberation and re-occupation of the Holy Land was a slap in the face to the rulers of the most powerful empire the world had hitherto seen. Dar al-Islam had been liberated. It was now Dar al-Harb, and had to be destroyed. Worse, the population had to be punished for accepting infidel rule. The liberation of the Holy Land was not something the Caliphs would take lightly and their reaction was predictable. War raged in the Holy Land for almost two centuries.

Their fury was not simply because the land had been liberated after their invasion and occupation of it. The Quran is based, loosely, on the Bible. It is a sort of half-understood pastiche. But, crucially, the most important figures in the Bible were retained by Mohammed as 'prophets'. The most important city to the Jews and Christians, Jerusalem, was written into the Quran as the most important city to the Muslims – even though Islam had its roots hundreds of mile to the east and south.

This was the justification that Islamic warlords used to invade and occupy the city and its surrounding territory. This caused the forced Islamification of what had previously been a Judeo-Christian territory.

In other words, the land and city had been made Dar al-Islam. But the Crusaders had made it Dar al-Harb again. It was inevitable that Islamic forces would try to seize the land and the city of Jerusalem itself, once again.

The Fatimid rulers of Egypt were unable to do so but they were defeated by the Abbasids under Salah al-Din (Saladin). In 1187, he recaptured Jerusalem. To be fair, Saladin was far more tolerant than the Fatimids had been, and Christians and Jews who paid the dhimmi – a special tax imposed on non-Muslims living in Islamic territory, allegedly for 'protection' – were not persecuted.

This was not the end of the Papacy's grand design to rule the Holy Land, but it was never able to recover. A moment should be passed in considering what the consequences were.

The Crusades had galvanised Christians all over Europe. Huge numbers of men joined them to travel the hard road to the Middle East and there, very likely, to die. Yet with military success came the confirmation of what the church extolled: the Christian God was all-powerful; he was the Almighty and could not be gainsaid. As long as the Papacy's forces remained triumphant, this message could not be challenged.

Salah al-Din, a brilliant strategist and military commander, gave the lie to that. Just as the Crusaders had once slapped the Fatimids, now he slapped the Papacy in return.

This was a shocking challenge to Papal authority which, at the end of the twelfth century, was absolute over Europe.

Islam was once generally tolerant.

One must not run away with the idea that it was somehow far better to be a European living in a Christian theocracy than to be an Arab or any of the other ethnic groups ruled by the Caliphate and living under it. Far from it. Slavery – albeit called 'serfdom' – was normal throughout Europe. Living conditions for the majority were harsh at best, with diseases rife. While the wealthy elite did well, for most commoners life was a Hobbesian grind: poor, nasty, brutish and short.

In many ways, the ordinary people living under the Caliphate were better off than European Christians. Sharia is indeed a barbarous and harsh code, but at least it was a proper legal framework. Once the brutal slaughter always associated with military jihad was over and those who survived had been cowed, Islam regulated its warriors in how they must treat their victims.

Religious minorities, as long as they paid the dhimmi, were usually left alone in the Caliphate; they had second-class status but they were not, generally, persecuted in the way that Jews were in Europe, for example.

Furthermore, this is the time of the greatest advances in Islamic art and culture generally. There were many secularists and indeed atheists who again, were tolerated. The great writer Omar Khayyam, a Persian, spoke of a life that was far from grim and devoid of earthly pleasure. Philosophers, mathematicians and astronomers worked and studied with a freedom that was completely unknown in Europe. But this period – we might call it a honeymoon – did not last.

Today, there is no doubt: life in an Islamic state is a hell on Earth. In Dar al-Islam, women are constantly abused and killed and homosexuals are routinely judicially murdered. (The latter despite the elevated prevalence if homosexual relations between Muslim men – or maybe because of it.) The slightest dissent will be punished with flogging or judicial murder. All science and technology, that cannot be bent to the furtherance of Islam, is illegal.

Nobody in their right mind, today, would want to live under the horror of Islam.

With the fall of Jerusalem the very first cracks had begun to appear in the monolith of Papal authority. It did not take a genius to see that either the Christian God was less infallible and almighty than had hitherto been believed, or that he had lost faith in the Pope. Shock waves rocked the Papacy and the Third Crusade was organised to retake Jerusalem. Although it did recapture some territory, it failed in this objective.

In 1202 the Fourth Crusade was organised and this had markedly different results.

For centuries the schism between the Catholic Church and the Orthodox Church had festered. In 1203, en route to Jerusalem, the Crusader leaders were diverted. Prince Alexios Angelos persuaded them to attack the Byzantine Empire in Constantinople and reinstate his deposed father. Most of the Crusaders, eager for the spoils of war, agreed. Only about ten percent of the knights who had set out carried on to Acre.

Constantinople capitulated after a show of Crusader strength and Alexios Angelos was crowned co-emperor. However he was deposed in January 1204 by a popular uprising. This meant that the Crusaders could not receive the monies they had been promised. They, along with the Venetians, decided to sack the city and set up the Latin Empire in its stead.

Consequences.

Effectively, the rape of Constantinople had four consequences. It cemented the schism between the Catholic Church and the Eastern Orthodox Church. It broke Byzantine control over important trade routes to the east. The reason the Venetians had been interested in the fight was to secure these for themselves. The Latin Empire was weak and immediately challenged by Byzantine resistance. This meant that military strength that might have been used to re-conquer Jerusalem was not available.

Finally, it broke the back of the Byzantine Empire. Despite regaining Constantinople and ending the Latin Empire, it fell into decline.

While these thoughts may have entered the minds of the European intelligentsia, and may have been discussed behind closed doors, for ordinary people, they were irrelevant. But something was to happen that made the questioning of the Church both more widespread and immediate.

3. War with Islam: ideology, not people

Islam is locked in a war with secular democracy and moderate Muslims themselves.

Ten days ago a Canadian, Robert Hall, had his head hacked from his body in a brutal public murder. Two days later, over 100 people were gunned down in a nightclub in Orlando, Florida; forty-nine died. Two days after that a married couple, both police officers, were stabbed to death in their home outside Paris and their infant child held hostage until the killer was shot by police.

There is nothing whatsoever to connect these victims, on the face of it. Nothing. A middle-aged professional, young people in a nightclub, serving police officers. They died in equally unrelated locations – the Philippines, the USA, France.

But they are connected all the same: they were all murdered in the name of Islam.

These are but the tip of the iceberg; all over the Middle East, Asia and Sub-Saharan Africa, in the same time, hundreds of innocent people were murdered – in the name of Islam. And most of them were Muslims.

These victims join the tens of thousands of others who have been murdered, raped, or enslaved in the name of Islam, just since 2000. If we go back to the 20th century, we find that millions were murdered, raped and enslaved in the name of Islam. When we call the roll of violent, murdering ideologies of that century, we always forget one; Nazism, Communism – and Islam.

Yet we may not speak a word against this. We may not name what we see, what is manifest, what is plain as day – that Islam perverts men into monsters who kill, rape and enslave in its name and expect a heavenly reward of unlimited, unending sex with 72 perpetual virgins for doing so. (The Orlando shooter was homosexual and we wonder what he imagined his reward might be; 72 Christians, perhaps – the pornstar, not the religion.)

A War Against an Ideology, not a 'Race'

Despite the blindingly obvious truth about Islam, we are not allowed to say a word against it. Why? Because Islam is mainly practised by people who do not have white skin. And the intellectual fascism of 'identity politics' insists that no-one of non-white skin colour may ever be criticised for anything.

This of course reveals the excruciating irony that 'identity politics' is itself a form of racism; but then, you have to have some intelligence to divine that. Bill Maher calls it the 'soft bigotry of low expectations', and Bill is right on point.

Well, enough is enough. Identity politics is indeed a form of racism and fascism, and a spade should be called a spade.

There is no 'war on terrorism'

This war began a long time ago and we ignored it. We misnamed it, pretended it might go away. We vacillated, imagining that our trinkets and compromises, our cavilling appeasement, might quench our enemy's thirst for blood. But all that failed long ago.

We are not 'at war with terrorism' – or rather that is too tautological a euphemism to let pass. All states, everywhere, are perpetually at war with terrorism. That is why a state exists: to protect the people from terrorists. But nobody says 'the King of France gave land at the mouth of the Seine to the Normans so that they could protect the country from terrorist attack'. They say, 'from the Vikings.'

To be at war against terrorism is a permanent and necessary part of a state's very reason to exist; to use this term to describe our current crisis is to deliberately deny the real name of the enemy.

It's a war against Islam.

We are not at war with a people, or a 'race'. We are at war with a Dark Age socio-political ideology that promotes injustice and is based on a pack of barefaced lies. This war is no different from the war against Communism. It's not about people. It's about ideas.

Islam is just a religion; just a set of ideas. It is an ideology invented to make some men rich and powerful by controlling women, children and all the weaker men. It's no less hideous, oppressive or murderous for being a version mainly promoted by men with non-white skin.

Islam stands against literally every single value that Western democracy believes in. Every value that European democracy – and that includes the Americas and parts of Asia and Africa, for better or worse – has fought for centuries to develop and preserve.

Islam hates women and gays, considers that children have no rights, animals have no rights. It insists that anyone who does not accept it as the literal truth should be killed. It hates art. It hates poetry. It hates music. It hates science. It hates secularism. It hates democracy.

Anything that could be considered civilised, Islam hates. It would rather turn the world back into a desert nightmare of brutality and discrimination where warlords do as they like. Where women are personal chattels of men to be raped when they are nine, or burned alive when they break its rules about marriage, or for refusing to be whores for jihadists. Where they have acid thrown in their faces for not covering them. Where homosexuals are thrown from rooftops then stoned till they die. Where the 'crime' of having an opinion is punished by death.

Armistice

The last war that European civilisation fought against Islam – a defensive war, just as this one is – lasted for a thousand years. This time the enemy is ahead of us. We now can see that there was no victory before the Gates of Vienna in 1683; just an armistice and we did not seize the opportunity it afforded us to smash the enemy forever.

Instead of striking the head from the serpent, we took our boot from its neck and let it go. We allowed it compassion – which is a part of our culture. But it is not a part of the enemy's and anyone who thinks that jihadists will spare the sword, should the world ever be unfortunate enough that they do seize the advantage, is barking mad.

Surely, if Islam is indeed a religion of peace, then no blasphemy could be greater than murdering, raping and enslaving in its name. Where, then, are the screaming hordes who protested against cartoons of Mohammed and called for the artist to be killed – for blasphemy? Those who called for the death of Salman Rushdie for the same? These men killed no-one, raped no-one, enslaved no-one; yet their 'blasphemy' was such that it merited death.

Why are the same people who called for this not out on the streets right now, demanding that the atrocities committed in the name of their religion must stop?

Such protesters are nowhere to be seen. One might even be forgiven for thinking that murder, rape and slavery are not 'blasphemous' at all, and that could only be because Islam – the religion of peace – actually condones them.

Do Muslims all support the jihadists? No, of course not, but the fact that the majority of Germans were not Nazis did not prevent the Holocaust; and the fact that the majority of Muslims are decent people, who do love peace, has not and will not prevent more killing.

If moderate Muslims are to neutralise the jihadist threat, then they need our assistance, because they too are under threat – indeed, they are under the greatest threat of any, since, after all, they live with the jihadists in their midst.

Muzzling Moderates

We need all the support we can get from moderate Muslims, yet this is confounded by Political Correctness. Partly, this is our own fault. We have allowed the Regressive Left to set a picket line around Islam, so that it may never be criticised, even by Muslims; just look at how they treat Maajid Nawaz, Ayan Hirsi Ali or Salman Rushdie.

This very ring-fence helps to muzzle moderate Muslims and to deliver them up to the jihadists. It isolates them from their natural allies – non-Muslim moderates – and pretends that this is 'defending a culture'. This attitude – promulgated by the Regressive Left, those 'useful idiots' – is pure racism in itself. It is, as Maher says, the 'soft bigotry of low expectations'. After all, how could we possibly imagine that people of brown skin could do better? And not only that, they must be allowed to do their worst without a word of protest.

Well if Islam, as a culture, has value, it is not in its ability to murder the innocent. Peaceable Muslim communities have already proven themselves to be rich recruiting grounds for jihadist murderers who have but rarely been turned over to the authorities and who, rather, are all too often hidden instead.

If there is a solution – other than massive 'ethnic cleansing', which nobody wants to see, even if it were possible – then it is in mobilising moderate Muslims to denounce extremism and violence. It is in standing with them against the jihadists. It is by funding their organisations and helping them to counter jihadism within their own communities. It is in protecting them from the threats they surely receive and ensuring that their voices be heard, by Muslims.

Furthermore, Islamic apostates – threatened with death by Islamists – must be protected and their voices must be heard. The Council of ex-Muslims of Britain, according to the UK Guardian, assists about 350 people a year to leave Islam in the UK, 'the majority of whom have faced threats…either by their families or by Islamists.'

The ghettoisation of Muslim communities turns them into pressure-cookers where violent extremists dominate. This is exacerbated, not hindered, by the politically correct Regressive Left.

In its towering conceit and racism, the Regressive Left considers it better that moderate Muslims be terrorised in their own communities by extremist Muslims, than that they be helped by non-Muslims. After all, goes Regressive thinking, they all have brown skin; they should be allowed to get on with killing each other undisturbed by white colonialists trying to enforce Western mores. Meantime, the Regressive Left gets on with really important things, like whether a man with a beard can legitimately 'identify' as a woman.

Why is it that public debate is always between an Islamic extremist, or a barefaced apologist for extremism, and someone of the political right, usually white? Because to expose the schisms within Muslim communities is to confuse the all-important message – white bad, non-white good. So what if moderates are sacrificial lambs? The Regressive Left couldn't care less.

Our strategy must therefore be twofold: on the one hand to completely disgrace the Regressive Left and its intellectual fascism of 'Identity Politics'. On the other we must massively support moderate Muslims, politically and financially, wherever they live, while denying any support or platform to Islamist extremists.

There is no certainty that we will win this war, even with the best of our efforts. What is certain is that if we continue to refuse to recognise what is happening and do not take immediate steps to counter it, then we shall lose it. Enoch Powell's 'rivers of blood' may yet come true; and none of us will be the better for it.

4. Unli sex: the foundation of Islam

Unlimited sex after death is the foundation of Islam; and in Islam the most obnoxious form is mainstream today.

This is dangerous because the aim of this form, Salafism, sometimes called 'Wahhabism', is the destruction of all civilisation and the return of the world to the conditions that obtained in the Caliphate a thousand years ago. To this end Islamic forces are rampaging across the globe killing, raping and razing to the ground everything that they find.

Yet we know that people are essentially altruistic. So how is it possible for a cult to motivate them to such focussed evil as it does?

The answer is in the control of sex.

When we researched *Why Men Made God* we spent a lot of time looking at extant and recently recorded matriarchies. We were struck by how peaceable they were and how calm and pleasant the men were. In these matriarchies the supply of sex is determined by women. Yet it appears that there is enough to satisfy the men and very little friction takes place between them, if any. This compares well to study of bonobos, *Pan paniscus*, our closest relatives, who also organise in matriarchal groups. The males are contented and non-aggressive.

This shows us the key to the Islam's power. By restricting the supply of sex, it causes competition and violence between men. It can then direct this violence to its own ends – typically conquest and destruction.

To do this, Islam first removed women's control over their own sexuality and reproduction. This remains the case today. Witness how in the Christian cults, any form of birth control – other than abstinence – is condemned. Look at how sex, in these cults, is condemned as a pleasure. This is happening for a reason, and that reason is social control.

And if you think that is bad, it's nothing compared to the hideous conditions imposed under Islam. In this cult, high-status men can have up to four wives. There is, generally, a slightly higher number of girl births (53% in favour of girls); but if high-status men can have four wives, this clearly means that low-status men struggle to find one.

Add to this the concubine system in which high-status men may keep as many female sex slaves as they like in addition to their official wives and it should be clear that for ordinary men there are very few women who might possibly be available. This has been exacerbated for certainly decades and probably far longer, by the practices of aborting female children or killing the newborns.

The inaccessibility of sex is further reinforced by the Islamic customs of making women invisible. Their faces and bodies are covered completely, so that men are denied even the pleasure of seeing them. The lengths to which Islamic 'authorities' go in this is ludicrous and would be laughable were it not real.

For example, Salman Rushdie recounts how Islamic clerics had decided that it was unacceptable for a woman to wear stockings even under a burqa, since the sound of her thighs rubbing together would inflame men.

Everything in Islam is about sex, yet nobody is getting any.

The natural consequence of this should be that men would have sex with each other, but Islam is wise to this and so sex between men is punishable by death. It happens anyway throughout the Islamic world, but the cult does its best to stamp it out, at least in public, and for those who don't matter.

Then, Islam attempts to eliminate male pleasure in sex using a barbarous procedure called circumcision which removes over half the sensitive parts of the penis. The specific reason for this is to reduce sexual pleasure. This is also practised in Judaism and in the more backward parts of the USA, for exactly the same reasons: the reduction of male pleasure in sex. At the same time Islam in particular sanctions Female Genital Mutilation which removes *all* pleasure in sex from women.

Why is this happening? The answer is simple: denying men any sexual release makes them more violent. This is why boxers refrain from sexual release prior to a fight. It makes them more aggressive. Islam needs violent, aggressive men to conquer the world, so it uses the same trick.

The other side of this vile equation comes, of course, in the afterlife. There is no trickery more sickening than the religious promise of reward after death, but this is far more vile than anything Christians ever came up with.

In Islam, the only assured way to enter Heaven is by dying in jihad, which means being killed in holy war. There are conditions to this: principally, one must not be killed by a woman. Furthermore, self-sacrifice, as practised by suicide bombers, is the ultimate, highest form of such a death and guarantees instant access to Heaven. To quote the excellent film *Four Lions*, a suicide bomber is 'in Heaven before his head hits the ceiling.'

This Heaven is not the vague place of lights and music that Christians believe in. The Muslim version is very specific. In this Heaven the newly dead warrior is welcomed by 72 girls who are indescribably more beautiful and sensuous than any human woman and who, in addition, have a virginity that is renewed every day.

These girls, these celestial purveyors of sexual pleasure, are called 'houris'. Now it has somewhat been lost by usage, but the correct pronunciation of the English word 'whore' is 'hoor' to rhyme with moor and poor, and not with door and floor. (A hoe is what you use to weed your lettuces.) This word is derived directly from the Arabic houri, and means the same thing – a female purveyor of sexual pleasure: a sex slave. Let's be blunt: a courtesan.

So let us look at what is happening here. In Islam, women are reduced first to property that may be bought and sold, as is the case in other patriarchal religions. They are then completely hidden, in life, from all men except their fathers or the high status men to whom they are sold.

Their hymens are made the measure of their property value and a woman who comes to the marriage bed with hers not intact may be stoned to death. There is a whole industry of hymen repair in countries where this abomination is the case and in Indonesia girls who wish to go to university and many other areas of life are obliged to undergo an examination to establish that they are 'intact'. While this abuse may make the stomach heave, apparently it is all right because it is for 'religious reasons'.

As a result of this, and the fact that half the sensitivity of the man's penis has been removed, the principal reward of sex – for those men for whom it actually happens at all – is the forcible removal of a woman's virginity. This is why Female Genital Mutilation exists – so that men whose genitals have already been mutilated may enjoy the tightness of the closed vagina – until, of course, motherhood fixes that.

Remember that the real meaning of 'virgin' is 'unmarried woman' which translates roughly into 'a woman who has not yet given birth'.

Having a child of course changes a woman, but in Islamic culture, the man's sexual delight may only come from a virgin (in the sense of never having given birth). This was why the Ottoman Emperors' concubines, were they so careless as to fall pregnant, would usually find themselves at the bottom of the Bosporus; their sexual quality expired, they had no further use.

In this culture, a woman is not understood to have pleasure in sex and instead it is her duty. We see something similar in attitudes in the more benighted parts of that most benighted of developed nations, the USA, where ignorance about sex is staggering.

For Muslim men the pleasure of a woman is all in taking her virginity. Once a mother – and having acquired the power that a mother has – a woman becomes valueless as a sexual partner and men will take another wife or a concubine. This is why the houris are perpetual virgins. The taking of virginity is the ultimate sexual reward in the patriarchal cults and nowhere more so than in Islam.

Rape, the forcible entry into a suffering woman, replicates what they believe to be the first act of sex, the loss of female virginity. Pain and suffering on the part of the woman are seen as intrinsic to sex and without it, sex is unsatisfying.

It is also why Islam approves of child brides – the suffering of a girl child penetrated for the first time is so much greater, and her opening is so much tighter. That permanent damage may ensue is irrelevant, since the 'prophet' Mohammed married his last wife when she was six and raped her at nine.

Just in this month a law proscribing child marriages and forced marriages (of women) was blocked in Pakistan because it was 'blasphemous' and 'anti-Islamic'. We need little more proof of the hideous misogyny of a ghastly cult than this.

So we have, in Islam, a refinement of the Abrahamic patriarchal mind-control systems. While many of the techniques used, such as male genital mutilation, occur in other cults, nowhere else do we see the full panoply, the distillation of control over sex into a method that makes ordinary men into rapists and murderers.

While it is true that not all Muslim men are prey to this, the poorer, less well-educated and more religious the culture they come from, the more likely they are to be.

Yet even here we must be wary: as Maajid Nawaz has pointed out, in the 1990s in the UK the choice amongst young Muslim men was not *whether to become* a religious fundamentalist but which flavour one should immerse oneself in. Unfortunately, for these people – principally men – Islam has become a badge of ethnicity, a common shield and buckler against the persecution perpetrated by a white elite.

The West would do well to note this. Bleeding-heart regressive 'liberals', in particular, have to understand that there is no 'intersection', no common ground between defending the rights of women and Islam. You cannot say you defend women while protecting a cult that overtly, deliberately and systematically abuses them.

The Salafist form of Islam, which Saudi Arabia has been financially supporting for decades, makes ordinary men into murdering, raping monsters, while turning women into chattels. If there is one consolation in the predicament the world now finds itself in, it is that plummeting oil prices should limit the power of this most noxious of regimes to export its evil, and with some luck may even lead to its destruction.

Nevertheless, there are, today, millions of Muslim men all over the world who literally and sincerely believe that the only hope they ever might have of enjoying sexual pleasure lies in dying while killing infidels and destroying all culture but the depraved one that spawned them.

The free world needs to take stock and defend itself. It is all very well to be generous; but when the wolf at the door fully intends to destroy you, it is sheer foolhardiness to welcome him in.

5. Sharia: Halal and Haram

The Muslim legal code called Sharia specifies everything that is 'mandated' and 'forbidden'.

In Arabic they are 'halal' and 'haram'. Sharia, contained in a manual called *The Reliance of the Traveller,* actually extends to over 1200 pages of text which specify every imaginable action or aspect of life. Everything from how to brush your teeth or how to put on your clothes, to how to beat your wife or kill your enemies. It is, literally, not just unnecessary for Muslims to think for themselves, it is haram (forbidden).

Muslims are obliged to follow Sharia all the time. There are punishments for transgressions ranging from fines to floggings to forced amputations to death. To reject Sharia wholly is *de facto* to become apostate, which demands a punishment of death.

Sharia is, by far, the most pernicious ideological evil that afflicts the world today.

Please do not take my word for this; I would rather you researched it yourself, for then you will know what Islam, with its debased code of Sharia, really is: the most anti-human and totalitarian ideology the world has ever seen.

So that you can do this research I have made a full copy of the Sharia code available. on my site.[2] Please download it and read for yourself.

A selection of examples, comparing haram (forbidden) with halal (permitted), is below. If you are one of those duped by the platitudes of Islamic apologists or the ridiculous 'regressive left', they may surprise you. They certainly give the lie to the fallacy that Islam is a 'religion of peace'. Sharia is much, much greater than the tiny number of examples below but I have made this list to show that it is more than not eating pork.

I originally made it using the words 'haram' and 'halal' but it seems to me that this is a form of dissembly, in using foreign, unfamiliar words. So I have used English translations instead. While 'forbidden' is a decent translation of 'haram', halal is more difficult. In all cases it means that the action is permitted, but in many it also means that the action is mandated or even obligatory. I have used 'permitted' and 'mandated'. The latter means that it is something that Muslims *should* do, rather than that which they may do.

(A deeper analysis of the gradations of 'haram' and 'halal', and the

---

2

minor differences in the interpretation of Sharia in the various sects of Islam can be found in an excellent piece by Bill Warner, published in 2009.)

> Philosophy is forbidden.
>
> Science and technology are forbidden unless they can be used as weapons.
>
> Modern Western lifestyle is forbidden.
>
> All music is forbidden.
>
> All poetry is forbidden.
>
> All representations – photographs, drawings, paintings, sculpture – are forbidden.
>
> All works of fiction are forbidden.
>
> Education in non-Muslim countries is forbidden.
>
> Giving money as charity to non-Muslims is forbidden – but taking it is mandated.
>
> Friendship with non-Muslims is forbidden.
>
> For a Muslim woman to marry a non-Muslim man is forbidden but for a Muslim man to marry a non-Muslim woman is permitted, as long as she converts and agrees to raise any children as Muslims.
>
> For women to show their faces in public is forbidden.
>
> Using women as concubines is permitted.
>
> Husbands raping their wives is permitted.
>
> Muslim men raping non-Muslim women is mandated.
>
> Muslim men marrying girls, Muslim or otherwise, as young as 6 is mandated; raping them at age 9 is also mandated.
>
> Sex with women outside marriage is forbidden but sex with slaves is permitted.
>
> Arguments against Islam are forbidden but preaching Islam is mandated.
>
> Anti-Islamic writers and beliefs, and their followers, are forbid-

den and should be put to death.

Expressing love for one's wife in public is forbidden but stoning women to death in public is mandated.

Smoking and drinking alcohol are forbidden.

Killing the innocent is forbidden but non-Muslims are not innocent by definition, so killing them is mandated.

Killing anyone who will not submit to Islam is mandated.

Following any law other than Sharia, despite the local law, is forbidden.

Allowing non-Muslims to permanently settle in a Muslim nation is forbidden but going to a non-Muslim nation for settlement purposes is mandated.

Killing Muslims during war, even by accident, by the adversary, is forbidden but killing innocent civilians of non-Muslim enemy nations, deliberately, in retaliation is mandated.

Men wearing clothes below the ankle is forbidden.

Disobeying a husband's orders is forbidden but beating a wife is permitted.

Dialogues at Islamic Shura Council, by the Ulema, or between Islamic scholars about how to run a country are mandated, but allowing ordinary people to voice their opinion is forbidden.

Condemning non-Muslims about anything is permitted but condemning terrorists amongst Muslims is forbidden.

Travelling the world is permitted but allowing non-Muslims, even charity workers, into Muslim lands is forbidden.

Shaving off one's beard is forbidden but shaving pubic hair is mandated.

Waging war against non-Muslims is mandated.

Laws of non-Muslim nations are forbidden but seeking justice from non-Muslim courts is permitted.

Allowing women to work is forbidden.

Democracy is forbidden, but using it to seize power and then destroy it is mandated.

Education for women is forbidden, except insofar as it might help her to run the household for her husband.

Apostasy from Islam is forbidden and punishable by death.

6. Why Islam Cannot Change

Why does Islam resist change and always revert to its barbaric, bloody, violent nature? The answer is because it has no choice.

Other faiths

Jews do not read the Bible as if it were literally true and in any case, the Bible is only one part of the foundation of their faith. The Torah, the body of literature at its centre, contains many other documents and traditions that inform Judaism. It is quite possible to be a Jew and at the same time an atheist. Many great Jewish thinkers and scientists, notably Albert Einstein, have been exactly that.

Practising Jews are expected to read the Bible but to make their own peace with God; and furthermore there is no promise of extra-terrestrial reward or punishment in Judaism. The reward for a life lived well is the return of the Promised Land – Israel.

This, together with their historically tiny numbers and the historic and ongoing persecution they have suffered, has tended to make them very tolerant, except in matters of the land of Israel itself. For example, while lapidation remains a punishment specified in the Jewish Bible, the Christian Old Testament, it has not been carried out for over 2000 years, as far as we know.

Israel is a democratic secular state famously friendly towards its gay and transgender populations, despite the scriptural injunctions placed against them. Women – though still reviled by Orthodox Jews – are respected by mainstream Judaism and are regarded as fully equal to men within the State of Israel.

Contradictions

Judaism is reasonable because there are contradictions in Scripture. It is impossible to equally believe everything this says when it directly contradicts itself, as well as observable reality. How could Jahweh possibly have created the sun three days after the Earth? Surely a day is a measure of solar time? Oy vey, it makes no sense.

The result of this is that most mainstream Jews see Scripture as a guide rather than as a rigid rule-book. This has tended to soften their attitudes. Although there are extremist fundamentalists who do not take this view, they are a minority and have no real power. Mainstream Judaism is inclusive, tolerant and receptive to new ideas.

Let's look at Christianity now before considering Islam.

Catholicism

The Catholic Church Fathers recognised the internal conflicts in Christian texts right from the beginning. During the hundreds of years that it took to define the official 'canon' of the New Testament – that is, which of the over 100 then extant books would be included – several compromises were attempted.

In the end, the Catholic Church took the view that the Bible was 'revelatory' and had to be interpreted by the priesthood. This followed the time-honoured tradition of priestly interpretation of divine revelation, which everyone in the Roman Empire was familiar with. For hundreds of years, lay people were discouraged from reading the Bible themselves.

Authority, in Catholicism, comes not directly from the words of the Bible, but from the priestly interpretation of them. This is called 'dogma'. And dogma can be changed.

Catholics no longer burn people at the stake for witchcraft, insist that the Earth is flat or that the sun rotates around it. While it might take the Church centuries to make these changes, they do happen. The Catholic Church even accepts Evolution and Big Bang Theory – carefully rewriting them as 'acts of God'.

Not only is the Church aware of the problem of internal contradiction, it is aware of the contradiction between the Bible and what can be observed; it is no accident at all that a significant number of scientists have been Catholics, including Gregor Mendel, the 'father of modern genetics', who was a friar.

Protestantism

Protestantism, whether of the Lutheran or Calvinist type, specified that each man – and they did mean men – should read the Bible and find his own truth in it. While Protestant church leaders have never been shy to shout their own interpretations from the pulpit, the essence of Protestantism is that followers must reconcile the contradictions between life and scripture, and the internal contradictions within the texts, for themselves.

This has led to a thoroughly disparate set of religious practices. The truth is that Protestants cherry-pick the Bible just as much as Jews and Catholics do. I see no queues to lapidate people for eating shrimps.

This means that, once again, most Protestants adapt to social change, to scientific knowledge and to technical developments. There are a few who deny their children medical help because of their religion, but even in religious states today, they are prosecuted.

Awareness of contradictions in the texts, and between the texts and life, then, are essential tools by which the ferocity of religions may be tamed. It allows them to be modernised in the light of new discoveries. There are always extremist fundamentalists, be they Hasidic Jews or the odious offspring of the even more repugnant Billy Graham, but they are not mainstream. They are fringe and they will stay that way.

Why is Islam different?

Islam, unfortunately, cannot do this, and that is why it is the most barbaric and dangerous major creed today. Yet the Quran is even more riven with internal contradictions than the other Abrahamic texts. So how has Islam managed to remain so firmly rooted in its most barbarous and cruel form? How is it possible for Islamic clerics to claim, as they do, that the Earth does not rotate on its axis?

In the first place, Muslims believe that the words of the Quran are, literally, the words of Allah, the infallible creator of everything. These words are neither revelatory nor metaphoric: they are the literal truth.

Secondly, Muslims believe that the prophet Mohammed was to be the last who would ever receive such heavenly wisdom. In other words, the Quran is the last, direct word of Allah, transmitted through the Angel Gabriel to Mohammed, and it will never, ever be changed.

So what about the internal conflicts? Unlike the Jewish texts or the Christian ones, the Quran is ostensibly the work of one man, who faithfully remembered every word told to him by Gabriel, the infallible agent of Allah, who is of course, himself infallible. Contradictions should be impossible.

Except Allah was, apparently, not infallible. He made mistakes and this gave rise to a solution that has forever crippled Islam's ability to evolve.

Abrogation.

This is called the 'doctrine of abrogation'. When Mohammed was – allegedly – receiving the good news from Allah via the Angel Gabriel, his followers noticed that, over the years, inconsistencies appeared. Mohammed – again allegedly – asked about this and Gabriel transmitted his question to Allah.

Allah's response was to say that when he gave a verse that contradicted an earlier one, he took back or 'abrogated' the older one. In other words it ceased to be the current infallible word of Allah. Only the later one was. Since Allah is infallible, however, the verses remained in the Quran.

So, Allah is infallible but changes his mind; but because the Quran is the last iteration of the word of Allah that will ever be given, according to Islam, then the last versions, whatever they are, are immutable for all time. They can never be changed.

Religious sophistication.

Religiously sophisticated Muslims are generally very careful not to discuss the 'doctrine of abrogation' with non-Muslims. This is made worse because the vast majority of the world's Muslims have never read the Quran, since it is in Arabic and most of them don't understand it. (There are translations into vernacular tongues but Muslim scholars scoff at these.) The consequence is that many Muslims do not even *know* about abrogation. But it is core theology.

The 'doctrine of abrogation' means that there are no contradictions in the Quran, even though there are verses, or Suras, that contradict each other, because *only the last one is valid*.

But how do we know which that is? The Quran is not ordered chronologically, but by the length of the texts. There is no way at all to know which came first, from the Quran itself.

The only way you can find this out is by reading the Hadith, or the commentaries on the life of the Prophet, which explain when each Sura was 'received'.

Religious authority in Islam

Authority in Islam is not from the Qur'an alone; it comes from the Qur'an and the Hadith together. The above shows how important it is to realise this. Furthermore, the doctrine of 'Taqqiya' instructs Muslims to conceal, lie and dissemble when dealing with non-Muslims, in the furtherance of the faith. This, again, is core theology, though it is habitual for Muslim clerics to practise it by denying it exists.

When discussing their religion with non-Muslims, such clerics always talk about the Quran. They will quote verses from it left, right and centre. They never talk about the Hadith, for it is here that the true nature of Islam is revealed. The Qur'an is hopelessly self-contradictory and confusing, with no narrative structure at all. It is only by studying the Hadith that it becomes possible to contextualise and, therefore, understand the Quran and indeed, Islam itself.

Clerics.

Muslim clerics and scholars are perfectly well aware of this and would prefer that non-Muslims did not read and understand the Hadith; this is because doing so will reveal, amongst other things deeply harmful to the PR image of Islam, that the harshest, most cruel and most violent Suras are invariably the later ones: those that still have force and are 'unabrogated'.

The later Suras are violent and intolerant while early ones tend to be peaceful and accommodating. This is because in the early part of his life, when he was seeking followers and was under scrutiny by the authorities at Mecca, where he lived, Mohammed was conciliatory. It was politically expedient to be. He had not enough followers to challenge the government and he feared that he might be punished if he were too aggressive. Mohammed had no interest in being executed as a troublemaker, and he lived in harsh times. So the Suras from this period tend to be 'soft'.

Flight to Medina

After Mohammed and his followers, sure enough, had annoyed the people of Mecca such that they were expelled, they fled to Medina, a Jewish city. Here, he and his merry band discovered banditry as a lifestyle and soon were getting rich by plundering camel caravans carrying trade goods. They then began taking whole towns and villages by force.

Be under no illusions: these were not heroes taking from the rich to give to the poor. These were criminals robbing, raping, enslaving and killing to make themselves wealthy and more powerful. The Hadith explain all of this in only-too-gory detail.

The later Suras are much more violent and warlike in reflection of this confidence and faith in violence. By this time, Mohammed was a successful brigand, plundering and killing any he challenged. Conciliation was yesterday but today was fire and sword. The Hadith identify which Suras these are.

Early vs. later Suras.

When pressed by non-Muslims, apologists will always quote the early Suras, even though they know perfectly well that these have been 'abrogated'. They are recognised as the words of Allah, but they have been cancelled out. So the fact that these may contradict later, violent Suras is irrelevant, since they are no longer the official word of Allah with effect today.

However, the same apologists will exhort Muslims to follow the later, 'hard' Suras precisely because these have not been abrogated and are thus the effective word of Allah.

There is absolutely no internal contradiction within the Quran, because in all cases of conflict, only the latest Sura is given any value. The others have been abrogated, or, as we have seen, 'taken back' by Allah and replaced. Only the last remains valid. One simply has to identify which is the later Sura on any given disagreement and then the point is settled.

This means that Islam has, as its underlying principles, violence and warfare, to the ends of increasing the individual wealth of Muslims and expanding the territory under the control of this benighted cult and, worse, that these ideals are permanently locked in forever.

This is because the last Suras were 'received' by Mohammed when he was a successful warlord and leader of a band of armed killers.

To call Islam a 'religion of peace' reveals the speaker as either a blatant liar or as ignorant of it. Unfortunately there are many of both.

Most of the world's Muslims do not speak or read Arabic, although they may be able to recite large parts of the Quran. They do so without understanding a word of it, but this is no matter since it is the sound of Arabic being chanted that pleases Allah. And even if they can read Arabic, the Quran is nonsensical without study of the Hadith.

Islam recognises that this is a problem, so it trains Arabic-speaking clerics, well versed in the Hadith, to preach to the masses.

Islam in retreat

Now you need to understand another issue that Muslims do not like to talk about. In 1683 the bloody tide of Islamic conquest in Europe was turned back by the defeat of the Ottoman hordes at the Siege of Vienna.

An allied army of European forces had hastily been put together to relieve the city. This included those of the doughty Polish King Jan Sobieski. He personally led the charge of the feared Winged Hussars, that finally broke the enemy.

This was not only the biggest cavalry charge in history, but without it the whole of Europe would have been plunged into darkness and you would not be reading this. (The Poles have never received adequate thanks for *literally* saving our bacon.) The Enlightenment, perhaps the most vaunted product of post-Renaissance Western culture, would have been snuffed out.

Thanks to the courage of the Poles, in defeating an enemy many times their numbers, over the next century the Muslim world was fractured and the faith itself was menaced by new empires – nearly all Christian.

Jihad is a powerful word in Islam. Up until the defeat at Vienna, it had unquestionably referred to the armed struggle to conquer more territory.

While Islam was at its lowest ebb after the triumph of Europe, it was altered to emphasise a 'spiritual struggle'. But this was pure convenience. The mullahs and clerics looked to the Hadith and saw that when Mohammed was under threat in Mecca, he preached peace and tolerance. So after the fall of their own empires, this is exactly what the clerics did themselves.

Stealth Jihad

Muslims are permitted, when they are so outnumbered that armed rebellion would wipe them out, to live in peace with their neighbours. This has been called 'Stealth Jihad'. This phase of jihad is indeed a spiritual rather than an armed struggle. It reflects Mohammed's early years in Mecca, when he and his followers were powerless and at the mercy of the other people in the city. In cases like this Muslims, following the example of Mohammed, should pray and live devout lives, lying low and preparing themselves for the time when their numbers are such that they can resume the armed struggle.

Stealth jihad is what the Muslim world reverted to after the defeat of its armies, but it must be realised that this can only ever be a temporary situation. The resumption of armed struggle is inevitable, a prerequisite of faith. Islam exists to conquer the world and make it Arabic; this can never be changed. When Islam is being complaisant, it is only because it is gathering strength.

It should be clear now that Stealth Jihad is not a softening of Islam at all, but simply a defensive measure. But remember, most Muslims do not speak Arabic and few are really familiar with the Quran, let alone the Hadith. The responsibility of deciding which message Muslims should follow, or even hear, falls on the clerics. For over 200 years they focussed on the moderate, non-violent – but at the same time abrogated – Suras.

A return to violence

Today, empowered by the wealth born of the developed world's thirst for oil, encouraged by the appalling obsequiousness of Western governments and positively bolstered by the sheer stupidity and ignorance of the 'regressive left', the clerical class that once preached the early Suras and encouraged the population to be calm, to submit to the power of others and to cause no trouble, is again preaching the Medina Suras – the ones that exhort violence and armed jihad.

It is vital to realise, right now, that so-called Islamist extremists are not: they are simply following the words and will of Allah now in force, which are contained ONLY in the later, unabrogated Suras. They are preaching and following the 'true' version of Islam, the later version, which is, throughout, bloody and violent and exhorts Muslims to kill, enslave and extort non-believers.

The cult these men (always men) preach is not extremist within the context of Islam. In fact it is the only true form; and it is to this that all Muslims must revert when they are strong enough to do so without risking extermination. Armed jihad and global conquest are not fringe extremism in Islam: they are its core values.

No contradictions

With absolutely no contradictions in the Quran, which the simple yet diabolical mechanism of 'abrogation' ensures, there can be no debate and so, no modernisation. When Muslim scholars argue, they are not doing so over the issue of which Suras are more valid. They only have to look in the Hadith to establish this. They are instead nit-picking over the nuances of meanings of words, or obscure calligraphs in texts. They know what Islam is about; there is no argument there. It is established, permanently, with no opportunity for alteration. And its end is world conquest.

The 'gentle face' of Islam is a sham, a ruse designed to persuade an unwary enemy, ignorant of the truth, that Islam will not spread war and violence; that it is peaceful and may be trusted.

This is an illusion. While individual Muslims may indeed be peaceful and trustworthy, they are the fringe. I celebrate those like Maajid Nawaz, who risks his life every day to try to soften Islam; but in a way, men such as he are indeed the extremists, in an Islamic context, for they are furthest from the established doctrinal basis of the cult. That is why they are so viscerally hated by other Muslims.

While we must – rightly – be thankful for good men such as he, it is not possible to be optimistic about the chances they have of successfully taming this monster.

7. Muslims we Must Support: Maajid Nawaz

Last week, Maajid Nawaz, a United Kingdom Liberal Democratic Party parliamentary candidate for Hampstead and Kilburn, became the centre of an attack from the Islamic fundamentalist right wing because he stood up for free speech. This is not, in itself, unusual; fundamentalists of any religious persuasion detest free speech. Nor is the chorus of death threats raised against Nawaz in any way uncommon from Islamic fanatics. However this case is important because it illustrates a divide which we must not only recognise but decide on which side we stand.

Nawaz' crime? After taking part in a BBC debate in which two students were seen wearing 'Jesus and Mo' tee-shirts, Nawaz tweeted the image, saying, "As a Muslim, I did not feel threatened by it. My God is greater than that."

For most people, that would not seem anything other than a reasonable point of view. After all, if faith is to have meaning at all, it must be strong enough to deal with criticism without resorting to violence. One would think. But, no: Nawaz' action immediately provoked a venomous tide of hatred from all over the world, partially orchestrated by Mohammed Shafiq, himself a Liberal Democrat activist.

Shafiq continues to insist that Nawaz should be removed as a Liberal Democratic candidate, though this now seems less likely after the personal intervention of the party leader, Nick Clegg.

Now this might look like a nasty little spat between two minor politicians in an also-ran party that is likely to be consigned to the margins at the next UK General Election, but it is far more than that.

Nawaz is director of the Quilliam Foundation, which promotes a modern, open-minded, anti-extremist interpretation of Islam, and Shafiq is chief executive of the Ramadhan Foundation, which promotes a narrow, fundamentalist, extremist vision.

Thus these two men sum up a debate that is central to Islam and by implication, vastly important to everyone else; yet this is not being talked about. One wonders why not.

Any student of the history of Western religion and culture must be struck by certain parallels that exist between Christianity and Islam. For over a thousand years, Christianity in the West was synonymous with

Catholicism. However, after the Renaissance and Gutenberg's invention of modern letterpress printing, this hegemony was challenged.

The Catholic church has never been a literalist faith. It always considered that the words of the Bible had to be interpreted, by a priestly hierarchy, and this interpretation is known as 'dogma'.

The Protestant Reformation happened because Bibles, thanks to Gutenberg, became widely available to read, for the first time. So-called 'Protestants' took a strictly literalist view: anything not written in the Bible was false, and everything that was written in it was true. For them, dogma was just the invention of men.

This led to the development of extremist, literalist forms of Christianity, led by preachers like Luther, Calvin and his student, John Knox, who returned with it to Scotland; and whence it was widely exported to the Anglophone world.

Knox's vision of his faith was little different from that of modern fundamentalist Islam. It was literalist, extremist and deeply misogynistic. It was this vision that sparked the appalling witch-burnings that became such a blight on Scotland's history in the 17th and 18th centuries. No colour, no images, no singing. All pleasure was sinful, women were demonised and men were in charge, absolutely.

This harsh and intolerant vision fell apart in the great schisms of the Scottish kirk in the 19th century, and was progressively replaced by gentler, more tolerant forms. Although the extremists still exist even now, moderation has become mainstream, even within Scottish Presbyterianism.

This dichotomy is exactly the same as the one we see in Islam today, between people like Nawaz, who promote a tolerant, inclusive, open version of faith, which, essentially, relies on interpretation and moderation, on the one hand, and those like Shafiq, who stands for a literalist, fundamentalist, extremist version.

The history of the development of Western culture, however, tells us that these are not equal, and that free-thinking and secularism are better, and more successful, than literalism and intolerance. The interpretative view is superior.

This is not academic. The Muslim population of many European countries is now approaching 10%. This is not enough for them to determine the future of Europe, but it is enough to provoke widespread unrest and, potentially, civil war. It has become the single greatest threat to peace in Europe that exists. It is therefore absolutely imperative that

European Islam wholeheartedly adopt the European tradition, evolved since the Renaissance, of tolerance, secularism, and free speech. If this does not happen, then violence certainly will.

This is why men like Nawaz are so important, and why we should all not only support them, but show them that we support them. It is in everyone's interest for Europe's Muslims to integrate properly into our culture, something which is deliberately being prevented by the fundamentalists. There is no chance that Europe will deport its Muslims, many of whom were born here. The ranting of the xenophobic right is neither helpful nor does it have any hope of success, other than in polarising a debate that should not be.

However, the disgusting grovelling and Political Correctness that pretends that there are no problems with Islam or the integration of Muslims into European society is just as destructive. There is a difference between extremist, literalist Muslims and moderates, and we must identify that difference, expose it and give our support to the moderates, many of whom are terrorised by the fanatics. The threats to Nawaz, or the fatwa against Rushdie, are real. They are designed to bully moderate, but less prominent Muslims, into silence.

Nawaz, and people like him, give hope to young Muslims that they can step out of a straitjacket of Quranic introspection and integrate properly into a secular state, where everyone's religion, or lack of one, is equally respected.

In other words, Maajid Nawaz is exactly the kind of free-thinking, mature Muslim whom we must support, because his very existence proves that not all Muslims are fanatical literalists; that there are Muslims with whom we can reason. The very last thing we should do is give any succour to the violent extremists and literalists that he is an alternative to.

We have a choice to make – do we want accommodation, tolerance and peace, or do we want increasing division, intolerance and violence? On one side stands Nawaz, and those like Salman Rushdie and Ayaan Hirsi Ali; on the other, all the banner-waving, screaming Islamic bigots and fundamentalists whose images we know all too well.

Islam is not homogeneous; there are deeply opposed strains within it. It is a function of a blinkered regressive-liberal Political Correctness to assume that all Muslims are the same. It is a reprehensible view which is offensive to all Muslims, just as much as saying that all Christians are the same; manifestly they are not.

In the same way as Christianity has American Southern Baptists, whose views are not acceptable in a modern democratic, secular society, there are intolerant strains in Islam which we should not accommodate. However, there are other strains which are tolerant, open and wise enough not only to integrate into the wider European culture, but to enrich it.

We have to choose which side in this debate to support, and we had better choose wisely. And quickly

8. The Realpolitik of Islam

It is now over twenty years since the fall of the Berlin Wall; for many young people, the Cold War, of which it was the most compelling symbol, is no more than a history lesson. In my desk here I have a small piece of concrete, with paint on, which was recovered from that wall and sold as a tourist trinket. It is perhaps the most telling one I have.

Our children do not, as those of my generation did, live in daily fear of being blown to pieces by atomic bombs or dying an agonising death from radiation sickness. They do not walk into their schools to find posters saying "Better Dead Than Red" on the walls, nor do they crowd around flickering television sets alongside their anguished parents, watching as Kennedy drew his line in the ocean and curled his finger around the trigger of nuclear Armageddon. And for this we should all be very, very thankful indeed. No child should have to live with nightmares like those.

The Middle East

The lifting of this Damoclean Sword did not, unfortunately, mean that our civilisation was free from danger. In dark and hidden places, new threats were gathering. The first, and most obvious, came from what we call the Middle East.

As is well known, during the Holocaust of World War Two a third of all Jews were murdered. Many of those still alive left Europe, vowing never to return. Some went to the United States, where they became, in many cases, powerful in business, science and the arts. Many others went to what was then the British Protectorate of Palestine, intending to set up a homeland for all Jews, to be called Israel.

It is an unfortunate fact, with more unfortunate consequences, that the land they occupied was not empty at the time. It was populated instead by Palestinians, an Islamised people descended from the Biblical Samaritans. They had every right, they believed, to call the land home. It matters little, now, that an arcane system of land tenure had allowed wealthy Zionist Jews to buy up land in Palestine, and become the landlords to sitting Muslim tenants.

After the horror of Dachau and Buchenwald, no Allied politician could deny the Jews what they asked, a pittance of desert. Wars were waged by Israel's neighbours to try to destroy the new state, but this, far from alerting us to what many in the Arab world considered an outrageous injustice, only showed how vulnerable Israel was, and encouraged us to support it militarily and otherwise. After these wars Israel annexed new land, seeking to develop buffer zones between its homeland and the neighbouring states who had attacked it.

We in the West forgot those who had been driven off, whose situation, living as they did for the main in refugee camps, was deplorable; at least, that is, until the formerly peaceful and prosperous state of Lebanon collapsed into civil war.

The concept of Realpolitik

We have to live in the world as it is, not as we might wish that it were. Clearly it would have been very handy if the land of Israel had been held as an empty desert for the Jews to return to. It would have simplified life greatly if Jerusalem were not so important to quite so many different, and mutually antagonistic, faiths. It would have been helpful if the refugee Palestinians had been given succour, new land to live on and financial support to restart their lives. And it would certainly have been handy if Islam did not insist that land once under shariaa may never be liberated from it. But Realpolitik provides no comfort on any of those. Realpolitik is not like that.

At the time, we in the West saw the Israeli conflicts as a sideshow, albeit one which the real global power-brokers, the USA and the USSR, meddled in as they pleased. It was still the Cold War and the Arms Race that dominated our strategic thinking. And still, then, the West had an imperialist mindset that assumed that the ultimate winner in any geopolitical confrontation would be the one with the most and biggest gunboats – or in this case, arsenal of nuclear weapons – and that the balance of power as it had been established at the end of World War Two would remain forever, propped up by the policy of Mutually Assured Destruction, or MAD.

Because of this mind-set, no-one seriously believed that the mighty United States would be pushed out of what was then South Vietnam. How could mere guerrilla fighters combat the might of a superpower, even if they did have one prepared to supply them with guns? It was a ridiculous proposal, yet one which, exactly, came to pass. We in the West might then have asked ourselves some hard questions about what was happening and where we were going, but by and large we did not. Vietnam was an aberration, not evidence of a trend. And yet, in 1979, Iran exploded in an Islamic Revolution that swept aside the Pahlavi dynasty – which had been held in power by the West – and set in place as its head of state possibly the most odious religious bigot since John Knox.

We still did not ask the questions we should have. The United Kingdom saw off an invasion of the Falkland Islands by Argentina in what was initially regarded by many as an impossible endeavour, yet which came to be seen as one of its most successful actions since D-Day. The United States, humiliated in Vietnam and again in Iran, managed to recover and executed several successful campaigns, notably the ousting of the Panamanian dictator Noriega. Gunboat Diplomacy still seemed to work, after all.

In the end, however, our friend Realpolitik stepped in. The dynamic balance of the Cold War era ended when the Berlin Wall was torn down. Germany was reunified, and then one by one, the states that had been enslaved by Stalin turned their backs on the Soviet Union and their faces to the West. Ultimately, not only did the Soviet Union itself collapse but the Communist Party, which had held power since 1917, was cast down. Catharsis was loose in the world and the balance of terror known as the Cold War, was finished for ever.

Complacency

Many of us were guilty of being rather smug, I remember. Surely now all was well. We had no more need to fear a surprise nuclear attack that would destroy everything we knew and loved. What power was there in the world that could approach, in its ability to be our dreaded nemesis, the awesome might of the Soviet Union? Even the Chinese, whom we still did not really trust, were now doing business with the West, and showed no inclination at all to threaten their best customer.

Everything was going to be fine; even the environmental crisis, and the approaching arrival of Peak Oil, a concept that no-one in 1990 had heard of in any case, could not rock the boat of our satisfaction. Sure, we had to clean up a few poisonous messes left behind by the years of Soviet domination, like the disaster of Bosnia. But even this only showed us how we could cope, and how powerful we in the West really were.

The European Union would become both larger and more integrated; its leaders wanted it to be an economic force to rival the United States. And the economies of the EU grew and grew; formerly poverty-stricken states like Spain became wealthy and modern, and we bent over backwards to assist the countries of Eastern Europe, previously Soviet satellites, into the fold, where they would themselves prosper. A new, static balance had been born out of the end of the Cold War, a balance secured in trade and economic success. And, as a result of all this, we allowed ourselves to drift into a false sense of security.

Yet peace and security were fragile things. In 1990, just as our triumph over the so-called Evil Empire, the Soviet Union, was approaching fruition, a rather nasty dictator, whom we had hitherto been assisting on the grounds that he was hostile to Iran, and, as the saying goes, 'My enemy's enemy is my friend,' upset the apple-cart.

Saddam Hussein, already in control of a significant part of the world's oil resources, decided that he would like some more and annexed Kuwait. One might query how we went about finding friends like him, and consider the wisdom of it.

My goodness, what an opportunity for our old standby, Gunboat Diplomacy – and this actually let us use the most powerful gunboats ever built, the US Navy's Iowa Class battleships, which had been 'de-mothballed' by US President Reagan, mostly as a Public Relations exercise. I mean, no-one believed they would be used in a real war, well, not against an enemy with a modern navy – and submarines – at least. But Iraq had no navy to speak of, and its air force was neutralised at the start of the conflict, so these mighty floating temples of destruction could pound away at land targets with impunity. Thus we were treated to real, live footage of real, live Imperial battleships raining the righteous wrath of the West down upon people so far away they were over the horizon.

As is well known, although Realpolitik – in this case horrific pictures of a bombed-out column of fleeing Iraqi soldiers, and a change of occupant at the White House – caused a delay in the process, in the end we removed Hussein from Kuwait, and ultimately his head from the rest of him…though that is believed to have been carelessness.

Many in the Arab world applauded our action in what is now called the First Gulf War. Hussein was an unpopular dictator with territorial ambitions and a powerful army. What Arabs did *not* appreciate was our continuing tendency to believe we could intervene in their affairs willy-nilly. Furthermore, Hussein was seen by some as a bastion against Israel, and America's action, in leading the campaign to liberate Kuwait, was seen as much as an assistance to Israel as the freeing of an Arab state.

The background

The Islamic world had been brought to its knees after the defeat of the Ottomans at the Siege of Vienna in 1683. However, in the 20th century, things began to change as a number of factors came together. The first was the establishment, by Kamil Ataturk in 1923, of the modern secular state of Turkey. This was ferociously resisted by Islamists, who founded something previously unheard-of in the Islamic world: a political movement expressly formed to counter the increasing secularisation of its sphere of influence.

Prior to this, Islam itself had been its own political party, but the collapse of the Ottoman Empire had left it leaderless, confused, and culturally unable to challenge Western secularism.

Thus was formed the Muslim Brotherhood, which has become synonymous with the political side of Islamic Jihad. While defeated in Turkey, it remained active, biding its time, infiltrating other states and studying its enemy. While the Brotherhood never openly takes up arms, it is ever ready to be the political representative of more violent Islamists.

The Brotherhood is a classic terrorist apologist, similar to the Communist Party or Sinn Feinn, in that it sets out to destroy that which it hates by infiltrating and defeating it. In the 1980s, the UK Labour Party found itself treated very much the same way by an ultra-leftist subgroup called Militant Tendency. These tactics are effective and have been proven time and again. The strength of democracy depends on the presumption that everyone taking part wants the system to work; it is therefore vulnerable to those who have another agenda.

Make no mistake, if ever a global caliphate were established and the world plunged into Islamic darkness, the Muslim Brotherhood would cease to exist. Its adoption of democratic political method is only a means to allow it to undermine and ultimately destroy that method and replace it with Islam and shariaa. That will instantly snuff out both secularism and democracy. Once democracy is gone, the Brotherhood would have neither platform nor purpose. Its activities in Turkey and Egypt today are clear evidence of its fundamental philosophy – once it has seized the reins of democracy, it shoots the horse.

There were two other major factors in the resurgence of Islam. The first was the end of the Imperial Era. For hundreds of years, European nations had controlled huge areas of the world and Muslims, like everyone else, had been obliged to toe the line. However the global change in power-structure that occurred as a result of World War Two meant that the old system had to die. Many territories where there were Muslim majorities became independent and, thanks to the activity of the Muslim Brotherhood, where Western secular democracy was imposed by the former rulers as a condition of independence, this was soon corrupted.

At the same time, the Arab world, which had for centuries been pauperised, became rich on the back of the modern need for vast quantities of crude oil to fuel the West's burgeoning economies. Countries like Saudi Arabia, with no manufacturing or other sustainable means of wealth-production, became fantastically rich. (Ultimately, of course, this source of wealth will dry up, and since the economies of the Islamic, and particularly the Arab, world are so dependent on it, running out of cheap Middle-Eastern oil may paradoxically be the saviour of the West.)

By the end of the 20th century, Islamic militancy had been growing for decades, fuelled by the black resentment the Islamic world has always harboured against the State of Israel, aided and directed by the shadowy hand of the Muslim Brotherhood and given both religious sanction and finance by wealthy Arab states like Saudi Arabia. Israel was the focus of their hatred, especially its policies towards the Palestinians and the land Israel had occupied after the Six-Day War. The settlement of these lands by Jews was deeply resented, and far away from the glare of publicity, plans were made to wreak vengeance.

Today

However, Israel had already proved itself too tough a nut to crack. As well as this, terrorist strikes against Israel were so commonplace they were paid little heed to by the West, the real enemy. These factors enhanced the attractiveness of targets deep in the heart of dar al-haarb, the Land of

War, where they were rich, fat and unprepared. The Islamists would use the very freedom of Western secular democracy to destroy it.

The practical politicians of the Brotherhood, who understand Realpolitik too, know that their intended conquest of the West is not something that can be achieved overnight, or even over a generation. However, bringing terror inside the borders of the hated enemy might at least cause them to flinch in their support of Israel. This, of course, is the same reasoning as Hitler, Franco and Mussolini used, to justify terror-bombing civilian populations in an attempt to cow their will. That it never worked appears to have escaped the Islamists.

On September 11, 2001, one such plot came to fruition. It provided Bush the son with the pretext to finish what Realpolitik had prevented Bush the father from doing: the humiliation and ousting of our former ally and protégé Saddam Hussein.

A hitherto little-known, Saudi-backed Islamist group, called Al-Qaeda, hijacked four airliners within the United States and flew them into the Pentagon Building and the World Trade Centre. The fourth plane was directed towards Washington. Although the White House was probably the terrorists' intended target, this could not be confirmed, because this plane's hijackers were overpowered by the passengers, the real heroes, who died in the crash.

The images of two planes flying into the Twin Towers, New York's most prominent skyline feature, and of the towers themselves collapsing, were transmitted live around a horrified world. Over three thousand people died in the attacks; a tragic drop in the ocean compared to the consequent loss of life, yet seminal and symbolic. Islamist militancy had come of age.

Twelve years after that event, which entrained American-led invasions of Afghanistan and Iraq, the former being very much less successful than the latter, despite the State Department spin, the West has other problems. A persistent global financial crisis with its roots in an untrammelled banking system which favoured risky, quick profits over safer, long-term strategies, has moved centre-stage in our concerns.

The consequence of economic crisis, at least in the West, has historically been an increase in our isolation. We become inward-looking and disinclined to consider threats from the outside world. This is just displacement activity, as happened in the years after the Great Depression, when Hitler and other fascist leaders were on the rise in Europe. Japan had became increasingly belligerent, staging horrific attacks on mainland China which the West, to its shame, chose to ignore. This was, lest we forget, the era of British 'appeasement' and American 'isolationism', both ideas which are today, rightly reviled.

While we have been so busy with introspection, however, our enemies have not been idle.

9. Islam: a danger to society

'Islamic extremism is a danger to society and a threat to public safety. It must be defeated wherever it is found'.

Well it's no secret that I think this is wholly true. Anyone who reads my posts on Islam knows that I consider it to be a sick, depraved cult based on male privilege, misogyny, homophobia, male paedophilia, 'honour killings', genital mutilation and violence.

Yet I did not speak the words above. The UK's new Justice Secretary, Liz Truss, was reported as saying them in the *Independent*.

Hallelujah! Is it premature to imagine that some common sense has at last been allowed to spring its green shoots in UK politics? Not so long ago, I would have been vilified for saying things like that, and I know people who have been banned from social media for it. That there is no more grim darkness than the regressive liberalism that infests such spaces has no greater confirmation. And today a minister of State says exactly what should have been said over a decade ago.

To acclaim this as a breath of fresh air would be the understatement of the week – a week in which, by the way, the toll of rapes and abuse of women all across Europe has continued to escalate. Rapes, needless to say, at the hands of Muslims – inspired by Islam, the creed of hatred and death.

Islam is a horrible, mind-controlling cult that fully intends to subjugate the planet. Its 'extremist' form – which is actually its only form – is, indeed, the greatest single threat to civilisation that exists. Of course it's a danger to society. No greater danger to society exists, except perhaps climate change.

In the UK, somewhat quietly, Theresa May's new Government has shown, on this point at least, that it might actually have some backbone. After over a decade in which British Government has been characterised by a spinelessness that a mollusc would be proud of, things do appear to be changing.

Truss also attacked those responsible for radicalising Muslims in prison: 'Preventing the most dangerous extremists from radicalising other prisoners is essential to the safe running of our prisons and fundamental to public protection.'

'Extremist' Muslim prisoners will now be held in secure units where they cannot infect other nominally Muslim inmates. Imams and clerics visiting prisons are to be vetted. It is a start, at least.

Reading this made me shake my head in sheer wonder. Was I still asleep? Was this a dream? A senior Government minister had AT LAST admitted the truth: Islam is a problem.

Yes, I know that she couched her statement in an anodyne form, in order not to scare too many politically-correct horses. That was why she suggested that 'extremist' Islam is a danger to society. But the fact is that anyone who actually has studied Islam knows that there is no distinction. All Islam is extremist and all Islam is a danger to society.

The only time Islam is not a danger to society is when it is secular. That is the Church of England Garden Fete variety; of people who identify as Muslims and maybe vaguely believe in Allah and Mohammed, but who have never read the Qur'an, nor understand the Hadith and their fanatical message of hate.

Muslims are like anyone else: there are good and bad. But Islam turns them into monsters who are a danger to society. That is its *raison d'etre*. It was created by highway robbers who wanted to justify their killings, rapings and taking of people as slaves. It was designed to recruit new members to a band of murdering thieves.

Therefore, Islam is the real danger to society. Without it, terrorists would have no ideology to justify killing, raping and enslaving other, peace-loving, decent human beings.

Danger to society.

Saying 'extremist Islam' is a danger to society – and somehow implying that some form of Islam is not so – is like saying that 'Extremist Communism is against capitalism.' It's pure dissembly. Communism is communism and Islam is Islam. The difference is not in the underlying creed but whether people take it seriously enough to start being a danger to society. In the case of Islam, we crossed that Rubicon a long time ago.

Nevertheless, we salute Liz Truss and the woman who is certainly behind her, the new UK Prime Minister, Theresa May. It is clear that she has decided to make some real changes.

May was a solid Home Secretary who performed well amongst much criticism from the ranks of the spineless yah-boo Eton boys. Her support for a UK withdrawal from the European Commission of Human

Rights is well-known.

Earlier this year she said: 'My view is this: if we want to reform human rights laws in this country, it isn't the EU we should leave but the ECHR and the jurisdiction of its court."

Her reasons? Well, among them is that it 'makes us less secure by preventing the deportation of dangerous foreign nationals.'

May was referring, of course, to the way that the ECHR 'had caused the extradition of extremist Abu Hamza to be delayed for years and… had almost stopped the deportation of Abu Qatada.'

The position of the vile regressive left on this should now be clear. It is determined to undermine Western culture. It has always coveted the destruction of the very system that allows its existence. The most convenient and most powerful tool it has is the rise of Islam, after 300 years in which it was in decline.

Communism, the favoured instrument of the regressive left for decades, is dead. Thankfully. But the regressive left, in its pathological quest for self-destruction, has found a new weapon – arguably even more violent, cruel and terrifying. That is Islam.

May's opposition to the ECHR is and remains that it prevents effective and decisive Government action against terrorism; and today, terrorism and Islam are practically synonymous.

Nobody's religion should put them above criticism or the law. Nor should any religion be protected from scrutiny and ridicule. And no religion can be allowed to preach the destruction of the society it exists within.

In the end, we shall have no choice: we must de-Islamify Europe. We need to return Islam in Europe to the garden-fete variety it once was.

Islam has revealed the truth about itself: it is a crawling snake. It intends to strike at those who have been generous enough to allow it in.

We have to draw that viper's fangs, so that it can no longer be a danger to society. We have to prevent it from being what it is.

I am a natural libertarian. I was raised on Thoreau and others like him, to believe that individual freedoms are paramount. But the line is drawn where those freedoms cause harm to others. There can be no doubt that Islam is harming non-Muslims all over Europe and, indeed, the world. By implication, it is harming Muslims too, by alienating them.

Nobody would be so monstrous as to suggest the eradication of Muslims, even were such a thing possible: but the emasculation of Islam is now a priority.

I hope that Truss and May will spearhead a long-overdue clamp-down on Islam, the greatest danger to society there is.

If we don't draw the fangs of this snake now, we will face civil war across Europe in a matter of years, not decades.

Religion

1. The 'Ontological Argument'= busted.

When dealing with religious apologists it's always better to nail them into the real world and insist on the same standard of evidence that is required for Gravity, Plate Tectonics or Evolution, because no apologist can ever provide these. Insisting on real scientific proof is a perfectly legitimate position, any time that someone is proposing the existence of something in the real world, including a god.

However, it is worth knowing about some of the more ridiculous philosophical ideas you might find used by apologists. I'd like to discuss a few.

The first is The Ontological argument. This is sometimes called the attempt to define god into existence. It was first proposed by Anselm of Canterbury (1033 – 1109). This original version was busted by Kant and Hume amongst others, but lo and behold, it resurfaced after several reworkings. While modern apologists are mightily proud of the shiny new gloss this has given the argument, it still devolves to the same thing:

> Any thing that can be imagined to exist, must exist, if it is imagined to have certain properties.

Clearly this is nonsense. However the dense fug of philosophical obscurantism is, as usual, used to hide the central argument, so let me expand what it says:

God is a being greater than which none can be conceived (unsubstantiated premise.)

The existence of god can be conceived in the imagination

The existence of god can be conceived in reality

It is clearly greater for a thing to exist in reality than only in the imagination

Therefore, since god is the greatest thing we can conceive in the imagination, then *it must exist in reality*.

Let me simplify: a thing which exists in the imagination must be real, if we can imagine that no greater thing than it can exist, since being real is 'greater' than being imaginary. So a thing having the property of [that than which nothing greater can be conceived] must necessarily exist. (Note: not possibly: necessarily.)

This kind of logic belongs in the schoolyard, yet some real grownups actually believe it. To call it anthropocentric drivel is an understatement.

By the way, this is not a Christian argument, though Christians often use it and it was developed by one. There's nothing in there to suggest it's the biblical god that we're talking about. This is not even a deist argument, since we could assign the property [than which nothing greater can be conceived] to anything. Try working through the argument using an orange, and you will 'prove' the actual existence of an orange than which no greater orange could be conceived, and that therefore such a citrus must exist. It is semantical balderdash, and a good example of how useless this sort of philosophy is at helping us to understand reality.

However, should you find yourself having to debate one of these twerps, the above doesn't work and security won't let you bat him (or her) about the head with a shovel till he (or she) grows a brain, then you might find the following useful.

Anselm begins: 'We believe that thou (god) art a being than which nothing greater can be conceived.'

This is a stipulation; it is the start point of this argument. And it is a great big whopper. Anselm's entire argument shows the clear hallmarks of having been worked in reverse, that is, from its conclusion to its beginning, which alone should rule it out of bounds. Well, it would in science, but apparently not in philosophy. Apparently that sort of stuff is quite okay in philosophy. Leaving that aside for a moment, let us pursue our Snark, and note the following:

The stipulation is completely unsupported and Anselm provides no logical or empirical base for it. It just is so because he says so.

Frankly, he could stop there and just say that god exists because he believes it does, and save a lot of fannying about, but no, not this one. Anyway, Anselm's target for his rhetoric – the invented and passive method by which he pretends he can demonstrate his 'proof', is an educated atheist, whom he calls the Fool. He says:

'But, at any rate, this very fool, when he hears of this being of which I speak - a being than which nothing greater can be conceived - understands what he hears, and what he understands is in his understanding; although he does not understand it to exist.'

This is the first part of Anselm's trick. Anselm is not developing a logical hypothesis concerning the existence of a deity, but a piece of declamatory rhetoric which he hopes will persuade the listener. This is why he uses the term 'Fool' which of course, is pejorative. Its use here is to deflect us from Anselm's sleight of hand; he has made a second unsupported assumption, that it is possible to understand what 'a being than which nothing greater can be conceived,' actually is.

Well, is it possible to actually conceive this being? What are the properties of such a being? Does it have mass? Does it have energy? Is it sentient? Where is it? Where did it come from?

'Conceiving' an entity means much more than just accepting an unknown value and proceeding for the sake of argument; it means assigning real, actual values – which in this case is impossible, since the being in question is allegedly infinite, and we cannot conceive an infinity – which is why we have the term in the first place; it's a usable substitute for something we can't understand or know, which we use to allow the argument to develop.

Anselm's 'being' here is actually equivalent to the term 'x' in mathematics: we may not know what 'x' actually means, but we can still use it. Similarly we don't know what Anselm's being actually is – we can't conceive it – but we can allow its hypothetical use without that, for the sake of the argument. So in this approach, Anselm's 'being' = x, an expression of unknown value.

This is completely different from conceiving a being such that we *can* comprehend the properties of that being. This is what we were unable to do earlier, and we'll call it y.

Anselm's trick, which he is about to use, is equivocation: he uses the term 'being greater than etc' interchangeably to mean an expression of unknown value which we have called 'x' which is trivial, and 'y' actually being able to conceive of this being, which we see is impossible.

Sometimes he uses one and sometimes the other, but he acts as if they were both the same. He has to do this, since if he were to be honest with his argument, then it would already have failed, because if he accepted that there is no way we can actually conceive his being, then the whole logical train would collapse. On the other hand, if he accepted that his 'being' was just a symbol, then his argument would have no weight. He has to cheat, in other words. Proving this is complex, but not hard.

Anselm goes on with some predictable piffle which is intended to show that there is a difference between something existing in understanding, and understanding that thing to exist. This is obvious. The Flying Spaghetti Monster exists in my understanding, that is, it is an idea in my head, but I do not understand it to exist as a real physical entity.

However, this is a straightforward bait-and-switch. We are given the above, a perfectly reasonable statement, because we are about to be slipped another huge porky and Anselm is determined we should not notice – because if we did, then his 'argument' crashes and burns. Again.

Here's the bait: he restates his stipulation in different terms:

'And assuredly, that than which nothing greater can be conceived cannot exist in the understanding alone'

Once again, he is deliberately equivocating between the symbol x above, which represents god, with an actual conception of god y, which is something totally different, and hopes we won't notice. He then adds the next line of his whopper, which is to say that god (that which etc) 'cannot exist in the understanding alone.'

Why not? The Spaghetti Monster does, with no difficulty. Anselm's reason is that this is because to exist in reality is greater than to exist in imagination, and we already (due to his unsupported first premise) got stiffed with the definition of god as that 'than which nothing greater can be conceived.'

And here's the switch:

'it can be conceived to exist in reality, which is greater.'

Clearly, it is indeed greater for a thing to have a real existence than to be a figment of imagination. But Anselm has switched from using x, a symbol referring to an unknown value, to using y, a real conception of such a being, in all its glory, which we have already seen we can't do anyway, which is why he had to use the x-symbol in the first place.

This allows him, in total, barefaced duplicity, to say:

'Therefore, if that than which nothing greater can be conceived exists in the understanding alone, the very being than which nothing greater can be conceived is one than which a greater can be conceived. But obviously this is impossible.'

So having got you to accept a simple x-symbol for an unknown quantity, he now says that this is actually a real conception of the being than which etc, and since if we could conceive of such a being existing other than in the imagination, ie in reality (here he's using the x-symbol) then such a being must really exist (using y, the real conception) because it would be greater than one which exists only in the imagination:

He seeks to prove that a being than which none greater can be conceived can be conceived to be greater than it is, which is obviously impossible, and the only possible conclusion is that the being must exist.

I'll do that again, using x to symbolise the unknown value and y to refer to a real conception, a known and understood value:

It is greater for x to exist in reality than for x to exist in the understanding alone. Yet if we take x to exist in reality, then we are saying that x is greater than x. Since we have agreed that nothing greater than x can be conceived, this appears impossible, (switch) so we conclude that y must exist in reality. The bait-and-switch is obvious.

However, we have already seen that the 'being' is incomprehensible. It is perhaps best understood as infinity, which is similarly impossible to conceive. It has no understood value at all, other than being 'greater than we can conceive'. But that is not what Anselm wants to 'prove'; he wants instead to prove that a real, actual god exists. So what Anselm is actually saying is that if we can accept x (an unknown value) to exist in imagination, then y (a known value) must exist in reality. This is claptrap.

This is why he had to use that weird definition or stipulation in the first place, because by a combination of a peculiar and misleading first premise and simple bait and switch equivocation, he has now deceived you into agreeing that his being must actually exist in reality. Note that proving that the unknown value x exists in the real world is meaningless: all you have said is that an unknown value greater than any known value must exist. Well, possibly, but that would give us no clue as to its nature. Anselm is not interested in that, he wants to prove a deity exists, and his deity at that. So what must exist (for him) is not x, an expression of unknown value, but y, a god with the qualities of godliness that Anselm accepts.

So the point to remember is that you must remain focussed on the definition of 'being'. It is either x above, or it is, throughout, a real conception of this being, y; Anselm's switch is not allowed.

However, whether or not we accept the definition of 'conceiving the being' as x (a token formula) or y (actually conceiving the reality of a god) does not change the outcome, happily.

Our apologist may accept that x was what was meant throughout, so you can say that he has not proved god exists, but only that an unknown value x exists in reality; now he has to define what it is, which puts him right back to proving the properties of a god, since you, like a good atheist, will insist that he does.

The apologist will probably see that one coming and insist, despite all the evidence, that what was meant all along by 'being greater than' was NOT an expression of unknown value x, but a real understanding of the nature of this being, y. This is actually useful to you, because Anselm's trickery had a flaw, which is contained in his stipulation that god is a being 'than which no greater can be conceived'.

Here we must ask a simple and legitimate question: 'Is such a being greater in every sense than a human?' (Do try to sound innocent.)

If the answer is 'no', then the apologist has now reduced his god to being within the compass of a human mind. He has limited it to human scale in at least some parameters. This god is not infinite, transcendent or unimaginable; it's no greater than a human imagination.

If the apologist does not concede defeat at this point, then we can hold his feet to the flame and insist that he explains in which parameters his being is greater than a human and in which it is not, and why. If he is unable to do this, that means he is unable to fully conceive of the being, and is using an expression of unknown value for it, x, which debunks his position under the first part above – meaning that Anselm MUST have performed a bait-and-switch. Either way, our apologist is in big trouble and it's time to press home the dagger.

On the other hand, if the answer is 'yes', Anselm's being is indeed greater in every sense than a human, then it follows that its power to conceive is also greater than a human's, so it must be able to conceive of an even greater being than a human could. This means it can conceive a greater being than itself, which in turn (following the ontological reasoning) means it cannot be the greatest being, since that which it can conceive must also exist in reality. Well, according to this loony-tunes philosophising anyway.

This immediately turns into an infinite series of regressions, with an infinite number of beings all greater than the one that conceived them. This is clearly a ridiculous logical fallacy: you cannot define a 'being than which no greater can be conceived' in a way that any such being can easily conceive a greater one. Honestly, this is playground stuff.

At this point, your man has no choice but to concede, well if he's honest – they usually aren't. If he now attempts to insist that what he meant by the 'being' was actually a hypothetical entity of unknown value – x – all along, then he has contradicted himself, and in any case all that he might have proved is that an unknown value of unknown properties exists in reality and is greater than any other unknown value of unknown properties – yahoo, could it be space itself? – and if he insists that 'conceive' means to actually understand what the term really means, then he is hoist by his own petard, as he looks at a tra;,il of ever-greater beings disappearing up the bottom of his absurd philosophising.

It is a neat dilemma, on the horns of which to impale. Do not let him (or her) wriggle off it, either.

A Kiss for Christmas
ROD FLEMING
Christmas Eve. John MacMaster is in a café in Paris. He has a gold-plated Luger and a bag of blood diamonds. Two men come in. That's when the shooting starts.
ISBN: 978-0-9572612-0-4

2. Christians is Bitchin'

Christians is bitchin' – again.

Well they do this every solstice, so it shouldn't be a surprise.

Personally I find the excessive emphasis on consumption, and the unstated presumption that one will go into debt to buy presents one doesn't want or need to make other people conned into the same bollocks feel a bit better, a pile of crap. For want of a better word.

So I won't be doing it. Sorry.

But I'm still up for a bit of Yuletide cheer; after all, we are talking about the one time of the year when the news is bound to be good – the days are getting longer…well…as long as you live in the (currently frozen) Northern Hemisphere anyway. I still find it kinda strange to find the entire Philippines covered in fake snow and sprouting giant artificial Xmas trees for, literally, months, before the big day, but then one thing I have to say about Filipinos, is man they do like to party.

We'll come back to those trees. But for now what about that bitching? Well, you know, I am a Scot, and all recent polls tell us we Scots are sliding into dastardly non-belief quicker than a Dundee lassie going down the Olympia Flumes, and I live in France, which is already a committed secular state. So nobody gives a monkey's here, it's all about eating and drinking far too much and regretting it later when that nice Hugo Boss suit refuses to fasten (again).

I don't, thank goodness, live in the USA, where apparently, some people (one imagines them to be mainly of the Christian persuasion) are once again, up in arms because we've 'taken Christ out of Christmas'.

You wot, guv?

We are aware, are we not, that the celebration of the solstice is one of the oldest annual rites that we have record of and pre-dates Christianity by thousands of years? We have heard of Stonehenge, Calainis, Newgrange?.....Oh, sorry, forgot.

Right, well, it's like this: The solstice is so called because at this time there are three consecutive days when it is impossible to tell the difference in the declination of the sun (that is, how high it is above the horizon) at noon, even using a modern vernier sextant. So the sun appears to stand still. Sol=sun, stice=still. See?

I know this to be true, I have tried it myself. December the 25th is the first day that the rise of the sun can be observed. Same thing happens at midsummer, the other way around.

Our ancestors thought a lot about this. For those who lived in temperate (now there's a damn misnomer if ever there was one) zones, the single most important event of the year was that the sun would begin to rise again, and to measure and confirm this they built amazingly sophisticated solar observatories, just like those at, well, Stonehenge, Calainis, and Newgrange, where masonry was erected that allowed only a sliver of light to pass through at dawn on the solstice days. This way, they could observe the direction the light travelled – one way until the solstice, and then the other when the sun began to rise, signifying the beginning of the New Year.

I know it would have helped if they'd had sextants, but apparently the aliens who built these monuments thought it would be easier to levitate 100-tonne stones into place rather than just give the natives a few gadgets to play with. (/facetious.)

Anyway, the point of all this is that Christ is a damn Johnny-come-lately. Anyone who has studied the Bible knows perfectly well that the 25th of December is not when he was allegedly born anyway. (It's the Feast of the Passover. Not even a winter festival, but a spring one, jings.) Then there were all the other 'dying and rising' gods – and goddesses, no sexism allowed here – who came before Yeshua bar Yeshua.

The thing is, they're all the same, agricultural deities whose significance is in the farming year. The Romans – who popularised Christianity at point of sword – just made the solstice Yeshua's official birthday because the Empire was already getting soused and eating too much even then – under the name of Saturnalia.

Come on, I mean 'Christ' wasn't even Yeshua's name! He spoke Aramaic, and 'Kristos' is a Greek word that means 'anointed one'. Same root and meaning as Krishna – whom some scholars believe to have actually been the model for Yeshua.

So we have a winter festival that has been celebrated for at least 5000 years, or 3000 before certain alleged events in Judah, a man whose actual birthday it isn't, and whose name wasn't 'Christ' anyway. I mean, 'take Christ out of Christmas'? Do me a favour and pass me the sherry, petal.

Call it what you like, it's the midwinter orgy. Been that way for thousands of years. And we all have the perfect right to drink and eat too much and enjoy our loved ones without being bitched at about the name we call it.

Oh yeah, I said I'd get back to the tree. Once again, out of luck, Christers. Trees have been sacred to the Goddess as long as we have written accounts, from Sumer on. In pre-Christian Europe, evergreen plants, particularly holly, were a symbol of her everlasting life. The holly's red berries were thought to represent her sacred menstrual blood, the original source of all life.

To the Norse, the oak tree was sacred to Thor (he of the hammer). When they became Christianised, the oak was replaced by the fir, and this tradition spread throughout Germany, Europe and ultimately over the world. Nope, doesn't seem to be a lot of Christ in there either.

Anyway, have a nice winter festival whatever you call it, and don't let religion get in the way.

A Kiss for Christmas
ROD FLEMING

Christmas Eve. John MacMaster is in a café in Paris. He has a gold-plated Luger and a bag of blood diamonds. Two men come in. That's when the shooting starts.

ISBN: 978-0-9572612-0-4

3. Hot Cross Buns – Cakes for the Goddess

Hot cross buns. That's what this article is about. So why do I have a picture of a Roman sculpture of a bull's head here instead of a nice snap of some hot cross buns?

Well, hot cross buns actually originated in Assyria as a part of worship of the Moon Goddess Ishtar. At least that is the earliest record we have of them. The Egyptians continued the tradition of offering cakes to their Moon-Goddess Hathor. They decorated the cakes with bull's horns, as the ox was the preferred sacrifice of the Goddess. The cakes, therefore, were symbolic of the sacrificed bull, whose flesh would be eaten by worshippers.

Hathor has been identified with Ishtar and Astarte. Astarte is Ashtoreth, who was worshipped by King Solomon, as mentioned in the Old Testament (1 Kings 11, 2), and to whom he erected a temple or shrine in Jerusalem. Ishtar, in her turn, is the Akkadian form of Inana, the Sumerian Queen of Heaven, a title that was inherited by none other than Mary of Nazareth. As I will explain in my forthcoming book, *Why Men Made God*, all Goddesses are the same, because there is only one goddess, she just has many faces. The eating of sacramental cakes is a widespread element in Goddess-worship.

This sacramental cake and its use in prayer to the Goddess is also mentioned, in the Old Testament, by Jeremiah (Jer. 7, 18) where he says, "The children gather wood, and the fathers kindle the fire, and the women knead the dough, to make cakes to the Queen of Heaven". Again Jeremiah (Jer. 44,19) says, "And when we burned incense to the Queen of Heaven and poured out drink offerings unto her, did we make cakes to the Queen of Heaven".

The Greeks turned Bull-buns into Cross Buns.

The Ancient Greeks carried on the ritual of offering decorated cakes to the Goddess, this time in the form of Artemis, the moon goddess... who is also a derivative of Inana through Ishtar. They called the cake a "boun", which is a form of "bous", the Greek word for ox, in reference to the horn-symbol on the cake. It is from "boun" that the English word "bun" comes.

The Greeks replaced the ox-horn symbol with a cross. This was done to symbolize the four quarters of the moon and to make it easier to divide the cake into four. The pieces were distributed to be eaten by worshippers at temples or shrines.

The Romans also ate these crossed cakes, at public sacrifices to Diana, their lunar goddess, who was just Artemis renamed. They bought them from vendors outside their temples: a practice against which St. Paul fulminated (1 Corinthians 10, 28). Two "buns", such as these were found in the ruins of Herculaneum, which together with Pompeii was destroyed by the eruption of Vesuvius in A.D. 79.

The pagan Anglo-Saxons adopted the use of these small crossed cakes in the worship of Eostre, otherwise known as Ostara, and by now the similarity of her name to Ishtar or Astarte should not be surprising. In fact, despite many detailed differences, the Teutonic mythology of northern Europe came from the same, older, Indo-European cultural beliefs as the Greek myths. The goddess of light and spring; it is from Eostre that the English derive the name Easter.

The custom of eating crossed bread or cakes became widespread across Europe, and the early church fathers adopted it and combined it with the Eucharist. The crossed bun or "boun" evolved into the Eucharistic bread or crossed wafers that St. John Chrysostom mentions in his "Liturgia".

So the beloved custom of baking and eating hot crossed buns, almost invariably seen as part of a Christian tradition, into which it has certainly been adopted, is in fact far older and dates from long before the invention of Christianity.

With the spread of Christianity as the official religion of the Roman Empire, all these traditions of eating and sharing buns decorated with a cross became established throughout Europe, remaining popular long after the secular Roman Empire collapsed. Today, it is practised in every Christian part of the world, although some of the more obnoxiously Protestant sects condemn it because of its association with Goddess-worship.

But then, so much of Christianity is based on reverence for the Goddess that to deny Her is impossible for any Christian.

4. Ley-lines: how an English Gent launched the New Age movement

Watkins' Ley-lines–a desire to see pattern.

Ley-lines were invented by an Englishman called Alfred Watkins, who spent much time cycling around the countryside near his home. In 1925, he wrote a book called *The Old Straight Track*, in which he described a revelation he'd had while looking at a map of Herefordshire four years earlier. He had suddenly seen a network of straight lines that connected points of human activity, such as

> "Mounds, Long-barrows, Cairns, Cursus, Dolmens, Standing stones, mark-stones, Stone circles, Henges, Water-markers (moats, ponds, springs, fords, wells), Castle, Beacon-hills, Churches, Cross-roads, Notches in hills,"

He theorised that in fact these showed the presence of a prehistoric network of paths, which had subsequently fallen into disuse, so that all that was left on them were the way-points, in the form of the markers described above. He also suggested that any 'true' ley-line began and ended at a hill. Watkins himself stopped using the term 'ley-line' in 1929, preferring to use the terms 'old straight tracks' or 'archaic tracks.'

Perhaps he was already aware that others had found in his ideas something he did not mean to suggest; he could hardly have foreseen that his theory would spawn an entire sub-culture.

The rabbit, however, was off and running. In 1936, a popular novelist called Dion Fortune wrote a fictional book called *The Goat-Foot God* which used the idea of lines of occult power running between megalithic sites such as at Stonehenge and Avebury, loosely based on Watkins' ley-lines.

World War Two intervened and perhaps people had enough to do during it and the period of reconstruction that came after; but in 1960 an ex-Royal Air Force pilot called Tony Webb took the lunacy up a gear when he wrote a pamphlet claiming that ley-lines were lines of force that alien space-ships used to navigate when they came to visit earth. Wedd was keen on popular fiction and a UFO-hunter. As a pilot, he would have been aware of innovations like the Decca Navigation System, in which beacons transmitted radio signals that could be triangulated to provide a position for an aircraft's navigator.

The Foundation of New Age belief

The seminal work, however, was a book called *The View Over Atlantis,* by John Michell, which played well into the Zeitgeist of the era. In it, Michell combined Watkins' ley-lines, which had no supernatural or astrological element whatsoever, with the Chinese concept of feng shui, in which a structure or site is chosen or configured to align with the spiritual forces that are said to inhabit it.

This combination of a plausible but false theory of archaeology with Chinese mysticism proved very popular, and *The View Over Atlantis* was described by the historian Ronald Hutton as "almost the founding document of the modern earth mysteries movement." However, Hutton also describes the book as being "quite unacceptable to orthodox scholarship."

Despite the obvious flaws in Michell's methodology, his book had a huge effect, and the cosmic significance of ley-lines became established within New Age culture. It was quickly linked with the Nazca lines in South America, which had also been ascribed to alien intervention.

Ley-lines were described as mystical lines of energy that formed a sort of psychic grid throughout the world, which those attuned could tap into and use; this was why so many churches were on ley-lines. They have been linked the Aboriginal Song Lines of Australia, and even represented as lines of cosmic force that descend from celestial bodies into the earth, and then travel along the ground. Indeed, an entire culture of so-called New Age thinking grew up based on this.

Naturally the academics and scientists who studied the idea, like Hutton, threw it out, since there is no evidence at all to support it. Watkins' initial revelation referred to Herefordshire in England, an area which is particularly dense in exactly the type of markers that he suggested were relevant. In fact it is so dense that if you take a map of reasonable scale and a ruler, and place the ruler between any two of these markers twenty miles or so apart, you will certainly find several markers either on the line or sufficiently near it to be within a reasonable margin of error.

However, this can be achieved using only the natural markers; so that pure chance could have established this network of 'lines.' In fact, the number of alignments that can be found doing this is no more than would be the case if chance were the agent.

This has been theoretically confirmed in several ways; a geometric analysis of 137 random dots on a plane will reveal 80 4-point alignments, and archaeologist Richard Atkinson mapped the positions of modern telephone boxes, to reveal similar alignments, which he called 'telephone leys'. His point of course, was that we *know* that the boxes were not set up on straight lines, so the fact that alignments do occur must be sheer chance. Thus there is no reason whatsoever to suppose any agency other than chance in the alignments between Watkins' 'markers'.

Nevertheless, while the use of Occam's razor might be tempting here, there remains the possibility that, as Watkins proposed, the lines were simply straight lines of sight between landmarks. Not unnaturally, if people were travelling along them, this would promote settlement; that is to say that even though the alignments could have happened by chance anyway, some of the man-made ones, at least, were deliberate.

But this too is a false proposition. Aeroplanes and ships may navigate along straight lines, but people on the ground do not, and that is because there are things in the way. Even in a wilderness as empty as the Scottish Highlands, it is simply impossible to walk a straight line for any distance. In southern England, which was at the time heavily forested, and remains full of rivers, hills and other natural obstacles, the problem becomes insurmountable. People do not travel along straight paths, they travel along the most practical ones. These may involve deviating from the line-of-sight route for miles to avoid marshes, dense forest, or rivers too deep to ford, to give but three examples.

Settlements do not grow up on straight lines either, but where there is advantage, such as on fording or bridging points on rivers, at the opening of passes between mountains, where there are natural resources to exploit or where the land is good for agriculture, where there is good water, in strong defensive positions, and so on, and people travel *between* these, not the other way round.

The paths that we choose will be conditioned by geography, and also by things like the availability of shelter from bad weather, not to mention the avoidance of areas where we might be set upon; as much a concern for the Palaeolithic man transporting a sack of goods for sale as for someone attempting to navigate central Glasgow on a Saturday night.

All that can really be said is that some prominent natural markers were almost certainly used by our ancestors as landmarks to help them navigate the countryside. They probably used man-made waypoints as well, such as those that Watkins proposed.

This is, after all, exactly how we navigate today. Ask anyone for directions and they will give a series of waypoints and instructions, such as these, leading from my house to the old village station: 'Go out the front door, cross the road towards the church, cross the yard, turn right at the little lane on the other side, turn left at the end of that, walk down the hill and the old station is in front of you.' Note the use of waypoints: front door, road, church, lane, hill; and of instructions: out, cross, turn, walk down.

What we would not do, however, would be to try to travel from here to the station in a straight line, for that would mean scaling a wall, flying over the Town House, climbing another, two-metre high stone wall, walking through a vegetable garden and a yard containing two large and not very friendly dogs, crossing a fence, and wading through a cattle-trough. Clearly to do so would be preposterous, and such a thing always was; we do not travel on straight paths, but by the most practical ones.

This proves, if further proof were needed, that Watkins' original theory, without which there would have been no book, and no spark to set off the subsequent brushfire, is false. All that happened was that he succumbed to the well-known human habit of seeing pattern and agency in everything.

Since the foundation is invalid, all the later theories are false too; but such is their attraction to belief that many people refuse to accept this, instead insisting either that the original theory is sound, in the face of all evidence to the contrary, or that even if Watkins were wrong, the lines of force that were later proposed, or whatever the viewer 'believes' is there, nevertheless exist.

What concerns us here is the way in which a set of beliefs have grown up, initially surrounding a proposition which we know the origin of and can easily demonstrate is completely without foundation, that proceed on to encompass beliefs which had nothing to do with the original, instead being later additions, but which use the original to support themselves. Consider Wedd's proposition that 'ley-lines' were lines of energy used for navigation by alien spacecraft, or Michell's weird juxtaposition of unfounded pseudo-science with Oriental mysticism.

So, from an observable phenomenon, that there are lines of sight between landmarks, and a reasonable proposition, that people use landmarks to navigate, has developed a hypothesis, at first sight plausible but false, that straight roads existed between landmarks, which has further spawned a belief, based in no fact at all, that aliens navigate the Earth along these lines. This then develops, now accelerating away from any contact with reality, to suggest that in fact these are lines of power in the earth, that they represent a cosmic connection with celestial bodies, and even a form of vitality within the Earth, or more.

Incredible though it may seem, many people believe all this to be true; indeed within sections of the so-called 'New Age' community, it is taken as proven matter of fact that ley-lines are indeed lines of cosmic power, and this is in turn taken as proof of celestial connections, earth-deities and planetary consciousness. And this despite the fact that at every turn, recognised experts in the field of history, archaeology, and statistics, used to having their work peer-reviewed, have subjected the original proposition and its successors to scrutiny and have debunked them time and time again.

This shows us that belief, once established, is not only very hard indeed to repudiate, but is self-propagating; that is to say, if you like, that belief begets belief.

5. God proposition: god true or god false?

The god proposition is supported not by fact, but by faith.

At the end of the day, the final word that the religiously-disposed have is to say that "It is so because I believe it to be so," before covering their ears. For them, this trumps everything.

This is the hook that caught Descartes when he confronted the issue, and then backed off very quickly. "I think," he said, "Therefore I am." This is fine. He is self-aware therefore he is sure he exists. He cannot be entirely sure that he exists as he perceives himself or that anything that is around him is as he perceives it, but he does make a very convincing argument, based on the progression of rational logic, that it is so (and thus takes several hundred pages to confirm what any pragmatist already knows. But that's an aside.) However, when confronted by the idea of God, it must exist, he says "Because he cannot imagine a world in which he does not." Oops. Well, it may have got Descartes out of the sights of the Inquisition, but it is an argument so feeble that it almost seems as if he meant it in the inverse.

But Descartes illustrates the point very well; God exists because those who believe in him say so. Now that leads us to two possible conclusions; the first is that religiously-inclined people are a bit soft in the head.

Clearly, if I say I believe I have a certain amount of money in the bank, that does not actually mean that I do, and if I proceed willy-nilly I may get a nasty shock the next time I get a statement or try to fill up my gas tank. Belief is no proof at all and to say that it is, definitely must bring into question the speaker's mental capacity. In other words faith is only valid to the person who has it.

The other conclusion is that God has actually been brought into being by the simple fact of being believed in, and at first glance this is certainly a more interesting possibility. However on closer inspection this proposition reveals a glaring weakness; since no-one can genuinely say that they know what is inside another person's mind, how do we know that we are all believing in the same God? Isn't it at least possible that we are all worshipping different Gods, since the act of our believing has brought them into being?

If we have to have gods, which I personally am not convinced about, I have no problem with this. Have as many as you like. However, for monotheists this presents another problem, since they are convinced that there is only one God. The question then is "Which one?" and we immediately see the schism that splits the monotheisms into violently squabbling camps reassert itself. The Jews are right because Moses received the word first. No, the Muslims are right because they received in last. No, they didn't, the Proddies did. And what about the Bah'ai? Or the Mormons?

Well, one might say that since there is only one god, that god must be the same god no matter who is looking. It sounds great but it has two huge flaws. The first is, "How do we know there's only one god," and if the only answer is "Because I believe it to be so," then we're right back where we started.

False Gods

In addition, leaving that aside, we then have to deal with the issue of false gods. You may perhaps argue that no such thing exists, but you would be at variance with most monotheists, and again, you would have the issue of proof – how do you know there are no false gods? This is important because the issue of false gods is central to the understanding of free will in religious terms, certainly as far as the main monotheisms are concerned.

If there are no false gods, then you're free to believe anything you like because it simply doesn't matter; god is god. Devil-worship is as valid as god-worship, since god is the devil too. Therefore free will is irrelevant; it doesn't matter whom or what you choose to worship, it's all the same thing.

Unfortunately for this utopian solution, one of the central claims of all religions is that they are a guide to moral behaviour. They set out to define what is right and what is not right in terms of the interpreted word of god. The trouble is, if all gods are the same, and someone happens to worship one that demands the sacrifice of newborn children, how can that be condemned in moral terms? You've just argued that his god is as much god as your god, and his god, he says, tells him he has to eat babies. You think this is ridiculous? What about if his god tells him he has to hack the arms off schoolgirls, or mutilate baby boys' genitals?

So now, instead of arguing about whose god is actually god, you end up arguing about whose vision of god is true and we are once again right back where we began.

Which gods are true though?

Alas, for monotheisms, there is no way out of this; either there is only one god, and whatever god you say you worship, that is still god, no matter what he demands, in which case the notion of moral accountability has just left the building, or there are indeed false gods, which means the issue is in deciding which are untrue gods and which are true. And if this latter be the case, than the violence and strife between the monotheisms can be justified by arguing that those perpetrating the violence are doing so in the name of the true god, and those who are subjected to it deserve no better, as they are followers of false gods.

Yes; well, if you must have a religion, you should choose one that is not predisposed towards such behaviour, and in the case of monotheisms, it is impossible to see how they can avoid it.

6. Is Witch-burning Back? The Religious Right Is.

Witch-burning is out of fashion in the West these days. Fortunately. But the religious intolerance that caused it is still with us and it's getting more strident. And in other parts of the world, religion is responsible for shameful acts of mutilation and murder on a daily basis.

The Internet has given voice to some whose opinions, frankly, should never have a public platform, and 'multiculturalism' that shameful abrogation of the moral values of our secular society, makes it increasingly difficult for anyone to express legitimate criticism of some of the nasty ideas put forward by people of religion under the disguise of 'faith'.

I am lucky to have been brought into a world where secularisation was ascendant. In every way, the light of science seemed to have the darkness of superstition in retreat. Even those Christians I knew did not suggest that the Bible was literally true, or the exact transcription of the words of a supernatural deity. For them, religion was a cultural practice and spiritual guide, or so it appeared. In any case the free and educated society that my generation argued and worked so hard for, surely would, in the end, render the very idea of formal religion obsolete.

When I first heard that there was a resurgence of the Christian right wing, and that this might threaten those freedoms, over thirty years ago, I refused to believe it. Surely no-one could seriously attempt to challenge Evolution, or the age of the planet, any more than they could counter Pythagoras' Theorem or contend that the Earth is flat, could they?

How depressingly wrong I was.

For decades, despite all the evidence, I believed that religious intolerance and sectarian violence were the result of political and social conflicts, rather than matters of faith itself. I believed that an improvement of living and educational standards would see the development of democratic, secular and tolerant, but most of all peaceful societies which recognised that faith was private, and everyone had a right to believe whatever they liked, as long as they harmed no-one and upheld the right of everyone else to do the same.

I now invite you to read the following comments, harvested from Facebook and all written by self-professed Christians:

"I say kill them all (atheists) and let them see for themselves that there is a God"

"Shoot them. Shoot to kill." (The target was atheists.)

"To ALL ATHEIEST DIE AN GO TO HELL HAHA IF I COULD ID SHOOT ALL OF YOU IN THE HEAD WITH A 12GUAGE" (sic)

"I love Jesus, and the cross and if you don't, I hope someone rapes you!" This was from a woman – so much for the gentler sex; and to follow up, her next statement was: "atheists, I hope God kills them all."

"They're atheists so it won't matter if you kill them."

These are the same Christians whose right to their beliefs I have always spoken up for, whom I have never once discriminated against because of their religion; yet they would, simply, kill me, because I am an atheist and so 'it won't matter'. At last I begin to understand how a Jew must have felt in pre-war Germany, and I can no longer pretend that Christianity is just a nice thing that nice people do on Sundays because it makes them feel good.

Nor can I pretend that at its heart, Christianity does not contain the same malignant intolerance that we recognise within Islam. On one side these cults may fly before them the dove of peace, but that is just the side they like to make public, and underneath it, one would have to be blind not to realise that many Christians are as intolerant as the most rabid ayatollah of Islam.

Despite that, I do recognise that not all Christians think like the most evil amongst them, in the same way that not all Muslims are suicide bombers: but just as it is rare to find a Muslim actually condemning Islamic terrorists, I hear no clamour of voices from Christians condemning those who threaten to kill, rape and torture me, just because I don't share their belief in a fiction that they cannot prove. The very opposite is true, and the worldwide web is now awash with ill-informed, anti-atheist bigotry and hatred.

You might argue that these are internet voices that may be safely ignored, but if the internet is blamed for helping spread the wickedness of radical Islam, which would impose the consummate evil of Sharia on the world, then in what way can it be blameless in its spread of hateful Christian bigotry? Today this vile and infamous defamy spewing from the Internet, and what tomorrow, if it is allowed to continue unchallenged? The mob at the door, the brick through the window, the tarring and feathering and then what – atheists hanging from lamp-posts? For all of these atrocities and more have been carried out by the Christian right, just in the last hundred years.

The only difference now is that today's Christian Fascists are not Catholic but Protestant, and their roots lie in the same version of the cult whose actions fifty years ago inspired the song 'Strange Fruit' – which describes the bodies of lynched black people hanging from trees in the southern United States; the very same place from which this new poison oozes.

The resurgent right-wing Christian bigotry, from the bible-belt heartland of the United States, is spreading its message of hatred and intolerance all over the world. We forget, now, that only eighty years ago the Ku Klux Klan had hundreds of thousands of members and millions of supporters; that it controlled politics in many US States. Its obscenity rose not because people turned a blind eye to it, its vile pronouncements, and its even more foul behaviour, but because, despite their later denials, they sympathised with its message: white, Christian, Protestant.

The very same vicious, bigoted people as were behind the Klan are once again on the march; now they are called 'fundamentalist Christians' but their principal targets are the usual ones of the religious right – liberal thinkers, atheists, homosexuals and women. If history serves to teach, then we know exactly what to expect of them.

Within the ranks of fundamentalist Christianity a group has arisen which actively seeks the end of the world, believing that they will escape and be 'raptured' up to Heaven. This claptrap would be utterly laughable were it not for the fact that the last President of the United States, one George W. Bush, is quite openly a believer in it, as are many other senior US politicians, and leaders of business and the media.

Apart from the massive egotism implicit in their position, that they are right and everyone else wrong, right wing Christians are a major force behind climate-change revisionism in the United States. Since the US remains the world's greatest polluter, these Christians, who, in embracing the so-called 'end times', see no reason to cut back on the profligacy that is killing the planet and instead do everything they possibly could to sabotage attempts to rescue it, are a threat to us all and to our children and our children's children.

In the light of this menace, I suppose the doctrine of 'creationism' seems a small matter; at least until you recognise the size of the pyramid of lies and deliberate misinformation that it is based on, anyway.

The twentieth century taught us that the powers of evil will manifest and grow when people tolerate them, and it is long since time, I fear, to decide which side of the fence we stand on.

I have always tried to be as tolerant of belief as I could, and have only asked that believers be as tolerant of my lack of it. But when I see literal death threats, when I see religious bigots openly try to bring about the 'end times', when I see them propose to stuff my children's heads full of absolute nonsense on the grounds that it will not challenge a fictional Bronze Age text, I know that this is a one-sided bargain.

In the secular haven that was Europe, and in particular in the United Kingdom, we have allowed ourselves to be lulled into a false sense of security. Even the rise of militant Islam has not, it seems, provoked us to take matters seriously, and, apparently because of some politically-correct taboo against challenging issues of faith, horrific cruelties like the circumcision of both male and female infants go unchallenged.

We abrogate these children's human rights when we allow their parents to mutilate them in this way. We would never under any circumstances permit such a practice for say, cosmetic reasons, irrespective of the desires of the parents: the children would be taken into protective care and the parents locked up. And this is exactly what should be happening, but it is not, because we are afraid of upsetting 'people of faith'. But why should we be afraid? These practices are abominable no matter who does the cutting of innocent flesh, which fictional deity they follow, or what their 'culture' is.

Evangelical fundamentalist Christianity is an evil and intolerant monster that intends, just as militant Islam would, to use the very rights and liberties that we and our forebears fought and died for, to destroy them and replace them with 'God's Law'. We know what that means, intolerance of all dissent.

Once, we railed against the Soviet Communist Party, and I was raised believing that the right to free speech was the most important right we in the West had. To defend this right, we built armies and nuclear arsenals and told our children that the one thing that was worth dying for, was that freedom of speech.

Yet do we speak out now, when we still can? For the menace is not some faraway evil empire, armed with enough weaponry to completely obliterate us, but an empire of evil that is being preached from pulpit and mosque in our very own towns and cities.

Do we identify this menace for what it is? Do we condemn the fundamentalist Christians when they try to sneak their outright lies of creationism into the classroom, when they praise the end-times or threaten death to atheists? Do we unambiguously condemn imams who make their women cover their faces in public, or who threaten death to those who mock their 'prophet'? No indeed, and instead, we even seek to stifle those who would condemn them and their despicable ideas and behaviour.

We are not allowed even to challenge those who challenge us, the debate is ended before it is begun, because this is a matter of 'faith'; but this must change. Religion, no matter whose, is a legitimate target for criticism, mockery and satire.

I don't believe that witch-burning, public stonings and beheadings, and the other contemptible abuses of humanity that are ever the sanction of religion against its critics will return to Europe; but that will only be if we speak out against it.

7. The Storytelling Ape

It's a striking thought that civilisation evolved here on Earth only 7,000 years ago. Since then, humans have achieved many really incredible things. But even in terms of our own – mostly unwritten – history, 7,000 years is almost insignificant; it's less than 4% of the time *Homo sapiens*, the storytelling ape, has existed.

For the other 96% of our time, we knew nothing of any advanced technology. We had no metallurgy and no agriculture. Everything we had, we found in the environment round us. And our footprint was incredibly light. We left almost no trace of our passing, which of course, has made it difficult to piece together our story. In the last couple of decades, though, with significant advances just this year, we have finally been able to construct a timeline of the human colonisation of the world.

Current research indicates that *Homo sapiens,* modern humans, first appeared on the plains of Africa, 200,000 years ago or thereabouts. For the first 150,000 years or so of our history, we remained in Africa. We all had dark skin, to protect us from the sun's UV. We were hunter-gatherers, and lived in small groups that may have been sedentary, remaining in one geographical area and exploiting it for food, or nomadic, endlessly following the herds of game.

We were talking and chattering all the time. We evolved with the power of speech. We have a hyoid bone, which allows us to stretch our vocal cords, and produce a variety of pitches of sound. Just as importantly, though, we have a dropped larynx. Behind our vocal cords is an empty space, which is what allows us to produce the modulation of speech.

These things did not evolve, and some time later we decided to make use of them; they evolved because we were already using them. We were talking. Why? Because it was a very successful evolutionary strategy. It allowed us to plan, to divide tasks, and to co-ordinate our efforts. This made us much more competitive.

Compared to *Homo erectus*, a close relative, we are small, lightly built, weak and slow. *Erectus* would have been a frighteningly effective hunter and may even have preyed on us in our early history. But *erectus* couldn't talk, at least as we understand it. They probably communicated vocally, but that's not talking. Simple communications only. The whole notion of oral culture – something we take for granted, like the air we breathe – is actually an incredible evolutionary step, and it is unique to us.

Almost certainly, from the earliest times of our existence, from the time we could first make a constructed phrase with a verb and a noun – the simplest grammatical structure – we used this ability not only to plan how to attack the wildebeest, but to tell stories. Mothers were talking to children, telling stories of where they came from, deep in our most distant past.

We don't just talk; we think in speech, at least most of us do, most of the time. Inside our heads, we are constantly churning through ideas expressed in words. Such a great part of our imagination is verbalised that we often forget that there are other ways to think, skills that artists and musicians, dancers and makers, scientists and mathematicians develop to the highest level, but which we all use, all the time.

Being able to talk wasn't a luxury: it was vital to our survival as a species.

About 74,000 years ago, something so nightmarishly devastating occurred that we could never have comprehended it, far less predicted it. A super-volcano in what is now Indonesia exploded.

This was no ordinary volcanic eruption. This was no Mount St Helens or Vesuvius. Nor was it Krakatau or even Thera. The eruption, which left a vast caldera we call Lake Toba, erupted around three thousand cubic kilometres of magma. That's equivalent to a cube of rock 31 kilometres (19.5 miles) long on each side, or to put it another way, significantly more than the entire volume of Mount Everest, calculated as a cone from sea-level to summit. A quarter of this material was blown into the sky as volcanic ash. Toba was a hundred times greater than the huge eruption at Krakatau in the 19th century, and by far the greatest natural disaster humanity has survived.

Toba very nearly killed us all. It was a truly apocalyptic event. A volcanic winter ensued, that lasted for years, when the sun was permanently hidden by clouds of ash and gas. This provoked a mini-ice-age, so that even when the clouds cleared, the climate was very different, drier and colder. And it stayed that way for perhaps a millennium. But most destructive of all, at least in the first part of the catastrophe, must have been the tsunamis.

Tsunamis are a special kind of ocean wave caused by earthquakes and volcanoes. Unlike normal waves, where only the water at the surface is moving, and that vertically, the whole depth of water in a tsunami is moving, rushing outwards from the point of origin at hundreds of kilometres an hour.

Anyone who has watched the terrifying footage of the 2004 tsunami that devastated southeast Asia will have some idea of their power, but although that was big, Toba makes it look trivial. Furthermore, Toba didn't just erupt and have done with it; after the initial blast and the first appalling destruction, the aftershocks and subsequent eruptions may have continued for months, sending wave after wave of super-tsunamis out to devastate everything in their paths.

A tsunami has a very long wavelength – perhaps hundreds of kilometres – and remember, the water in it is *actually moving*. It's not really a wave so much as a mountain of water. So a tsunami hundreds of metres high could also be hundreds of kilometres long. This means that coastal areas would not only have been flooded, but flooded again and again, as successive tsunamis thundered in. With no way for the water to escape back to sea, it would have surged further and further inland. And this was no local event; the Toba super-tsunamis would have hurtled out in all directions until they hit a land-mass.

And when they hit Africa, they hit us. This was the crunch. This was the moment when humanity itself came close to extinction.

Science disagrees about how many of us were left after Toba; cautious estimates suggest a few thousand, but many geneticists think our numbers came down to a couple of hundred breeding pairs. Similar bottlenecks that occurred in other African species, for example cheetahs, chimpanzees and lowland gorillas, confirm the evidence of our own gene-pool; a near-extinction event hit us all.

After the floods receded, there would have been only death and hunger. The survivors, who must have been on high ground or near it, would have seen, where once there were limitless reaches of fertile grassland teeming with life, a devastated, post-apocalyptic landscape where everything had been killed. The lack of sun would have made the recovery slow, and the fall in Earth's temperature would also have resulted in drought, as more water was held in the polar ice.

The grassland, once so rich in game, would have taken many years, perhaps generations, to recover, with the soil hopelessly salinated and no sun to warm it or rain to wash it clean. The huge herds that once grazed there must have all but disappeared. From a time when we could be assured of food for the morrow and a comfortable life, we were reduced to survival on the scant pickings that this appalling disaster left us, while predators, maddened themselves with hunger, saw us as easy targets. Our Paradise was indeed lost. We survived, but only just.

I believe we did so because we were talking. We communicated. We formulated strategies, we assigned roles, we consulted the elders, we made decisions. When we met other groups, we could exchange precise information, and our scouts could tell us exactly what they had found. But perhaps most important of all was something so simple that we even forget it.

We told stories to each other, and to our children. And those children, in turn, told them to theirs. These stories contained all the collected wisdom of those who came before us, which we too had learned at our mothers' knees. We invented oral tradition and it saved us. All the things we needed to know – which plants were good to eat, where they grew, the techniques of hunting, where the game travelled, and the terrible story of the flood itself – were encapsulated in story. Certainly they were elaborated and woven into myth, but that is how oral tradition works.

The story of humanity is much more than just the milestones of our genes, or the geography of our expansion; it is the story of story itself. Our culture, which is based on our incessant chattering and our big brains, is what defines us.

We are not just the Toolmaking Ape, nor even simply the Talking Ape; we are the Storytelling Ape.

8. Jesus? I have a better story than that...

Today marks the first day in one of our greatest annual cultural events: the winter solstice. From now until the 25th, the sun will appear to hesitate before it once again begins to climb into the sky. That of course, is the reason so many solar deities have their birthday on the 25th – Mithras, Dionysus and Christ being but three.

But what you may not know is that while many of these three 'dying and rising' gods, every one of them an agricultural deity, are clearly men, the very first was not; she was a woman.

The earliest version I have found is in the Sumerian tale of the goddess Sul or Sud. This is not a Sumerian name and it's unclear where she came from, but that doesn't matter. As befits a goddess, Sul was staggeringly beautiful and at the peak of her fertility; she knew it was time for her to choose a partner.

Sul liked to bathe at dawn in the canal outside the city, and became aware that she was being watched. She told her mother, and her mother went away and found out about it. When she came back she was distraught. Apparently, the god Enlil, the Lord of the Air, had taken to hiding in the reeds at the other side of the canal to spy on Sul.

Now Enlil was what we Scots call an 'orra chiel.' He was not blessed with the graces. He didn't actually have a mother and father in the conventional sense, since he had been formed from the sigh of love that would forever separate the Earth, Ki, from the Sky, An. So Enlil, though as handsome as a god should be, had never been taught the social skills he needed to win a bride. He was clumsy and tongue-tied, and rough and ready in his ways.

So Sul's mother forbade her daughter to go bathing in the canal again, telling her that if she did, Enlil would surely rape her.

Sul, in typical style, for a Sumerian goddess anyway, reflected on this, and the next morning had her servants do her hair and face, put on her finest jewellery, then went for her customary bathe, naked, in the canal.

Enlil, watching, was so overpowered with desire that, as Sul's mother had predicted, he swam across and had his way with her. As a result of this, Sul became pregnant with the moon god.

And this is where the story gets interesting. Sul, incensed, insisted that Enlil be tried for rape in front of all the Sumerian gods and goddesses, the Anunaki. (These were not space aliens, by the way; tinfoil hats off, please. They were called the Anunaki because they were the mythical children of An and Ki, that's all.) Anyway, the punishment for rape was death, and Enlil was judged; he died and went into the Underworld.

But Sul had fallen for him. So she herself descended into the Underworld to seek him out and bring him back to life under her protection. She met Enlil three times, and each time he was wearing disguises; only on the third did she recognize him and together the pair walked out of the Underworld and back into life. They were married, and Sul became Ninlil, Lady of the Air.

Now this story, which is as charming as all the Sumerian stories, makes several very important points. The first is that a woman has the right to wear whatever she likes, and behave exactly as she likes, including bathing stark naked in public while wearing all her jewellery and make-up, without fear of rape or molestation. Another is that a woman's word alone is enough to convict a man – and to sentence even a god to death. But it also says that love can forgive anything, and that this, too, is within a woman's gift. Finally it also says that love, and the strength it gives, can even defeat death itself.

So remember – the very first 'dying and rising god' was not a man, but a plucky and determined woman who herself passed into the darkness of death, not once but three times, to save the man she loved. I think that's a pretty damn good story, actually. Maybe we should tell it to our children at this time of year…

9. Singing the World into Being

I first read about the Songlines in the late Bruce Chatwyn's eponymous book, and even then the concept fascinated me. The Songlines are massively complex, but essentially devolve to the creation mythology of the Aboriginal Australians.

In this, every animal had an anthropomorphic first ancestor – so there was Kangaroo-Man, Koala-Man, Lizard-Man and so on. Each human tribe is also derived from one of those ancestors. In the dawn of time, these ancestors walked through the world, literally singing it into existence.

The words they sang are the Songlines, handed down through the millennia of human life on the continent.

That on its own is a pretty amazing idea. But then I realised that these Songlines were more than just myth. For a start, they reached from coast to coast of the continent, across many different tribal areas. Secondly, they criss-crossed each other with enormous frequency.

As a Creation Myth it was right up there with the most spectacular I had ever come across, and left the Biblical one (a watered-down version of a far more interesting Sumerian tradition) looking dull and unimaginative.

Through Chatwyn and later reading, I realised that the Songlines are not forgotten but are a part of contemporary Aboriginal culture. The men still learn them, word by word. Each tribe learns the parts of all of the Songs that apply to its tribal area, but more than that, each tribe has a totem animal, and so a totem ancestor, the original 'man' of that animal. This Songline they learn in its entirety.

The Songlines are fascinating. They're not hypothetical. They don't describe mythical places or events or heavens or hells, but the real world, in which we live. They are a living geography.

This was all pretty astounding, but it got a lot more so when I read a paper, years ago, by J B Haviland, about the Guugu Yimithirr (GY) language. This is one of a group of related Aboriginal languages. It's the one that gives us the word 'kangaroo'. This language is fascinating because it does not have 'egocentrically relative' directions.

Let me explain. In English and all other European languages, we use terms to describe location that are related to ourselves or something else. We say 'in front of me', 'behind me', 'to the right or left of' and so on. We also use locators that use the same system, but related to something else, for example another person or an object – say the house. 'The church is in front of my house.'

GY doesn't do this, nor does it have words that would allow speakers to. Instead of these relative directions, based on the position of ourselves or another object or person, they use cardinal directions – to the North, South, East or West. So to an Aboriginal thinking in GY, the church is not in front of the house, but to the South of it; and the snake is never behind you, but to the North, South, East or West of you.

Now we are able to use and understand this terminology; however, apparently many Aboriginals think we can't, because in general, we don't, unless we are being very formal or precise. The point is that GY speakers *never* give relative directions, only absolute, cardinal ones.

Think about that a moment. Aboriginal men learn all the Songlines of their area, which describe in fine detail the land they live in. These Songlines are in a language that places everything in terms of absolute position and direction. Everything.

This means that every person who has learned them is carrying around a virtual map of the entire territory, with everything accurately located in it, *in their heads!* No wonder they could wander around for weeks and never get lost, which amazed the European colonists. They needed compasses and maps to do what an Aboriginal could do just by singing..

Now that is pretty damned impressive.

But it gets better, because the Songlines are not static. They change – or at least they are changed – whenever the landscape changes. People walking the Lines, singing them out loud, alter them when, say, a flood has caused a river to divert its course, or some other physical change has happened. Then, they sing the new version to their tribal brethren and the update enters the culture. This they do at ceremonial meetings called Corroborrees, which are normally closed to anyone other than fully-fledged adult tribesmen.

(Women are not present, nor do they learn the Songlines, but that discussion is for another day.)

This just has to be one of the most remarkable cultural phenomena that exist; it is a highly sophisticated, communally held, virtual model of the world which is reliable and constantly updated – and not one graphical map exists within it. It's similar to the way landscapes are plotted out in computer games – not with visual representation, but with code. It allows a person to travel not only throughout the land their tribe inhabits, but following their own Ancestor, right across the Australian continent and back, and never get lost or have to ask for directions, always knowing where water, shelter or game can be found.

Furthermore, because this is a part of their creation mythology, their religious belief, walking the Songlines is not merely a pleasant jaunt in the country, but a deeply spiritual experience, like a pilgrimage. It is a reaffirmation of the creation mythology, of the religion and culture itself. And as long as Aboriginals walk and sing, their culture will persist.

Amazing. It just blows my mind every time I think of it.

10. Pursuing the Goddess

Since 2002 I have been researching into something that I felt more than anything else. Something was nagging me. At the time I lived, as I do now, in France, and the signs of Goddess-worship were all around me. Cathedrals were full of images of the Goddess, the art replete with them. I could see this but I couldn't define it, I couldn't understand what it meant.

When I returned to Scotland I was a very busy man for a long time, building a house and trying to make ends meet from my freelance work, and also my own mother became ill and died, so the research went on hold. But it was always there in the back of my mind, and as I travelled round Scotland, that epicentre of dry Presbyterianism, I saw again and again the unmistakable mark of the Goddess all over the architecture and in the symbolism.

The Goddess was the principal focus of my Masters' Degree research and even though I came a long way, I didn't reach the answer I sought. When I came back to France I began to write, but in April of 2012 I had to stop. I was getting too confused.

My research had spanned the entire world and the whole of recorded history by that time, and I still hadn't made the breakthrough. I put my notes and files aside.

Most of the rest of 2012 was a bucket year; I sailed my yacht round Scotland and then went to Asia to blow the proceeds of her sale; along the way, I fell in love. Recharged, in 2013 I began to research again, but this time, for reasons I couldn't be sure of, except that I am a firm believer in just following my nose, I found myself studying the Bible, which I had not done for decades. I was once again pursuing the ever-mysterious and elusive Goddess, whom I thought must reside in Eve and Mary, and of course she does. But there was something more, something I was just not seeing.

In the end, brain fever set in and I decided to put these notes too, to one side, and concentrated on less intellectually demanding projects, which resulted in *French Onion Soup!* being finally completed. But the Goddess was always there and I knew she would call me back sooner or later; I knew there was something she still had to tell me, something that perhaps she had been trying to tell me all along, but my mind had not been open enough to accept.

I had a teacher once, who really was not a very good teacher at all, but he did impart one piece of wisdom to me in the years I knew him; he extolled the merits of the 'fresh eye'.

'When you're stuck,' he said, 'Put it away. Cover it up, hide it. When you come back you'll have a fresh eye, and that will make things clear.'

Well, he was right, and for this one veracity, I might forgive him all his waspishness and jealousy; though perhaps not for his rejection of objective reality in favour of Postmodernist mumbo-jumbo.

Two weeks ago, after the New Year, I went back to my drawers of pages, notebooks full of scribbles and my digital folders swollen with documents. I began reading over what I had already written about the Goddess, and…there it was.

On Friday, I found it. The speck of dust that crystallised the super-saturated solution. The key that unlocked the door. The secret code that, when applied, made sense of everything, where there had been no sense before. Just like that. Click.

On Friday morning I was looking at a pile, nearly 300,000 words, of notes and hypotheses that just…were completely confusing. Today I am looking at a satisfyingly complete view that explains the whole of Western culture, from the earliest records we have, till now, and is fully supported by the evidence.

Okay, so, fair enough, I still have to turn this into something readable, but now the lights are on. I'm not feeling my way forward in the dark any more, listening to the Goddess' voice whispering half-heard, inexplicable mysteries, like an archaeologist exploring a huge catacomb, his candle guttering and flickering fantastic shapes on the walls. I found the switch and bingo, hahaha! It's ferking obvious now, plain as the nose on your face. All the colour and glory clear to see, all the complexity of interwoven cultural collections. It's as if I had lit a 1000-watt halogen lamp inside the tomb of a lost pharaoh for the first time in millennia, and was overwhelmed by the revelation.

Like they say, it's easy when you know. Years of research in so many related fields, enough books to sink a ship, most of the important cathedrals in France visited (and not a few elsewhere) and one, little, tiny detail that I had assumed unimportant turned out to be the key. It wasn't unimportant at all; it was THE important.

Without it, nothing made sense, and with it, everything does. Which I think says something about being completely open when doing research, having no preconceptions and just following the evidence.

I think I feel quite good about this. And if you want to find out exactly what the secret I discovered is, you'll have to wait till the book is finished. It will be worth it.

The book, Why Men Made God, was published by Redefining the Sacred in 2015.

ISBN: 978-0-9572612-2-8

Why Men Made God
R A Fleming & K Burkowski
Why do we have the religious beliefs that we do? What are the roots of faith? How did our religions evolve and how did they influence our cultures? Why Men Made God leads you through the fascinating history of human belief

ISBN: 978-0-9572612-2-8

11. Something Greater

I'm sometimes asked if I don't feel that I am missing out, by not believing in 'something greater'. It's a valid question and one that I think all atheists should ask themselves. But the answer, at least for me, might also be of interest to others.

Yes, I am part of something greater, in a very real and immediate sense. It's not so much a question of believing but of accepting the evidence in front of me. I am part of the Earth. The Earth is not just a core of molten iron covered in a crust of rock and water, with an outer gaseous atmosphere, though it is these things. It is a living system, an entity. And I am – we are all – part of that entity.

Consider what you are: you are composed of billions of individual living things called cells. All of these living things co-operate in such a way that the whole survives. This is a very successful evolutionary strategy for the genes that make them – and you. Every cell in each individual human body – just like all other multi-cellular animals – contains exactly the same DNA as all the other cells. We have, recently, come to understand how parts of our DNA control other parts, so that each type of cell plays the role it should.

The maverick ecologist James Lovelock proposed that the Earth was an interconnected living system. I agree. Certainly the Earth does have an inert core – but so do we; our skeletons are made of calcium carbonate, which is limestone, and pretty inert. Massed around that is all the astonishing variety of cells that constitute us. In the same way, massed around the mineral substrate, the Earth's biosphere has incredible variety, with millions of species of plants and animals, all interacting and evolving.

Is the Earth sentient? Of course. The core and mantle are no more sentient than our bones, but no-one, I hope, is arguing that skeletons have feelings. Poor Yorick would be distraught. Instead our nerve cells feel – and for the Earth, every animal possessed of a nervous system feels.

Does the Earth think? Yes, of course; we, and the other higher animals, are the thinking part of the whole, incredible living space-ship that we are a part of. We are the Earth's brain. Our thoughts are hers. We humans, indeed, are the flight computer, and it would be wise of us not to make too many mistakes.

Is the Earth a part of me? Of course, just as I am part of it. Everything that I am comes from the Earth. My body is composed of compounds formed from the stuff of the planet; she owns me, I don't possess her. And those materials are not given, but loaned, for I will as surely return them one day as I take, and use, them now.

And yet, it is even more incredible than that, for what you must realise is that in the beginning, the Big Bang, there were only three elements formed, the lightest – hydrogen, helium and lithium. Some of this, because of gravity, became stars, which are huge fusion reactors. Everyone knows that the stars turn hydrogen to helium, but this is not the only fusion reaction going on, only the one we see on the surface.

Inside stars, other, more complex fusion occurs, and in the largest, high-mass stars, every element that we know, along with others that decay too quickly to survive, is formed by fusion reaction in enormous heat and pressure. When these stars die, they blow themselves outwards, seeding the universe with the heavy elements that make planets and life itself. We are, literally, stardust. The wonderful Carl Sagan first told me of this when I was young and it amazes me as much now as it did then.

So, you ask if I am part of something greater? Oh yes, I am not only part of the most unimaginably great thing that we know, the Universe, but my particular organism, the Earth, is just one of countless planets. Many are also living things, possessed of sentience, of life, of other beings who are right now looking up into the glittering night sky full of stars and asking themselves 'Am I part of something greater?' Beings who, perhaps, will go indoors as I just did, put another log on the fire and settle down with their thoughts. I wonder what those thoughts are like? Would I find them beautiful, or terrifying, or just incomprehensible? I am pretty sure I will never find out.

For the last twelve years I have been researching our early beliefs and how these have filtered through to today, and our modern cultures. That research is the basis of the new books I'm writing now. One thing that has struck me again and again is how close the earliest beliefs we know of were to the truth.

Our ancestors believed that life came from the Sea. The Sumerians, for example, believed that the first deities, Ki, the Earth, and An, the Sky, were born in eternal lover's embrace, deep within the Sea, which they called Nammu. They understood Nammu to be female, and to have existed for eternity.

And we do come from the sea, though it took many thousands of years for us to scientifically establish this; all life comes from the Sea, and we carry it around with us. The fluids in our bodies are saline, but far less salty than today's oceans – why? Because, 375 million years ago, when our first terrestrial ancestor, Tiktaalik, a fish with eyes on top of its head and fleshy pectoral fins, containing the same bones as in are in our arms, first struggled onto dry land, it did so from an ocean that was much less salty than today's. Our tears are the taste of the long-gone sea that birthed us, our original Mother.

Our foremothers revered the Moon, and this too has carried forward. For the Celt, time was counted in nights, and we still have 'fortnights'. And what is a month if not a 'moonth'?

For our ancestors, as they picked and foraged their way along the shoreline, three things must have seemed so closely related that, taken together, they formed a statement so powerful that it is still with us: the monthly cycle of the moon, the monthly cycle of the tide, and the monthly cycles of women were all related, and that could only mean one thing: god was a woman, and women were of her.

For our ancestors, human women were possessed of the goddess' powers, since they alone could make life. So the sea, and rivers, became sacred to us, because we knew that within their bodies, women used a magical water to make babies, water which flowed out of them when they brought life forth.

When we moved inland, following the rivers, to the interior of continents, we lost touch with the sea – though how long our reverence for her persisted is clear in the Sumerian and following mythologies, other myths from all over the world, and even into the Bible.

Then the land became our Mother, and again we revered her as the Earth, the Sumerian Ki, or Ninhursag. She brought us her riches and we were grateful. First these were the herds of wild fauna and the fruits and vegetables that we lived on, and later the riches were from agriculture, which gave us civilisation. Rivers were her amniotic fluid, and to bathe in them was literally to be reborn in the grace of the Mother – as happens today, and every other day, to the millions each year who make pilgrimage and immerse themselves in Mother Ganges, as once I did, too, long ago.

We are used, perhaps, to the idea that the Ganges is sacred to the Hindus, but perhaps less aware that in Europe, the Celts believed the same, and every river was sacred to them, a manifestation of the Goddess herself; this is a belief that is found all over the world.

Perhaps my Christian friends should remember what they are actually doing, as they splash the holy water on their babies' brows, or allow themselves to be plunged under water and 'reborn'. From no male sky-god does that water come, either literally or metaphorically, because it is of the Earth, and it is of the Mother. To be baptised is to be reborn from the Mother, doused in her amniotic fluid.

I don't have a problem with any of this. I know I am of the Earth and that it (perhaps one shouldn't personalise her too much) is incredibly greater than I am. I don't believe she has supernatural powers, but the fact is that the natural ones she certainly does have are utterly dumbfounding.

I know I came from her, and I know that to her I will return and this does not in any way fill me with dread, for I am absolutely certain that there is neither punishment nor reward after death, only an eternal sleep as dreamless as the one I slept before I was born. She is the Mother, the Living Spaceship, carrying us on her back as she hurtles along at mind-numbing speed. Everything about her strikes me mute with sheer, unmitigated awe.

So yes, I am part of something greater, and I wouldn't have it any other way.

Travel

1. Boracay, A Hidden Tropical Paradise

The beach at Boracay.

Boracay is a bouquet of impressions. Triangular sails silhouetted against the sunset, tropical forest all around, an avenue of palms along the beach.

Pure white sand, clear, unpolluted tropical water, adventure excursions, fun night-life and a laid-back atmosphere – not to mention exotic dancing girls. All this at prices that remain reasonable. Does this appeal? Well, instead of Phuket or Bali, consider a trip to Boracay instead.

Boracay (pronounced bor-AH-cay) is an island in the Western Visayas region of the Philippines. It's a popular resort amongst Filipinos and other Asians. It has an amazing beach, lots of eco-tourism and adventure sport, and great night-life. However it is relatively unknown by Western tourists, and remains fairly unspoiled and friendly. Plus, for Brits and other Anglophones, English is almost universally understood and very widely spoken, as it is throughout the Philippines.

Getting There

There are two practical routes to Boracay, whether you're going direct from Manila or visiting Cebu, the capital of the Visayas region, first. The simplest and cheapest is to fly to Kalibo on the island of Panay.

Kalibo Airport is just over one hour's flying time from Manila's

Ninoy Aquino International Airport (NAIA), and there are flights from Cebu, which also has international flight connections. There are several domestic budget carriers, including Zest, Cebu Pacific and Air Philippines.

From Kalibo, take an air-conditioned minibus to Caticlan-Tabon Boat Terminal. This trip takes about two hours. From the terminal, take a motor-trimaran or banca to Boracay Island itself, a voyage of around twenty minutes. Once on the island, there are few taxis, so take either a tricycle, which is a motorcycle and side-car with a roof, or a 'bus' (really a pickup truck with seats) to your hotel. If you have booked through an agent or telephoned the hotel to say you've arrived, they should send a courtesy vehicle.

The alternative is to fly to the small airport at Caticlan itself, and take the ferry to Boracay as above. However, these services are far less frequent and much more expensive than those to Kalibo.

The Resort

The main resort at Boracay stretches along about one mile of beach, from Station One in the north to Station Three in the south. The deluxe hotels are mainly in Station One, with midrange and budget accommodation elsewhere. The resort is on the western side of a narrow isthmus in the centre of the island, with the town stretched along inland in typical resort strip-development style

The Beach

Once there, the first place to hit is the beach, to unwind from the travelling. This is one of the finest anywhere, pure white sand gently sloping into crystal blue water. Even at the height of the season, however, the crowds are numbered in the hundreds, not thousands, and the convoluted journey there suddenly seems like a real plus point.

An avenue of palms separates Boracay beach from the buildings, but there is no traffic along the narrow road, pedestrians only. In fact nearly all of the resort is free of wheeled vehicles, which really makes the place seem relaxed, compared to other resorts where the endless bustle

of cars and motorcycles is an ever-present source of noise and stress. In Boracay, life is at the human pace.

The beach itself is off-limits to the vendors and the smiling armed security men (a common feature everywhere in the Philippines) ensure that they stay on the road.

As soon as you set foot on the beach you can feel the relaxation taking over. Boracay really is a tropical paradise, and as you survey the scene, the glorious white sand beach, the crystal blue-green sea, the waving lines of beach-front palms and the blue hills in the distance, the traditional outrigger boats with their colourful triangular sails, this truth is inescapable.

Beach-front bars provide luxurious recliners and umbrellas on the beach itself and most don't charge, though it is polite to buy a drink or two. Towel hire for the day is about eighty pence. Why not treat yourself or your loved one to a manicure and pedicure, for about £5, or a massage, for about the same? Waiters, smiling hugely, circulate around the recliners. There's no surcharge for drinks or food on the beach. In a nice touch, the beach itself is a strict no-smoking/no-litter zone.

Shopping

In Station Two there's an open-air shopping area called D'Mall, with lots of small cantina-style restaurants serving traditional Filipino cuisine, as well as the ubiquitous Jollibee fast-food outlet. Prices are reasonable, with a main course, soft drink and dessert ranging from £2.00 to £3.00 each. These places are clean and the food is good. Most offer 'unli' or unlimited rice, so you can eat as much as you like. Further along in Station Three the restaurants are a little more upmarket, though still good value, and in Station One there are European and international-style restaurants with prices to match.

D'Mall has a forest of small boutiques selling shoes, clothes and accessories, beach and swimming equipment, and has several ATM machines. The police station is also located here. Boutique prices are fair but compare to Manila malls.

If you want cheaper, then walk back away from the beach to the main road that leads through Boracay town, which is full of more traditional Filipino shops and restaurants.

My travelling companion, after a quick check of the competition, decided that she couldn't possibly be seen on the beach in the bikini she'd brought, so I duly traipsed around the beachwear shops with her. In one, while she disappeared into a changing-booth with a few minute scraps of material, a gaggle of young Koreans arrived and did the same.

Moments later I was surrounded by a half dozen girls, all wearing about six square inches of cloth and comparing each other's choices, while completely ignoring me as I intently studied the ceiling. I was rescued when my friend asked me to give my opinion on hers.

Vendors work the beach road and will try to pressure-sell, but Filipinos are amongst the most laid-back of Asians. Many sell jewellery, much of it made from pearl. The prices are attractive but if you're tempted, make sure the pearls are genuine by gently biting them – fake pearls usually slip on the teeth. (All the ones I tried passed the test.) Others sell everything from sunglasses to sun-hats to flip-flops to cigarettes and soft drinks.

Activities

If just lying on a tropical beach while being pampered and occasionally immersing yourself in comfortably warm water gets too monotonous, Boracay offers plenty of other activities. Parasailing is the most thrilling, as you are flown up into the air suspended from a kite towed by a speed-boat. There are organised diving trips to suit all abilities, and dive-equipment hire for those with the proper certificates. Island-hopping day trips begin at £15 with lunch included. There is horse-riding and a even a pro-designed golf resort.

Traditional Philippines sailing boats called paraw are available for hire, with crew, from £25 per day. These will take four passengers upwards, and it's a very relaxed way to visit local scenic highlights like Crocodile Island, Puka Shell Beach, Panoly Beach and Crystal Cove. Alternatively, if you fancy a shorter sail, there are plenty of paraws working along the beach, with prices from £8 per person for an hour.

Nightlife

In many ways, though, apart from the magnificent beach, what makes Boracay great is the night-life. As the early tropical evening falls, the strip along the beach transforms into a neon palm-tree wonderland and the beach-front bars begin to fill up.

Filipino beers cost around £1.30 for a 330ml bottle. American and some European beers are also available, but I highly recommend Red Horse, made by the San Miguel brewery (you didn't know San Mig was Filipino?).

Simple cocktails start around £2.50, but many bars do a two-for-one deal on the first drink and, instead of wasting time with a second glass, they just make it a double, so if you're cruising from bar to bar, you may end up more tipsy than planned. There are even organised pub crawls, which set off around 8pm from various points along the beach road. Just look for the crowd and follow it.

Don't miss the spectacular fire-dancers, who gyrate energetically while spinning flaming torches, often grabbing members of the audience and turning them into a bemused part of the show. But it's all done with good humour. This is the Philippines and if there's one thing they know about here, it's having fun.

Sitting in Sand Bar, a marquee permanently pitched on the beach, I watch as a girl is led from her seat and one of the dancers, grinning, comes close behind her, swinging fire-torches within inches of her face.

The girl's eyes widen and her mouth gapes in horror, while her friends roar with laughter and throw 100-peso notes into the bucket another dancer is carrying.

Ladyboy firedancer at Sand Bar.

After a short while, though, I realise that there is something unusual about the female dancers. It turns out they're ladyboys, young transsexuals. I chatted to one, Maria, the attractive, curvy brunette in her mid-twenties who had just terrified the girl. Speaking in excellent English, (although with a noticeably husky voice,) she explained that several dance troupes like hers worked the bars along the beach, doing a forty-five minute show in each.

"There's so much prejudice against us, even in a place like this, it's hard to get regular jobs. But we dance for tips and make more than the bar staff." She shrugs. "The tourists love it, so the owners are happy."

A member of the audience becomes part of the show.

Sharing the take with the others in her troupe, Maria, a native of Boracay, makes £15 or more a night. That's enough for her to rent a nice room and have a comfortable life. She slips my 300 pesos (£5) contribution into her dress top beside the neat fan of notes already there, and grins cheerfully before heading back to work.

Three cocktails each for myself and my companion, and a plate of sisig (spicy fried minced pork) to share, at Sand Bar, came to 900 pesos, or £15. Add in tips for the dancers and it was still a great evening's entertainment for very little expense.

By the way, tipping is not mandatory anywhere in the Philippines. Tip if you think the service was worth it, or when the recipient has no other means of payment, like the dancers.

There's music everywhere along the beach, with plenty of live bands both in the more conventional bars and set up under the palm trees. It's all free, but once again, tips are appreciated.

Filipinos are famously talented musicians and, apparently, can turn their hands to any style. In just a few minutes' walk, I heard reggae, rock, jazz, soul. (The one modern style I didn't hear was country, for which I am extremely grateful.) Everywhere is the same: great music, nice atmosphere, and while it's certainly busy, it's not uncomfortably crowded. Most of the tourists, probably 75%, are Asians, either Filipinos on a short break or Chinese, Japanese or Koreans here for a longer stay; everyone is incredibly polite.

Maria.

Commercialism is inevitable in a successful resort, and here it is definitely more noticeable than on other Philippine resort islands, like Palawan. Compared to Phuket or Pattaya in Thailand, or any southern European resort, though, it is relaxed, low-pressure and chilled. There's plenty of opportunity to spend money, but I never felt I had to. Even the street-vendors were relaxed, which is unusual.

The Flip-Side

It's not all up-side though. For families with younger children, there's very little to do on Boracay. There are no lifeguards on the beach and dedicated child-friendly facilities are restricted to those you can find at the hotels. In any case, just getting there would be a harrowing journey for them. For older, less active people, there's also little provision, other than the golf resort, and even getting about may pose problems, since the beach road is just sand.

Sunset at Boracay Beach.

A Fantastic Place for Couples

However, Boracay is great for anyone teenage and up who likes to mix beach life with active fun during the day and plenty of lively entertainment at night. It's a fantastic place for couples, singles or families whose kids are a little older and can appreciate the adventure. Plus the beach itself is unquestionably one of the most beautiful in Asia, which means the world. It feels very safe and I saw no drunkenness or bad behaviour.

Given the quality of the natural attractions and the wide range of activities and excursions available, coupled with the vibrant night-life, and the good peso exchange rate, Boracay is not only a great destination but a relatively cheap one.

Typical Boracay Accommodation Prices:

Boracay is an established and popular resort, so prices are in general a little higher than other Philippines provincial destinations.

Budget hostel:

from £10/ per person per night. Very basic level of accommodation, shared dorm and bathroom. Suitable only for backpackers.

Midrange:

From £25/per room per night: Fan cooled double room with en-suite. Breakfast usually not included, wifi and other facilities may be available. These can be very nice but in hotter seasons may be uncomfortable.

From £35/night upwards: double room with en-suite, wifi, air-conditioned, usually with breakfast. Up to two children can often stay at no extra cost as long as they don't use extra bedding, but a breakfast surcharge will be applied. There will usually be a swimming pool and restaurant.

Deluxe:

Up to £400 and more. The full range of facilities expected from top-quality international-standard luxury hotels is available. Bear in mind that internet booking agencies mark up prices, so it may be worth contacting the hotel direct.

Money:

There are ATM cash dispensers in D'Mall that will take either Visa or MasterCard. Using these is probably the most convenient way to get spending money. But be aware that they sometimes run out of cash!

However, remember that your bank may charge for ATM withdrawals, and so may the local bank. Further, you're limited in how much you can take per day, so you can't just take out a lot in one go to save fees (which in itself is hardly secure.) It makes sense to actually pay for larger purchases with the card rather than to draw cash to use for shopping.

There is still a lot to be said for traveller's cheques in the currency you will be using. Firstly, there is protection built in and they should be replaced quickly if stolen. As well as this, having a specific amount is a handy brake on the temptation to hit the ATM every time the funds go down, without realising how much you're spending! If you use a good currency-exchange tracker like xe.com, then you can arrange to buy when the exchange rate is in your favour. One commission only is paid.

The alternative is to take cash either in your local currency and change in the Philippines, or in pesos bought at home. This will probably give you a small margin on the ATM exchange rate and as with traveller's cheques, you can buy your pesos when the exchange rate gives you the best value. However, carrying large amounts of cash is never a good idea, so I suggest keeping it in the hotel safe.

http://www.boracayonline.com/

2. Philippines Diary: Jeepneys

Jeepneys at Waterfun, Taguig.

Most people have at least heard about jeepneys, the ubiquitous, colourful and incredibly noisy backbone of the Philippines public transport system. For those who have not, you'll catch up.

The first jeepneys were in fact modified Willys Jeeps that the Americans left behind. The enterprising pinoys lengthened the chassis and fitted seats. Now they are custom built with stainless steel, all-enclosed bodywork and diesel engines.

Most jeepneys are 20-seaters; 18 in the back and 2 in the front, guv. This makes them unquestionably the friendliest form on transport on the planet, because actually there's only enough room for 16 in the back and we are talking kitten-hipped pinoys here.

This ensures fairly intimate physical contact as you are wedged in between people on either side. The conductors – called 'barkers' – will make sure you're wedged in too, banging on the outside and telling the passengers to squeeze up. Entry to the main passenger 'cabin' is through the rear, but there are two seats up front by the driver. These are not any more spacious, but the view is better.

(I have only once had a conductor look me in the eye and say 'You're too big.' I laughed it off as a matter of principle. If you're one of those colossal USican things, best get a cab.)

The next thing to be aware of is that there is only about 1.5 metres of headroom, so if you're much over six feet, you will bang your head off the roof even when seated. For everyone, the low height means entering and leaving the jeep in a crouched position, of which more later.

Once wedged in between your new friends-for-life…well, at least for the next few minutes of it anyway…comes the small matter of fares. These range from a low of four pesos to a maximum of sixteen, in Manila. In rural areas, where the rides are much longer, they can be up to 50 pesos.

If you board at a terminus, a conductor will either take the fare as you enter or he'll come onto the jeepney to collect it. (I have only once seen a woman doing this job.)

If you board en route, however, things are slightly different. Etiquette demands that you call out 'Bayat po,' to the driver before handing him the fare. This he will take while driving and sort out your change and return it, also while driving. It's quite a feat. Unless you tell him otherwise he will assume you want to go to the terminus, so if you don't, say so. This also means he'll stop to let you off at the right place. Since otherwise you won't have a clue when to get off, this amounts to Good Thinking.

Now the observant among you will probably already have picked up on a problem: what happens if you are not sitting right behind the driver?

You're wedged in, right, and negotiating a forest of knees crouched into a hunch while rattling along in this, let's be honest, fairly basic machine would be impractical anyway. (At least if you lose balance you won't fall far.)

Well, there is a system. You call out 'Bayat, po' just as if you were sitting behind the driver and wave the fare in his direction. One of the other passengers will take it and pass it forward till it reaches the driver. In exactly like manner, your change, if there is any, will be returned to you. Naturally etiquette demands that you participate, so when someone thrusts money at you, pass it in the appropriate direction. It should be obvious enough.

Now all this is very well, but how do you decide which jeepney to get on in the first place? Well, they all ply defined routes for which they are licensed by the relevant city authority. The route will be painted on the side of the jeep itself…so, not obvious at night or when one is coming towards you. However in the windscreen there will be a small destination board with the terminus the jeep is heading for on it. These are only about 20cm x 8cm, so you'll need sharp eyes and at night, a sixth sense. Best to ask if unsure.

Hailing jeepneys is easy, just wave your arm at an approaching one. If it has vacant seats, the driver will stop, if it doesn't, tough. There will be another along soon.

To get the driver to stop and let you off, the standard method is to tap one of the stainless steel overhead rails with a coin. Sometimes there is a pull-cord by the handrails which will flash a light in front of the driver, and if all else fails, shout 'Para, po' and he should get the message. There are no real jeepney stops, the driver will just pull up as quickly as he can.

If you are unsure of where to get off, it's sometimes better to ask a fellow-passenger, because jeepney pilots usually have limited English. This is fine, since Pilipino hospitality demands that you, a guest, should be properly looked after. I have even known locals to pay my fare and then alight with me, point me in the right direction and hop on the next jeep to continue their journey.

Getting off a jeepney is almost as entertaining as getting squeezed into the seat, especially at a terminus where everyone else gets off too. Here, you will leave in crouched stance, following the crowd in single file.

This means that your face will be around a foot away from the person in front's bottom. Depending on your preference, choose to enter the line after a boy or a girl…

I told you it was a friendly form of transport.

3. Arayat Escapade

Mount Arayat at sunrise.

A couple of weeks ago I went to Mount Arayat National Park in Pampanga, here in the Philippines.

I'd been invited by some friends to spend the day, with a walk in the mountain park in the morning followed by socialising later. This meant first taking a bus to San Fernando and then another, local bus. We wanted to be there for sunrise, which is why I found myself sitting in a taxi at 3.30 am, hurtling through Quezon City at speeds in excess of 100 kph. It was a good adrenaline rush to start the day.

I took a Victory Liner coach from Cubao. Many of the coach lines have terminuses there, and the other that serves Pampanga is Genesis. (Yes, the Biblical one; this is the Phils.) The fare to San Fernando is 102 pesos. You can pay on the bus but during office hours there's a ticket office which they prefer you to use. You can also get refreshments in the terminus.

As ever, food and drinks vendors boarded the coach to ply their wares before we set off. The journey time to San Fernando is roughly an hour, depending on traffic, following the North Luzon Expressway (NLEX). Be sure not to get off at the first stop in San Fernando, wait till you get to 'interchange'.

Azumi.

I was to meet my friend Azumi Ballesteros and some others for the morning walk, but in the end only Azumi and another girl called Chin showed up. Two others had said they would come but hadn't, and this had clearly annoyed Azumi; she has a sparkly nature, quick to anger but as quick to forgive.

After exchanging greetings we boarded another bus, which took us close to the Park entrance. Then, in true Pilipino style, we boarded a trisikel (a motorcycle and sidecar) for the last part of the journey.

Unfortunately, Azumi hadn't checked the opening time of the park, which was 6 am, and we arrived at 5.30. No matter, the security rustled up some chairs in front of a television to divert us while we waited, and even made us hot drinks. I think mine was tea, but I'm not sure; as ever the main thing I tasted was sugar. It's one of the charms of this country, though; everybody shares, even if they have a sweet tooth that would make a Westerner's eyes water.

At six the official ticket-seller arrived and we began our walk up the hill. The first part is a steep and very uneven staircase called the Hundred Steps. It's far more tiring than it should be, because of the difference in the heights between the steps; fortunately there's a good handrail which

Pic Rod Fleming

allows the less than super fit (eg me) to haul themselves up. I noticed that Azumi and Chin had no problems though. Ah, youth.

After the Hundred Steps, the trail debouches (love that word) onto a metalled road for half a mile or so, and then becomes a rough trail through the forest again.

The Philippines jungle is actually a delight to walk in. There are very few nasty insects, unlike jungles elsewhere, to bite and make life misery for the walker, and even the flies are not numerous. I don't know why this is, but Philippine jungles feel fresh and healthy, even when the temperature climbs.

But one always has that sensation, as in any jungle, of being watched by myriad hidden eyes. I imagined how soldiers must have felt – and still feel – campaigning through country like this. I thought I was being watched by hundreds of shy animals, but the eyes could easily have been those of a predator or a hostile enemy. To patrol in country like this would be nerve-wracking. I grew up during the period of the Vietnam War but it was only much later, when I began to visit jungles, that I realised what that must have been like and why it was so traumatising for the US soldiers.

Chin relaxing.

We were chatting about this as we walked and Azumi agreed.

'My friend told me it's really dangerous here.'

'Is it? Why?'

'There are NPA (New People's Army) hiding in the forest,' she replied, with her characteristic lisp. Involuntarily I looked around.

The NPA, or in Filipino, Bagong Hukbong Bayan, are the armed wing of the Philippines Communist Party. They appeared in the late 1960s and during the Marcos era their ranks were swollen by young people disaffected by the dictator's brutal regime. Ever since they have been responsible for a trickle of killings, kidnappings and other banditry. I am aware that, as a European, I am a target that they might consider to be worth cash money; the fact that nobody would pay it would mean I would disappear.

While I shrug off Azumi's worries, it's true that you could hide

hundreds of armed guerrillas in this jungle and not only would nobody ever know, they also would be completely self-sufficient. The jungle is literally a larder. There is fruit hanging from the trees to pick and vegetables grow everywhere. The wildlife is rich and while we, as noisy townies, see only birds, there is certainly an abundance of game.

I confirm this in discussion – Azumi translating – with one of the park wardens, who double as guides. He has stopped us to ask where we intend to go and suggests a viewpoint a few hundred metres higher up. I mention the NPA and he nods. 'Maybe. You must be careful and stay on the path.' I personally can't see how this would make me less likely to be kidnapped, but I let it pass.

I point to the densely-forested peak of Mount Arayat itself, looming above us. He makes a face. 'It's four to six hours up there and back. And you can't go alone, you need a guide. We can sort that for tomorrow, but I'm booked today.'

As well as the NPA, it turns out, whose presence the warden is being coy about, a more mundane danger exists. The path is not well marked and the unwary can wander off it and get completely lost. He explains that recently a party of Germans did just that and it took six hours of search the next day to locate them.

'They were out in the jungle all night,' explains the warden. 'Now we don't let people go up without a guide.' I can see that Azumi is quite satisfied with this answer, although I'm not quite. Being a nosey journalist.

Why so dangerous in the dark? I suppose there are animals but there are no large predators; the most dangerous terrestrial fauna here are snakes and I remain unconvinced about the NPA. I think the real issue lies in the Filipino's terror of the dark. I have encountered this before.

Filipinos are deeply superstitious and believe in a range of truly nightmarish supernatural beings that populate the night. These are not casual beliefs in the way that some people think it's unlucky to walk under ladders or go anti-clockwise round churches. These are real, visceral beliefs in a spirit world that is not only immediately present, but a genuine threat to humans. These spirits, which range from the kapre, a dark-skinned, cigar-smoking, but usually harmless man[1] who sits up trees watching people, through the engkanto, and to the truly horrific aswang, a genus of ghouls that feed on people, only appear at night.

I am pretty sure this is the real reason the warden is so emphatic that it is dangerous to be out in the jungle in darkness; compared to the monsters of the mind that infest the darkened jungle, the NPA are small beer.

Research into these fascinating ideas, which I'll go into another time, throws light on the Philippines' history. Although the originals of the demons existed long before the Spanish came, these colonial overlords used them to terrify the people out of living in the forest and come to live in the towns where they could be better controlled. They slaughtered natives – who may or may not have been campaigning against them – mutilated the bodies and put them on display, claiming that it was the work of the aswang and other creatures of the night.

This, apparently, worked and to this day Filipinos are extremely nervous about being in the forest after dark.

The friendly warden led us a little further up the path and pointed out the viewpoint, then struck off on another trail. Despite the terrors of the night and the poor pay, this was a man with a great job, I reflected.

Azumi, Chin and I reached the viewpoint at around 11, by which time the day was heating up. The most prominent feature was a massive rock, black basalt, which must have been blown out by Arayat when it last erupted. Looking around I could see dozens of other, similar rocks. The destruction wrought by these must have been enormous. This individual rock must have weighed 300 tonnes or so; the power needed to blast it up into the air from the crater itself, at least two miles away, is truly humbling. Mother Earth is not just the nurturing goddess that brings life, but the Dark Goddess of death and destruction. To the Sumerian she was Ereshkigal, to the modern Hindu Kali; but she has always been with us, her body the dread portal into death. Arayat, thankfully dormant for now, is where she spews her vengeful anger.

(Arayat is considered to be the home of goddess Mariang Sinucuan, the archrival of Namalyari of Mount Pinatubo.)

1 It is widely believed that a tree at the entrance to Malacañan Palace, the Philippines President's official residence, is inhabited by a kapre, whose role here seems to be of supernatural protector.

At the rock we sat and some sticky sweet rice cakes, called malagket, which Azumi had brought. I can attest to the sugar content of these and confess I couldn't eat all of mine, while the girls munched away happily.

Azumi and I climbed to the top of the basalt. The view was magnificent, even though it was a little limited by the heat haze. I could see Olongapo to the southwest, and, closer but still distant, San Fernando. Azumi pointed out other towns.

After a relaxing break we set off down the path again. It was very broken and obviously, in times of rain, serves as a temporary river. I had noticed, on the way up, large deposits of manure that looks like they originated in something that was not quite a cow and neither a horse, and to my delight we discovered the source: a carabao. This is a kind of buffalo, and here it was being used by the licensed charcoal-burners who exploited the fallen wood to transport their produce back down the mountain.

We watched as one, a female, was hitched into a cart. She seemed very placid and later we discovered more wandering loose. Nobody seemed to bother.

As we reached the lower levels we became aware of the heat; on the slopes the breeze had kept us cool, but here the trees were much bigger and sheltered us from it. There were many more people around by now and, as usual, everyone greeted us politely.

Once down near the entrance once more we stopped at one of the 'cottages' under the trees and the girls set out lunch – barbecued fish, meat and salad. I took a few pictures and we headed off to get a bus back to San Fernando.

4. Manila: Skinny Cats, Transports of Delight and Beautiful Women

Jeepney and taxi in Manila.

Apart from Manila itself, the conurbation of Metro Manila includes other cities that would themselves be enormous by any other measure: Makati, Pasig, Quezon, Cavite, and others. So transport is a major part of Manila life. But this is Asia and, unlike Europe, there is no organised public transport. There are no service buses, no trams or metro systems organised by local government. Everything is run privately, and the sheer amount of private transport provision is staggering.

Given that I have not yet see anyone carrying a passenger on his shoulders, and horse-and-cart solutions are reserved for the tourist area of Intramuros, the old part of Manila, the most basic, though not always the cheapest, means of transport is the gloriously named 'pedicab'. This is a bicycle with a side-car.

The main problem with this solution, leaving aside the thorny moral issue of whether it can be right for a 14-stone Scotsman and an admittedly much lighter Filipina to be push-biked around by a sweating 9-stone Pinoy, is the complete lack of suspension on these contraptions. Since the roads in Manila resemble the Somme after a barrage, this means a bone-jarring ride that risks lumbar impaction.

Still on three wheels, the next step up in luxury is the *trisikel*. This is a motorcycle and side-car, which at least does have springs and shock absorbers. However, the presence of the engine, usually no larger than 125cc, spurs the intrepid pilots to extreme feats of passenger carrying.

In Manila, where the tricycle side-cars don't have rigid roofs, I have still seen six people aboard one, and in the provinces, where they do have such roofs, ten. (How do you get ten people in a tricycle? Easy. Four in the side-car, two behind the driver and four on the roof.)

I imagine that clutch replacement is a routine maintenance task on these machines. However, the basic nature of the transport does not necessarily mean that it is cheaper. Tricycles don't have meters and it is wise to negotiate a price for the trip in advance, and to know what a taxi would charge, or you may find yourself paying as much for a cramped bone-shaker on a wooden seat as for a pleasant air-conditioned cab ride.

Moving from three to four wheels, the next transport of delight is the world-famous jeepney. These very distinctive vehicles look like overgrown jeeps with passenger cabs. Fares are cheap but since each jeepney travels a particular route that is marked on a board (which may or may not be legible) using the service is fraught unless you have a good knowledge of the geography.

On board a jeepney.

Jeepneys come in a rainbow array of colours, liveries and decorations. The all seem to have names and are a genuine example of folk art, rich and diverse. The one thing that every jeepney I have seen has in common with its kin is that the tyres are as bald as William Hague, as smooth as racing slicks, even down to the spares. The saving grace, if there is one, is that traffic in Manila moves so slowly there is little risk of aquaplaning even in a downpour.

Related to the jeepney are vans, usually Toyota minibuses with air-conditioning and actual glass in the windows, and the fabulous FX, which is a large SUV with, usually, 8 seats. These are also pretty well priced.

However the most convenient, comfortable and consistently reliable ride is the taxi, and fares are reasonable. A 45 minute journey from Ermita in Manila to Pasig City costs 450 pesos, or about £7.50, and most in-town rides are around 100 php or £1.50.

By the way, if you are flying in for the first time to Ninoy Aquino, Manila's airport, make sure you get a taxi chit from the security guards at the exit. This will give you a taxi ride into town for 500 pesos; without one, it will be 850.

Once arrived in Manila, other things will slowly become clear. Everyone speaks at least basic English; but often it is more basic than you might think, due to the Filipino's natural enthusiasm and eagerness to help. It is easy to become mired in a hopelessly lost conversation where your interlocutor is talking about something completely different from you, and there is no way to get things back on track, at least without being rude. This is Asia and loss of face is not something people enjoy.

There is a distinctly, and somewhat unnervingly, European flavour to everything, though this is very much Asia, baby. This is due to the long Spanish colonisation. Filipinos even sound Spanish when they are speaking in English, and Tagalog, the main native tongue, has borrowed heavily from it. But don't be fooled: this European veneer is on a powerful and vibrant Asian culture, and you don't have to scratch deep to find the truth.

In India, it's rats, here it's cats. And the cats are incredibly skinny. They're everywhere, and every bin and refuse dump is crawling with them. I guess it keeps the rats down anyway…these cats look like they've been starving for months. They behave like the well-fed cats Europeans are used to, but beware: rabies is endemic in the Philippines and cats are a vector. Do not be tempted to pet them. In any case, the locals won't like it; they view them as pests. Filipinos love their pets, but there is clearly little charity for stray felines.

And then there's the women. Whatever mixture of genes caused it, for the Philippines has known several eras of colonisation, the girls here are frankly drop-dead gorgeous. Not tall, but very beautiful. And they can be forward too. On my last visit, I was waiting for a plane at Puerto Princesa with my companion and went to buy drinks. The girl serving at the counter, who was about 21, came out and began flirting very insistently, even though she must have seen that I was with someone.

Her older colleague just shook her head at the younger woman's brazen behaviour and said, "She wants a friend," to which I replied, "Sorry, taken," and hurried back to the relative safety of my seat before temptation, for the girl was, of course, stunning, led me to places I should not go.

This is certainly not an isolated occurrence. Young Filipinas like older Western guys, and routinely flirt. The fact that they are in themselves a standard of beauty, with their mixture of Hispanic and Asian blood, just makes this all the more thrilling. Filipinos of both genders are genuinely charming, open, nice people and they have remarkably few sexual inhibitions, especially given the power of the Catholic Church here. I am not suggesting that Filipinas are loose – they are not – but they are not shy either, and will happily smile and chat with a stranger. It does make for a pleasant stay.

A devastatingly cute Pinay. They're everywhere.

5. The Goddess in The Philippines

The Goddess is a big deal in the Philippines and goddesses are out in strength there this week. The occasion is the closing rounds of the Universities Athletic Association of the Philippines (UAAP) women's volleyball tournament, held at Smart Araneta Coliseum in Quezon City.

Teams with names like De La Salle Lady Spikers and Ateneo de Manila Lady Eagles, the Tigresses, the Lady Warriors and the Lady Bulldogs battle it out in front of huge, enthusiastic and thoroughly partisan crowds. And these girls aren't kidding; this is serious stuff.

The audience is mainly young – but everywhere in the Phils is mainly young. That's only to be expected in a country where the population has increased by a factor of ten in fifty years. And there are as many men here as women. Filipinos are as passionate about volleyball as Scots are about football.

This is hard sport and women are seen as true warriors. It's a quality of the Philippines that is so often forgotten. It doesn't matter where you go here, strong, self-assured women are everywhere. Men, when you do see them, seem to be mainly the ubiquitous armed security men, taxi-drivers, tricycle-drivers, manual workers. Everywhere else, the face of the Philippines is a smiling woman with sparkling teeth.

Women here are completely unashamed of their sexuality and physical beauty and flaunt them all the time. They are fully aware of their sexual power and unafraid of it. There is no sense here that women should be hidden away, as if their sexuality would corrupt.

However there is no doubt who chooses the partner here; it's the woman. Listening to any phone-in chat show quickly confirms this. Her sexual favours are hers to dispense and, in a culture that, despite its profound Roman Catholicism, increasingly affords women control over their own reproduction, their independence is clear. It is the men here who seem shy, bashful even, at least when in the company of women.

Oh, Pinoy men are extremely friendly and love to party. You come across a bunch of guys and they'll pull out a chair for you and four hours later, through a haze of Red Horse, you discover that these are your long-forgotten best buddies, an integral part of your life.

But if there's a woman in the crowd, it's different. They'll shut up and let her invite you to sit. I had a fascinating illustration of this one afternoon in Laoag as I waited for a tricycle to take me into town. It was hot and there wasn't much shade; my companion, perhaps wisely, had decided to take a siesta. A group of the hotel staff were sitting outside around a table, three men and one woman; like most Pinays she was tiny. Yet it was she who came over, insisted that I moved into the shade and fetched me some water. This was not subservience or some bizarre deference to a white Westerner, but because this was her space. Just by being there, she adopted it. The men were deferring to her, and obviously, courtesy demands that a stranger not be left standing in the afternoon heat.

I found this fascinating and began to look out for it…and the evidence was everywhere. On a jeepney, the driver of which is, as usual, a man, I am confused by the fare. There are men on the jeepney, but it is a woman who sees that I wish to ask something, and immediately takes control of the situation.

'Hello sir,' she says, a silence begging the question. 'How much to Robinson's?' Without batting an eyelid, the woman, who is perhaps forty, replies, '16 pesos, sir.' I count out the coins into her outstretched hand and she checks it, and passes it to the driver, accompanied by a flurry of Tagalog. He nods and drives. 'He will stop for you sir,' says the woman, reading my mind. She gets off two stops later, but sure enough, at the Robinson's Mall, the driver says 'tsup tsup' and pulls over to let me off.

This is normal. Pinay women are assertive and strong, sexually confident, often with a high standard of education – 60% of graduates are women – who quietly but firmly arrange the space around them. Combine this with a religion that puts the Goddess right at its heart, and the result is clear. If there is a modern, city-based culture where the Goddess walks, this is it.

I have many friends in the Philippines and a good few are on my Facebook contact list. Frequently they make some religious reference, and I usually check it out. One led me to a site where a well-known preacher was berating the people, saying that their form of Marianist Catholicism was what had brought successive natural disasters upon the Philippines. It made me think. Despite the obvious shortcomings of the logic, I could see what he was getting at. This is Goddess worship; there's no place I know of where Inanna, Isis and the baby Horus are more deeply revered. Okay, so they changed their names but that means little. Archetypes, after all, are archetypes.

In addition, despite the in-your-face prevalence of Roman Catholicism, the huge number of churches, the Jesus and Mary posters everywhere, the figurines and the Biblical texts, there is another cultural source that must not be ignored. The Philippines is in southeast Asia, and underlying the apparently Westernised, Christian worship is a strong and deep-rooted animism.

Animism is usually described simply as the belief that everything has a spirit that gives it life. This is only a partial truth, however. The basis of animism is Goddess worship. The Goddess is the Earth, and the trees, the rocks, the rivers, and the spirits that live within them are also part of the Earth, and of the Goddess. The Philippines has an extremely well developed mythology of fantastic creatures which emanate from the Goddess and haunt the night. The night, of course, is the time of the Goddess, and here walk the Aswang, the terrifying, shape-changing and bloodsucking beasts of Philippine folklore.

Of course, we can see immediate parallels in the cultures of southern Europe, and in the West, in Ireland, Scotland and elsewhere; what is Nessie but an Aswang with a Scottish accent? Yet in the West these things are increasingly fairy-tales rather than folklore, and very few people except in the most remote areas actually fear shape-shifters today.

Not so in the Philippines; while sophisticated Manila-dwellers sometimes turn their noses up at such rural beliefs, they are quickly caught in the lie. I live in a 16th century fortified town house with a spiral staircase and watch-tower complete with gun-ports. Every single

Filipino I have known well enough to describe it to, has, at some point in the conversation, earnestly asked, 'Don't you have any ghosts there? Are you sure?' They're not kidding. These spirits frighten them – and so they should, for they are terrifying.

The 'chthonic swamp' of the Goddess, as Camille Paglia put it, is very close here. Outside of the major cities, it's even more so, of course. The Philippines' population may have mushroomed over the last half-century, but it is still a huge land area and vast tracts of virgin jungle still exist. And jungle is very much the home of the Goddess and her spirits, both fair and foul.

Taming the Goddess, it might reasonably be argued, is what civilisation is all about. One way that this is done is to incorporate her into a broader pantheon, and that is exactly what Catholicism does. Inanna is everywhere in the beautiful and sexually confident young women, who never shy from a stranger's gaze and who are so direct and forthcoming.; but she is also Mary.

If a Pinay girl likes you, she will let you know. If she has to do business with you, she is polite and formal and absolutely not deferential. Isis is in all the mothers, the venerated ones. And she is mirrored in the faith: 'Mama Mary pray for me' is a mantra. The first point of contact isn't Jesus or God but Mary, the Queen of Heaven, a title borne by both Inanna and Isis.

Why? Because the Goddess is dangerous. Preachers may rant about God sending catastrophe, but the people know better. God may be doing his damnedest to keep the wild, elemental forces of the Goddess at bay, but it's a losing battle. The untrammelled force of creation that is unique to the Goddess, that makes woman and Earth sisters, is beyond any male control. Oh the jealous warrior-god may rant and rail, but his power is feeble compared to the Goddess'. Here the evidence is everywhere, for earthquakes still happen, typhoons still happen, tsunamis still happen, and at every turn the lesson is made plain: the Goddess takes back that which she has given.

But there's a direct route to protection, one hidden below centuries of violent repression but still very much alive: propitiate her. Venerate the Goddess and perhaps in her tempestuous and mercurial tantrums she will pass you by.

And this is exactly what happens. Hardly a week seems to go by in the Philippines but some sort of religious festival occurs, and at each, lovingly crafted representations of the Goddess are paraded through the streets of towns, villages and cities across the land. Everything stops;

great cities like Manila grind to a halt, the traffic eerily silent – this is Asia, after all – as the drivers patiently wait for the processions to pass so that they may be on their way. Candles, universally, are the light of these exquisite expressions of devotion – for candles are fire, and fire was our first defence against the beasts that haunt the night.

Jesus himself is the sacrificial lamb – not to atone for some bizarre concept of 'sin' that the Goddess holds in utter contempt, but to the Goddess herself. We give you this man-god that you will love and protect us, and spare us in your anger. See how we have hoist his body high; he is our offering to you.

That is all Christianity has ever been: a recognition that the cult of the jealous Jewish sky-god is totally ineffective at protecting us, for the Goddess can still wreak havoc at her will. There is no idea of 'freedom of choice' or 'free will' in the sky-god allowing such human suffering; he allows it because he has no choice, for he is not in control. Instead, the Goddess is, and she always has been, as she remains today, untamed, for even with our fantastic technology we cannot control her. We are the fleas on her back, powerless to prevent her scratching, whose pathetic talisman, the sky-god, is useless at protecting us.

That is why the people pray to Mama Mary. They know who she is. They know that she is the Earth and the force that created all life on it. She can and does, take back what she gives, in the blind, undirected passion of her elemental dance. And the relationship of women to the Goddess is very clear; as She is powerful, so are They.

If nearly eight millennia of the subjection and suppression of women, to the point of total disenfranchisement and even forbidding them to allow themselves to be seen, proves one thing, it is this: it doesn't work. Reducing half the population to second-class citizen (or worse) status by power of violence hasn't changed a damn thing. Disasters still happen, and you and I will still die. The Goddess takes back what she has given, and no fanciful invention of men can stop her.

6. Ladyboys in Pattaya

So you're planning to meet some ladyboys in Pattaya? Read this.

The whole of south-east Asia is remarkable for its highly visible populations of transsexual women. These are not at all the same as you may be used to thinking of, if you are a Westerner. They're not like Bruce 'Caitlyn' Jenner. (See my discussions on Blanchard for more details.)

Ladyboys in Thailand and across Asia are not like that at all. They are beautiful and very sexy. They are extremely feminine in appearance and manners. From their early teens they use female hormones, often birth control pills which are freely available without prescription. These can turn them into staggeringly beautiful women. And the fact is that many men are powerfully attracted to them.

Ladyboy Phenomenon in Pattaya.

I was recently asked how things were in Pattaya, so if you're thinking of going there to meet some TS women, the following may be useful – or at least more useful than most of the garbage you'll find on transphobic 'backpacker', 'ex-pat', or autogynephile sites. We're definitely trans friendly here, as long as you are the right type. I'll do something on the other major hotspots some other time, but the general rules apply there too.

The phenomenon of highly feminine, sexually attractive transsexual women has become increasingly well known over the last two decades, mainly through the internet. Transsexual porn, for example, is extremely popular, but only amongst men who identify as 'straight'.*

Unfortunately a great deal of the information available is either badly researched or flat wrong.

Why Asia?

The destination of choice for men, who desire to investigate further their attraction to transwomen, has become Thailand. Pattaya, along with Phuket and Bangkok, are the favourites. Thailand has a very well developed tourism sector, with many hotels and short-term apartments at very reasonable prices.

Pattaya is easily and cheaply accessible from the West by air and does not require prior visa approval for most Westerners – you get a month automatically on entry. As well as this it is relatively inexpensive, fairly relaxed, warm, sunny, many people can speak English and there is excellent infrastructure and communications. Together, these make it popular with all types of tourists as well as more hard-core travellers.

Thailand is an ideal destination.

Thailand is therefore an ideal destination for the ladyboy-attracted man who wants to find out more. 'What happens in Thailand stays in Thailand,' is the saying. As long as you don't make the actual news, nobody will ever know what you get up to – although they may presume you are seeking out sex.

Action in Pattaya is constant all year round, although in the low season, Western summer, things can be a little quiet and it will be rather hotter and wetter than from November to March. Pattaya attracts a lot of Russian family tourists – I can only imagine what might be going on inside their heads – but they don't get in the way.

Only around 10% or so of the sex workers in Pattaya are ladyboys, as transsexuals there are usually known (they all call themselves that) but they are obvious. Ordinary Thai girls, even sex workers, are nowhere near that forward, or, frankly, that gorgeous.

(By the way, don't call ladyboys 'kathoey'. Depending on pronunciation and context, this may be offensive.)

You will see ladyboys serving in restaurants, in shops, working in hairdressing salons – I think every salon in Asia is majority LB – as well as in banks, travel agencies and such-like.

Besides this, there are well-known, glamorous ladyboy cabarets in Pattaya. Tiffany and Alcazar are the two best nown, both with large theatres, but there are many other venues from auditoria to intimate clubs. They're not everyone's cup of tea, but I recommend visiting at least once.

(Please note: the girls who work in these, certainly the more upmarket ones, are usually NOT available for paid sex, or at least, not on the premises. Don't cause embarrassment.)

1000 ladyboys.

However that leaves plenty of choice. There are estimated, at the last figures I saw, to be as many as 1000 transsexual sex workers in Pattaya, of a total of 10,000 or so including natural girls and gay boys. These girls either work in bars or freelance on the street, while some do 'escort services' through websites.

Generally, contracting with bar girls is safest because they work under a person called a *mamasan*. This is usually an older woman or ladyboy whose job it is to manage the younger girls. The mamasan will make sure the girls behave when they are with clients (you have to behave too). So if there's an issue, you can go see mamasan and get her to sort it.
Bar fines.

However, you will have to pay a 'bar fine' to take a girl out of the bar. The logic behind this is convoluted and it's really just the bar's cut from her sex work. How much depends on the bar. 300 – 500 short time is reasonable, but I have heard reports that this is going up. If so, that will just put business in the hands of freelancers.

The girl will ask for 1000 – 1500 baht short time, although, if you appear green, she might chance for more. Don't pay it; it's a buyer's market.

You will find yourself targeted by girls (of both types) so be polite but firm. In some bars, ladyboys can be extremely direct and may shock you. Expect to have your genitals in someone's hands early on, and someone's genitals in yours. However, don't be rushed and if you don't fancy a particular girl, just say so.

Protocol, with bar girls, is to buy a 'lady drink' while discussing your plans for the evening. These are more expensive than regular drinks and she gets the extra as a tip.

If you are interested in having sex with her, tell her so and move to the conclusion, otherwise she'll think you're not serious and may just disappear. (You have no idea how quickly a six-foot LB can either vanish or suddenly materialise right beside you until you have seen it done.)

Also, try to define what will be on the menu before you make the deal. I won't get into too many details but, for example, if you want a post-op, ask. Same if you are only interested in a pre-op. (Most are pre-op.) The usual sign is to make a snipping gesture with index and middle fingers. There are other gestures for specific sorts of entertainment. You'll figure it out.

Many bars in Pattaya have rooms, usually around 300 – 500 baht, where the fun happens, otherwise your girl will know a place where the price will be similar. It's not really usual to go to your hotel for short-time unless it's very close by – cuts into the sex time – but it is for long-time.

Short-time, by the way, should be a leisurely hour, more if she's having fun. And these girls are not miserable sex slaves. Most of them really enjoy what they do and if a girl likes you, she'll let you know. You will enjoy what she does too.

If you're thinking of taking a girl back, check your hotel is girl friendly beforehand. Most in Pattaya are, but better to be sure. Many girls are reluctant to do long-time in the early evening (they can make more money with quickies) but at the end of the night might be quite up for it – nice hotel bed, proper shower and breakfast on you.(Well, lunch; good luck getting one of them up before 2 pm.)

Expect to pay 1500 – 2500 baht depending on the time and how much of a slob you are.

Your girl might be quite pissed by the end of her working night, since part of a bar girl's job is to get as many lady drinks purchased as possible and she has to drink them. The later you wait, partly because of this, the more likely it is that you'll get a rate – but also the more likely that another cruiser will snaffle her.

Other men will just cut in and if you haven't made a deal, that might be it, she's gone and all the money you spent on lady drinks goes out the window. Just make sure she's not a total zombie when you finally get her out; but if you can contain yourself, great morning sex will be on the agenda.

Remember that while these look, feel and act like beautiful women, they are motivated by a male sex drive that is just as powerful as yours is.

She may be asked to leave her ID card at the concierge desk, most probably, and this is definitely in your interest. A good hotel will require that you accompany her to retrieve it, so she can't make off with your new Nikon while you're asleep. Always use the room safe for your valuables, however.

If you take a bar girl home for long time remember the bar fine meter is running till you take her back. Get confirmation on how much from mamasan BEFORE you take the girl out.

Do I need to mention, you must use a condom? Well you must.

This applies even if you (think you) are in a long-term relationship with a bar girl. You don't know who else is in there. Be sensible and be safe. (Now if you have a real relationship with a girl, which you are not going to establish in a 2-week trip anyway, it's different. But by then you'll have more experience.)

Freelancers.

After 10 pm or so (LBs are just unusually gorgeous vampires) there will be loads of ladyboys on the street in Pattaya, not just in the bars. Their prices are similar to bar girls but no bar fine – and no mamasan to run to if there's a problem.

You will certainly, at least in Walking Street, see many well-known faces, as the producers of porn seek their models here. However, you might pay much more for the services of a girl who is no hotter or more talented than any other, but just has done a lot of porn. Your choice.

Finally, you can meet girls online. The principal site is Thai Friendly, which has literally thousands of girls subscribed. (Facebook is also popular but the profiles are mostly in Thai, so you may have difficulty.)

Not all the girls are seeking casual paid sex. Some are in fact looking for longer relationships. But there are plenty who would still be interested and it will say so on their profiles.

Transsexual dancers at Alacazar Cabaret in Pattaya.

Do be aware though, that you are effectively asking someone you have never even seen in real life to come and stay in your hotel room for however long. Take sensible precautions and it might be smart to meet at a short-time hotel; she may also feel more comfortable with that.

(Note also that the same concern applies to the girls; if she's dating rather than just coming for paid sex, expect to be asked to meet somewhere public and don't be surprised if she arrives with 'a friend' who may be a large gay man. She's just being sensible too.)

My advice to a first-timer would be to stick to bar girls until you find your feet. But having said that, nearly all the freelancers are fine; one thing that you will find, if you do this, is that Asian TS, call them what you will, are amongst the nicest and most fun people you will ever meet. The crack is DO NOT GET DRUNK and treat them with great respect. It's Thailand, respect is a big deal. It will also be paid back.

Then there is the question of love. It is easy to get sex in Asia without paying for it. In fact, I used to wonder why anyone would, till I discovered the old adage 'You don't pay the girl for sex, you pay her to leave afterwards.'

Now I will be honest, being genuinely in love with an Asian TS who really loves you too is the most wonderful, rewarding experience. There is nothing she will not do for you. The sex will be mind-bendingly good. Most ladyboys have a great sense of humour and are strong characters – they have to be. She can probably cook like an ace and will delight in looking after you. But the payback is commitment. You have to be ready to give that.

Asia is full of stories of Westerners who have had all their savings taken by a gold-digger who is actually running a string of men. So be careful. These are lovely women but they have real needs, supporting the rest of an enormous (by Western standards) family being one of them.

They see milking Western men as a legitimate career; they don't see it as fraudulent, as any cursory check of the relevant sites will prove.

Now it's up to you. You can just buy sex in the marketplace; or you can have casual fun, and it will cost dinner and beachwear and salon visits and so on, and maybe the buffalo got a bit sick this week. There's probably not that much in it.

Or you can get serious. But serious is really serious, and these girls will give you their hearts on a plate. If that's not what you want, you have to tell them.

You need to know what you want up front and not let passion – or for that matter alcohol – cloud your judgement. I can highly commend the experience of being in a committed relationship with an Asian TS, but it's not for everyone. Try to be cool and if you're only going to test the waters and find out about yourself, follow the old adage – 'no getting lubbed up'.

Back in Pattaya, watch it on Beach Road after 1 am. Just be careful and if you feel you're a bit tipsy, get a tuktuk or a taxi home. Don't walk alone there if you can avoid it.

Also, you're meant to carry your passport at all times in Thailand but this is risky; better make a colour photocopy and carry that along with your hotel reservation receipt. If you are asked (very rare) you can politely explain it's at the hotel. (This is one area where the Philippines is better; here, if you extend your visa, you'll get an Alien Registration card. That is all you need to carry, leaving your passport in the room safe at all times.)

Police.

Be aware that there is a difference between Thai Royal Police and the Tourist Police. If you have trouble go to the Tourist Police FIRST. They have a cabin in Walking Street. They are generally more sympathetic and speak good English – indeed, most are ex-pats themselves. If you go to the Thai Royal Police and they reject your claims, that's it and the Tourist Police can do nothing to help you, even if you have a legitimate grievance. It's a 'face' issue.

Also, anything you agree to will be held to be a binding contract in any dispute. So mind what you say. If you are in a dispute with someone and you believe you are right, keep shtum and insist on calling the Tourist Police.

The old Pattaya 'jet-ski' scam is still ongoing, for example. Here, an innocent is hired out a jet-ski with significant damage which may have been covered up to make it look less obvious. He takes it back and bingo, $500 USD bill for repairs, while the owner is brandishing a gun.

Keep calm and get the Tourist Police. The scammers are all known to them. But if you agree to pay the damage in the heat of the moment or because you are intimidated, you'll be held to it. Stay polite, say nothing and get the cops.

Always avoid violence and stay calm.

Being calm is big in Thailand. If you appear aggressive, you'll just get it back with interest.

Be very careful never to get into a violent exchange with any Thai. This applies just as much everywhere in Asia. 'Face' is hugely important across the region. I don't care if you're a 120kg 6'4" Yankee Doodle or whatever.

Apart from the fact that they might well be armed, all those little Thai guys do Muay Thai or I dunno what. And even if you do manage to get the better of one, you know something? He's going to come back with 20 of his chums and hospitalise you if not worse.

The best thing you can do, if you fuck up like this, is to get on the next plane out. They might not come today, or tomorrow, but they will come, and you will be consuming sustenance through an intravenous drip for the rest of your trip – or maybe your life.

Don't imagine that just because they look cute, ladyboys can't defend themselves. They're as strong as men (unsurprisingly) and will whip off a stiletto-heeled shoe and beat you round the face with it if they have to. Play bonny and play safe.

Finally, if you want all this in safety and to meet a nice group of girls in a relaxed, no-pressure environment, try Sensations Bar in Soi 21. Also, if you don't mind staying a little out of town I can recommend Gino House. It's quiet, clean and discreet.

Oh, and, I should warn you: once you have discovered ladyboy love you will never go back.

Note: Strictly, the name for men attracted to TS women is 'gynandromorphophilic'. Practise saying that, then you'll have a riposte for the Ozzie morons. As in 'Gay? Far from it, you kangaroo-shagging arsehole, I'm gynandromorphophilic.' Try it.

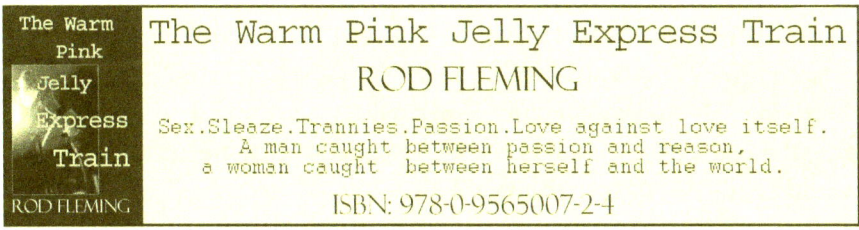

The Warm Pink Jelly Express Train
ROD FLEMING
Sex.Sleaze.Trannies.Passion.Love against love itself.
A man caught between passion and reason,
a woman caught between herself and the world.
ISBN: 978-0-9565007-2-4

Author's note

I thought it would be easy. I thought, look, I'll just stick together a selection of stories; from *Rod Fleming's World* and make them into an eBook. Then, I thought, I could give the eBook away to loyal fans for Christmas and maybe get a print book out of it too.

That was Christmas 2016 and here we are in October 2017. But the compilation has, at last, been finished.

It might have been quicker to rewrite the whole darn thing but hey, I thought it would be easy. Part of the problem lay in the fact that many of my views have diametrically changed over the time sine the blog began. That meant I had to remove some of the older posts altogether and update a good many more.

I have tried to be honest. The material presented here, though proofed and edited again is substantially the same as it was when first published. Some of the posts on the blog are now completely different from the original versions found here.

In broad terms, while still a Huxleyan Agnostic (that is, I do not believe in a deity but accept that I cannot prove that one does not exist) I have become much more sympathetic to some expressions of Christianity, especially Catholicism and the tradition I was brought up in, Scottish Presbyterianism. While these are very different religions, they both contributed enormously to the Europe and the Scotland I was born into and so, to the formation of me. Post Renaissance European Culture is the finest culture the world has ever known; it is more open, more just, more representative, more egalitarian and more freedom-loving than any human society that has ever existed. It must be protected, and if the Christian Churches will stand up to fight the threat it now faces from Islam and a resurgent Marxism, then I am on their side. My enemy's enemy is my friend. So some articles that displayed a degree of impatience with Christians have been excised and I would make my peace with them.

When I began the blog I was sympathetic to the claims of Feminism, but five years of exploring the foetid depths of that cult have shown me the error of my ways. Feminism is just Communism under a fancy new name and it is every bit as wicked. It is determined to destroy European culture, the finest in the world. So a good few articles had to go there too.

On Sex and Gender, again, my position has evolved. I am as supportive as ever of True (HomoSexual, HSTS) Transsexuals. As regards Pseudo (non-homosexual or autogynephilic) Transsexuals (AGP). then, as far as the Western type is concerned, I regard many of them as dangerous and ruthless bullies. They appear not to care what damage they do in order to further their political ends. (Very few AGPs in Asia even think about politics; they are, by and large, a far more pleasant group of people.) The damage done by the Western variant extends, now, to harming children and that must stop. So a few other articles ruled themselves out, though some slipped through.

(I did not, in the period covered, deal with the most modern issue, transtrenderism, where being trans has been reduced to a lifestyle choice -- but one that ruins lives. I will be addressing this in the blog.)

What's left is, I think, a good distillation of hundreds of articles on the site. This book reflects a range of my writing and I hope it will bring new areas to readers who habitually arrive as a result of a search or who browse by category.

I hope you enjoy it.

Books by Rod Fleming

French Onion Soup! ISBN: 978-0-9565007-3-1

The first book in this series, *French Onion Soup!* tells you about about arriving in France, wine, food, the *affouage*—a unique way of gathering winter fuel—French lawyers, renegade mules and many other areas of Burgundian life, in a quirky and hilariously funny style.

A Little Shop of Horors. ISBN: 978-0-9565007-8-6

Creeps and chills from a selection of modern horror stories guaranteed to make you think twise about turning out the light. Most are set in Scotland with authentic background details and tap into the rich folklore of the country. Just right for a winter evening!

Why Men Made God. ISBN: 978-0-9572612-2-8

The Egyptians, Greeks, Romans, Celts and northern Europeans all had pantheons of gods and goddesses. What changed and led to the idea of just one, all-powerful God? Why was the original Goddess abandoned in favour of a sequence of sky-fathers? Who wrote the Bible and why? What impact does that have on us today?

Why Men Made God answers these questions, in a pacy and easy-to-read manner, backed up with science. With Karis Burkowski.

The Warm Pink Jelly Express Train. ISBN: 978-0-9572612-3-5

Brian Macmaster is a journalist licking the wounds of a divorce in Paris. He meets a transsexual prostitute who leads him into a spider's-web of intrigue, deception and extortion. *The Warm Pink Jelly Express Train* is a sexy, powerful, relentlessly paced novel that is not only a page-turner but also explores one of the most fascinating taboos of contemporary culture.

A Kiss for Christmas. ISBN: 978-0-9565007-7-9

Christmas 1981: Europe is in turmoil, the *Human League* is top of the charts, it's pissing stair-rods in Paris and Johnny MacFarlane has just got back from Damascus with a load of smuggled blood diamonds.

   Harry, the most notorious fence in Paris, offers him a special surprise: Hermann Goering's gold-plated 9mm Luger. Johnny goes back to the bar to pay his tab, when he gets another surprise: a bullet. That's when his world explodes.

The Children of Aldebaran. ISBN: 978-0-9572612-1-1

The time of the Big People is past and the world is ruled by the Animals. Silas Farsight, a young otter who looks forward to a life as a lawyer in the forest village, is horrified when his cousin is kidnapped by a gang of ferocious cats. With his indentured clerk Stoatwise Cuttleworth, he sets off in pursuit.

   His cousin, Magda, is being taken to the Dark City, where an evil beast known as the Great Cat is plotting imperial domination of the Free Animals. Silas must rescue her. His adventures lead him to the Sea Otters, a wild and mysterious people, of whom he knows only myth and legend. Yet it is with them that he will find his own true destiny. A fast-paced and exciting fantasy adventure.

Poaching the River. ISBN: 978-0-9554535-0-2

It's a typical sleepy afternoon in Auchpinkie, a tiny fishing village on the east coast of Scotland. But all that's about to change. The action races to its riotous climax, as local hero Big Sandy poaches the River Pinkie in a daring adventure, the public convenience is destroyed by a freak explosion, and the minister is baffled by the sudden religious conversion of two formerly heathenish young lads. *Poaching the River* will make you laugh and cry out loud.

The Spring Run. ISBN: 978-0-9572612-5-9

Spring is coming to the village of Auchpinkie on the east coast of Scotland. With it, women's minds turn to romance and men's to something else — poaching. But it turns out these are actually very closely related. *The Spring Run* is a hilarious and charming romantic comedy set in a world full of larger-than life characters. (This is a standard-English translation of *Poaching the River.*)

Buying

You can buy my books as paperbacks or as e-books from any good retailer in most of the world, including Amazon, Barnes & Noble, Waterstones and all major e-book retailers.

Alternatively, please navigate to my site at http://rodfleming.com/ where you will find direct links to purchase them online..

Visit my Amazon author page!

https://www.amazon.com/author/rodfleming

www.ingramcontent.com/pod-product-compliance
Lightning Source LLC
Chambersburg PA
CBHW052014290426
44112CB00014B/2234